THE MATCH OF MY LIFE

THE MATCH OF
MY LIFE

Compiled by Ray French

Foreword by Garry Schofield

HEADLINE

First published in 1994
by HEADLINE BOOK PUBLISHING

10 9 8 7 6 5 4 3 2 1

British Library Cataloguing in Publication Data

French, Ray
Match of My Life
I. Title
796.333092

ISBN 0-7472-0972-3

Typeset by
Avon Dataset Ltd., Bidford-on-Avon, Warwickshire

Printed and bound in Great Britain by
Mackays of Chatham PLC, Chatham, Kent

HEADLINE BOOK PUBLISHING
A division of Hodder Headline PLC
338 Euston Road
London NW1 3BH

Contents

Acknowledgement

Many thanks to Steve Mascord for his help in researching the details supplied by the Australian players in this book.

Foreword

There is no finer feeling for a rugby league player than to leave the field at the final whistle, relax in the comfort of the dressing room, soak in a hot, steaming bath and reflect upon an outstanding performance. Though essentially a team sport, rugby league offers a player the chance to become the hero of the hour by virtue of his running, his passing, his kicking or his tackling. And yet most players would freely admit that, rather than the adulation of the crowds, pride in their performance is the greatest spur to producing their best efforts in a match. The majority of matches in a long and successful career are quickly forgotten as time erases the memory of that once-magical defence-splitting pass or the perfectly timed burst on to the ball. Some games, however, by virtue of a player's individual brilliance, the unusual circumstances surrounding the match or the unique atmosphere in which the game is played, linger longer in the memory. These matches, precious to any player with a pride in his performance, may not necessarily stamp themselves as extraordinary contests in the recollections of fans but, for personal reasons, they often represent the match of a player's life.

Such matches are invariably contests of the highest intensity which bring out the best in any player – a Challenge Cup final at Wembley, a vital championship decider or a thrilling Test match where the honour of a country is at stake. But a seemingly unimportant league championship clash or even a harmless end-of-season exhibition game can prove the stage for a player's greatest performance or his most memorable moments in an illustrious career.

As can be seen from the games chosen by my colleagues and myself in this book, those games that stand out in the memory can often be varied and surprising. All are, however, special to all of us, being the most memorable match of our lives. I hope you gain as much enjoyment from reading about the games as we did from playing in them.

Garry Schofield

1

Introduction

One of the most rewarding aspects of speaking to players about the 'Match of My Life' has been the pleasure which their accounts have given me.

To listen to my boyhood heroes, Tom Van Vollenhoven, Billy Boston, Lewis Jones and Alan Prescott, recount their heroic deeds and, above all, their feelings in the white-hot atmosphere of a Championship, Challenge Cup, or Test clash gave me a sharper insight into what made them so special when, in later years, I played alongside or against them. To learn, at first hand, just what thoughts were passing through the great Wally Lewis's head when the Australian skipper was plotting Great Britain's downfall in the third Test at Central Park, Wigan, in 1986, and to appreciate the challenge and satisfaction experienced by Great Britain's Garry Schofield, a year earlier on the same ground against New Zealand, only added to my enjoyment when sitting in the commentary box for BBC television. And to relive Wigan wing ace Martin Offiah's amazing ten-try haul in the Premiership semi-final clash with Leeds in 1992 reminds me of the drama experienced by all of us in the press box as we constantly checked and re-checked watches in those final dramatic 12 minutes in the hope that he would equal or beat the sport's record of 11 tries set by Hull Kingston Rovers' 'Tich' West 89 years ago.

As an ex-player I can, perhaps more than most, appreciate just why a player should choose a particular match to be his most memorable. The choice must always be personal and individual to the player and the reasons for his choice vary greatly. Though my own playing career embraced Championship and Challenge Cup final winning appearances, county and international action, and the honour of slugging it out (literally!) against the likes of all-time greats John Raper, Artie Beetson and Bobby Fulton in the green and gold jersey on the Sydney Cricket Ground, my own most satisfying 80 minutes came nearer home, at Knowsley Road, St. Helens in a Championship semi-final tie against Hull Kingston Rovers in Saints' cup-winning season of 1965–66. The fans, my team-mates and the opposition may have long forgotten the match but it will always be firmly etched in my mind.

The matches included here in my selection are all held dear to the hearts of the players who have chosen them to be the 'Match of My Life'. I am sure their accounts will add to the nostalgia and enhance the memories experienced by those readers who were lucky enough to be present on the terraces and witness personally the players' deeds.

Who knows, the selection of memorable matches in this book might even tempt the reader to consider his own 'Match of My Life'. Now that would be an interesting choice, wouldn't it? Some, hopefully, are included within these pages.

Ray French

Dean Bell

Australia 6 New Zealand 13
Test Match, Lang Park, Brisbane
21 July 1987

Born 29 April 1962. Within days of former Wigan coach John Monie's appointment as supremo of the newly formed Auckland Warriors, the shrewd Aussie tactician was laying plans to tempt Dean Bell to lead the first-ever New Zealand side into the Australian Winfield Cup in 1995. The Wigan skipper's tough professional attitude to his game, his hard, uncompromising centre play and, above all, his undoubted qualities as a captain made him a priority for any coach attempting to start up a club from scratch. One of the first players to take advantage of the relaxation of the ban on overseas signings in 1983, Dean, or the Mean Machine as he was known at Central Park, travelled from Manukau in New Zealand to Carlisle, Leeds and Wigan via Eastern Suburbs in Australia, all the time sharpening his attacking skills and earning a reputation as a fearsome tackler. Representative honours and, eventually, the captaincy of his country came his way between 1983 and 1989, when he retired prematurely from international rugby to concentrate upon his career with Wigan.

Without doubt the unparalleled success at Wigan in recent seasons and the acquisition of their many Championship and Challenge Cup honours owe much to the respect in which the softly spoken Bell is held by the players. He never shirked the heated exchanges, and invariably led from the front by example.

To appreciate the depth of feeling between the players in an Australia v. New Zealand Test match, one has to understand the competitive edge and, at times, the open animosity generated by the media and the public of both countries. The rivalry is intense and, certainly from New Zealand's part, is fuelled by a feeling that the Kangaroos, in sporting terms and especially in rugby league circles, have in the past tended to look down upon and dismiss the efforts of their near neighbours. Few Kiwis can appreciate or accept the supremely confident and at times downright arrogant approach of Australia's players and their public to their opponents in a Test match. Kiwi teams have often been made to feel inferior alongside the Green and Golds by a vitriolic press campaign or a comment from an Australian player and, accordingly, have often suffered psychologically in their pre-match preparation. Young Kiwis, making their debuts in the magnificent surroundings of the Sydney Football Stadium or the fiery cauldron of Lang Park in Brisbane, have been known to have lost the psychological battle before even stepping on to the pitch. Not so Dean Bell, a player with a steely mental approach to his opponents and with complete confidence in his own abilities.

The atmosphere generated around the one-off Test match at Lang Park between Australia and New Zealand in July 1987 served only to make the Kiwi centre even more determined to succeed and humiliate the enemy. The eventual outcome of the clash and the quality of his performance in both attack and defence stamp the match as perhaps the most satisfying of any in his long and distinguished career.

The Australians are always hostile to the Kiwis in their pre-match build-ups. Any visitors to Brisbane are invariably given the full treatment before a match, a kind of softening up in the press. Many players are affected by it, but it can spur you on and make you more determined than ever to do something to shut them up. When you can, then it is a great feeling. There is no greater satisfaction than to play well at Lang Park and beat the Aussies on their own ground. We did just that and our treatment before the match helped to make it the most rewarding of my career.

In the absence of loose forward Hugh McGahan, on duty in the Winfield Cup with North Sydney, Dean Bell was chosen as captain to lead a relatively inexperienced New Zealand party on a short pre-match tour of Queensland and Papua New Guinea before playing the one Trans-Tasman Test of the year in Brisbane. In partnership with new coach Tony Gordon, then a completely unknown force at international level and the inexperienced successor to the highly successful Graham Lowe, Bell led a very young but talented squad of players. At the time only three members of the tour party were playing overseas with British clubs: Mark Elia at St. Helens, Joe Ropati at Warrington and Bell himself at Wigan. There was much young talent with emerging Kiwis such as Shane Cooper, Kevin Iro, Adrian Shelford, Gary Mercer, Ross Taylor and Shane Horo, all of whom eventually found fame overseas, eager to win a Test jersey. However, despite an impressive set of results on the mini-tour, with wins over Northern Rivers and Queensland and a 36–22 victory over Papua New Guinea at Port Moresby, where Bell himself scored two tries, there was a feeling that life would be difficult in the heat of the forthcoming Test match.

We played well in our mini-tour and developed a good understanding and team spirit, but there was very little experience in the side. We were a young side with many making their first appearances in a Kiwi jersey. We were perhaps a little vulnerable in the pack where we didn't have the biggest

5

of forwards. In contrast, the Aussies were a supremely confident bunch and had a star-studded array of backs capable of destroying the best of teams. We were not over-confident but we were fired up and determined, and Tony Gordon had prepared us well.

The home side had every reason to be confident, such was the quality of their backs: four of Australia's greatest-ever midfield backs, Gene Miles, Brett Kenny, Wally Lewis and Peter Sterling, were wearing the famous green and gold jersey, while Garry Jack at full back and Dale Shearer and Michael O'Connor on the wings were hardly novices. Such were the expectations of the Australian public of its national side, and so readily accepted was the outcome of the match, that Lang Park was barely half full, there being only 16,500 fans scattered around the terraces and seated in the grandstands. Those 16,500 spectators and millions in New Zealand and Australia watching on television were in for a shock.

Loose forward Hugh McGahan, released from his Winfield Cup duties for the occasion, assumed the captaincy of the Kiwis, thus releasing Dean Bell to concentrate entirely on his centre role and to settle down youngsters Kevin Iro and Gary Mercer alongside him in the threequarter line. But the opening exchanges were fierce.

The big Australian pack made them very firm favourites with the bookmakers, and the forward exchanges between Greg Dowling, Wayne Pearce, Bob Lindner and our own forwards were tough. The temperature on the field at Lang Park is always high, and there were a few scuffles early on among the forwards. We settled down better than they did and concentrated on the football. It paid off for us.

Thanks to the pressure exerted on Australia in midfield, and especially around the play-the-ball areas, where Kiwi hooker Wayne Wallace and halves Clayton Friend and Shane Cooper hurried the Aussie ball receivers into mistakes, little was seen of their gifted attackers in the opening quarter. It was left to New Zealand to trouble the scoreboard operator and to Bell to provide the inspiration and the excitement. The Wigan centre was part of a brilliant six-man, 80-yard handling movement which swept upfield from near the Kiwis' own line when Kangaroo centre Brett Kenny mistimed an interception and was left floundering. Bell's quick thinking and footballing sixth sense were soon to provide his side with a spectacular try when, in full flight, he raced down the touchline to combine with wing Gary Mercer for a try.

The try was a typical piece of New Zealand adventure. I managed to break loose in the centre and made my way down the touchline. I appeared to be clear but I wasn't, because Australia's Dale Shearer shadowed me and

6

hemmed me in. As he waited for me, I drew him towards me and then flipped the ball over my shoulders to where I knew Gary Mercer would be. He caught the ball and sidestepped Shearer before crossing the line to score. It was a big surprise to the Australians but was a huge boost to us.

In Bell's opinion, the New Zealand team contained 'honest toilers rather than stars', but those toilers, and Bell in particular, blunted Australia's attacking edge, restricting them to just one Peter Sterling try and a Michael O'Connor goal with a display of ferocious tackling. Though not the biggest of midfield defenders, then standing at 5 feet 10 inches and weighing just 13½ stones, Dean Bell had acquired a reputation for uncompromising tackling. Wally Lewis, Gene Miles and one or two of the Australian forwards felt the full force of the impact as, spurred on by the possibility of an upset, he crashed into them with sickening and monotonous regularity. His example resulted in his team-mates marshalling a blanket defence against any Brett Kenny- or Wayne Pearce-inspired raids, with the result that Australia became more and more frustrated as the game wore on. Insists Bell:

I was selected as the man of the match, I think not so much for any individual brilliance but more for my general all-round play, both on attack and defence. I was involved in a few good runs and bursts of attacking play, and I really enjoyed the tackling. We upset the Aussies, knocked them out of their rhythm and, though in Kenny, Lewis and Sterling they had three of the best tacticians and passers of a ball in the world, they could do little against us.

A try for powerful prop Ross Taylor, courtesy of good running and handling by Sam Stewart and a young Kevin Iro, who had announced his arrival on the international stage only days earlier with a record 20 points on his debut against Papua New Guinea, was enough to give the Kiwis a famous win. Half-back star Shane Cooper's drop goal and the powerful Iro's second goal merely rubbed salt in the wounds. The shouts from the New Zealand players, the leaps into the air and the fists raised at the final whistle were the outward signs of the joy in the Kiwi camp at this unexpected but richly deserved win. The significance of such a win and its importance in the development of rugby league in New Zealand were not lost on Dean Bell, always keen to savour a defeat of his near neighbours!

Australia are the world champions, and it is always very difficult to beat them, however they play. They don't get the tag of world champions for nothing. Defensively they are so strong and have such strength in depth that, unlike New Zealand at the time, they can always bring top-class footballers into the team.

They have always stayed ahead of everyone else in the game, never rest on their laurels and are so intense and thorough in their training methods. Winning becomes a habit, and they have it. The win was so important for the younger players, who could believe in their own ability, and so good for New Zealand. The feeling in the dressing room after the match was terrific, it felt so good to be part of a winning team.

Dean Bell, in recent seasons as captain of Wigan, has become more used than most to winning championships and cups. His performance at Lang Park for his country, and the performances of he and his colleagues overseas for New Zealand and various Australian and British club sides, has helped to raise the profile of Kiwi rugby league in the 1980s and the 1990s to heights never previously attained. It is fitting that, as he prepares to lead the Auckland Warriors into their first season in the Australian Winfield Cup in 1995, the former Manukau threequarter still retains that fierce pride in his own ability and the desire to see his country succeed which took him to victory in that tense atmosphere at Lang Park seven years ago.

The quality of the Australians' game comes through the tough competition in their Winfield Cup. They are used to intense competition every week. In England, perhaps only Wigan v. St. Helens games or matches against Leeds or Widnes reach such intensity. New Zealand rugby has improved rapidly in recent years because many of our stars are now playing professionally in the Australian and British leagues. The arrival of the Auckland Warriors will be a wonderful boost to our chances at Test rugby, for every week now New Zealand's top players will be involved in tough matches against Australia's top sides. There were only three of us playing for an overseas club in the team that beat Australia in 1987. Hopefully, in future, we will be able to compete at Test level on more than level terms.

AUSTRALIA Jack; O'Connor, Miles, Kenny, Shearer; Lewis, Sterling; Dowling, Simmons, Tunks, Pearce, Niebling, Lindner. *Subs*: Johnston, Davidson.

NEW ZEALAND Williams; Elia, Iro, Bell, Mercer; Cooper, Friend; Taylor, Wallace, Shelford, M. Horo, Stewart, McGahan. *Subs*: Freeman, Lonergan.

Scorers Australia   *Tries* Sterling. *Goals* O'Connor.
        New Zealand *Tries* Mercer, Taylor. *Goals* Iro (2). *Drop Goals* Cooper.

Referee Neville Kesha (New Zealand).

Billy Boston

Leeds 13 Wigan 11

Challenge Cup First Round, Headingley, Leeds
9 February 1957

Born 6 August 1934. When William John Boston, a former Welsh Youth international and Cardiff Internationals Athletic club player, decided that, at 18 years of age, he would consider offers to join rugby league, the chase to his mother's home in Tiger Bay, Cardiff, resembled the old American Gold Rush. Workington Town, headed by all-time great Gus Risman – himself a former pupil of Boston's Cardiff school – Hunslet and Wigan headed the list of clubs eager to compete for the pacy, powerful winger. That Wigan won the hunt, and for a fee of £3000, was one of the best-kept secrets in the game, for Billy 'B', as he was later known to the Lancashire club's fans, was under pressure to continue his illustrious rugby career in the armed forces with the Royal Corps of Signals at Catterick in Yorkshire. However, in a team containing such illustrious players as league international centre Phil Jackson, and England union stars Reg Higgins and Phil Horrocks-Taylor, the young Boston immediately shot to prominence with an amazing 126 tries in a season. The secret could be kept no longer and, with the army's permission, the Tiger Bay tornado made his debut at Central Park in October 1953, eight months after his signing, against Barrow 'A' team before a crowd of 8000 fans.

Though his service commitments restricted him to just half a dozen first-team games that season, such was his promise in the new code that he was sensationally included in the Great Britain touring party which headed for Australia and New Zealand in the summer of 1954. By the time the Wigan wing returned home, he had more than justified his daring selection with a then record 36 tries from 18 appearances and a record-equalling 4 tries in a Test match against New Zealand. The name of Billy Boston was soon to reverberate throughout the rugby world, a name revered for the owner's thundering runs down the touchline and the shuddering, shattering crash tackles that enveloped and halted, quite dramatically, any opponent down the flanks.

In a career that spanned 18 years, including 11 matches with Blackpool Borough in his final 12 months, Billy Boston amassed over 571 tries, registering the fastest-ever century of touchdowns in just 68 games. At both club and international level, where he gained 31 Great Britain caps and scored 24 tries between 1954 and 1963, he was a constant menace to the opposition, but always respected by them for the quiet and unassuming manner in which he conducted himself both on and off the field.

The sight of hundreds of fans, forced by the pressure and numbers on the terraces to crowd behind the goalposts and stand in the in-goal areas, was an indication that something special was happening at Headingley on that dry, clear day in February. The rain of the previous few days had eased in time for the supporters of both clubs, Leeds and Wigan, to decide that here was a match which just couldn't be missed. Those of the huge 38,914 crowd, however, who were not in their places 20 minutes before kickoff did miss this rugby treat, as the Headingley gates were locked. Over 5000 despairing fans were left on the outside with no way of looking in. Those who were locked inside waited in eager anticipation for the contest between the two giants of rugby league.

Wigan, in the process of building a new side that would later take them to six Challenge Cup final appearances in the next nine years, and fortified by the recent signings of ex-Swinton scrum half Rees Thomas and giant, 17-stone former Leigh prop John Barton, had won their previous 12 matches. The home side, Leeds, had cruised unbeaten through their previous 11 matches, and the whole of Yorkshire willed them on to defeat the might of Lancashire. Yet by far one of the major factors in determining the size of the crowd and the attendance of so many neutral spectators was the appearance of two of league's greatest-ever players and two of the biggest personalities ever to trek north from the valleys of Wales, Wigan's Billy Boston and Leeds' Lewis Jones. Both were in outstanding form, and either was capable of winning the match on his own by virtue of one dramatic intervention.

Billy 'B' was in such spectacular tryscoring form that in the 1956–57 season he was to top the league's tryscoring charts with 60 tries, while the 'golden boy' from Llanelli, Lewis Jones, was to shatter the game's record number of points scored in a season with 496 points from 194 goals and 36 tries – a record that still stands today. Both aces were surrounded by a galaxy of international stars, and the stage was set for the showdown. According to Billy Boston, the atmosphere was electric.

It was a perfect day for rugby, mild and cool, and the crowds were right up to the sides of the pitch. Many Wigan fans couldn't get into the ground, and I know some who gave up hope and went to Elland Road to watch another Welshman, John Charles, score a goal for Leeds United. But at Headingley the atmosphere was intense, and it took a while for our coach to pass through the crowds in the streets around the ground. Leeds had their star attraction in Lewis Jones, and we knew that we had to mark him very closely or he could do a lot of damage. The betting with the bookmakers was even money, but we were still very confident.

* * *

After the opening skirmishes, Wigan fans were even more confident as their big pack of forwards proceeded to monopolise the ball and lay siege to the Leeds tryline. Winning the ball from six of the first seven scrums and – under the unlimited-tackle rule whereby a team could retain possession until an offence was committed – keeping hold of it for long periods, the Wigan six were ideally blended to mount wave after wave of attacks. In prop Brian McTigue and Frank Collier, then playing at loose forward, they had two of the best ball players in the business, artists with a ball in their hands and able to prise open the tightest of defences with a short pass to a colleague in support. Strong-running forwards Norman Cherrington, Bill Bretherton and the giant battering-ram, ex-guardsman John Barton were invariably in attendance to give the Leeds line a pounding. Leeds supporters gasped when Barton was held inches short of the line and Wigan's skipper Ernie Ashcroft was hurled into the corner flag when the tryline seemed at his mercy.

All Wigan's hard work was undone, however, when, in a rare Leeds raid, the mercurial Jones struck with his usual clinical efficiency and with more than a hint of flair which stamped him out as unique among points-scorers. In the tenth minute, the graceful Leeds back raced on to a loose Cherrington pass and kicked the ball towards the Wigan line. Using his instep to propel the ball twice to the tryline, he used his acceleration off the mark to beat Barton to the ball and finished off the opening try with a spectacular dive. He nonchalantly placed the conversion between the posts; the Leeds hero had justified the faith his fans had in him. Within two minutes, Wigan's idol Billy Boston replied with a piece of magic himself.

Receiving the ball on the wing, about 60 yards from the Leeds line and seemingly hemmed in on the touchline, Wigan's powerhouse passed Leeds' former England rugby union star Pat Quinn with a surprising burst of speed, and in typical Boston fashion elected to run through Leeds' second row Bernard Poole and full back Jimmy Dunn. Former Royal Signals team-mate, Dunn, crashed to the ground, a victim of an unstoppable runaway 15-stone scoring machine, while the gallant Poole was simply bounced out of the way when he came into contact with Billy Boston's powerful hips. Cherry and white bob-caps flew into the air, the din of the once-fashionable wooden supporters' rattles clattered around the ground, and the excited fans crowded over the straw which lined the touchlines to slap the big, bustling Welshman on the back. Wigan's own star had replied in spectacular fashion and, though centre Eric Ashton was to miss the conversion, the bookmakers' predictions were proving right.

I was marking Pat Quinn on the wing. He was a very big man, and I knew that it would be difficult to run through him, so I used my pace to test him on the outside. He lacked a yard of pace. Jimmy Dunn, my old army friend,

11

was at full back, and their second row Poole was covering on the touchline so I had little option but to run at them. I was pleased with the try because when I got the ball I didn't have much room in which to work.

The tackling, as was to be expected in such a close encounter, proved fierce, with many high tackles becoming the order of the day. And yet, for all the ferocity and sickening impact made by the forwards, the discipline was maintained on both sides by tiny Oldham referee 'Dickie' Thomas, who barely stood as high as Leeds loose forward Harry Street's waist. For all the tough personal battles in midfield it was a simple, fair tackle by David Bolton on Lewis Jones which eventually caused the Wigan half back to leave the field, reduce the visitors to 12 men for the whole of the second half, and allowed Jones to orchestrate even more havoc in the Wigan ranks. Twice the Welshman moved the ball wide to Pat Quinn's wing, where the ex-England union star was twice bundled unceremoniously into touch by the rugged Boston. Long, raking kicks to the corners troubled Wigan full back Don Platt and set up the situation for further Leeds pressure. But, once again, it was Jones' fellow countryman who reminded Leeds that their progress to Wembley would not be straightforward.

Lively Wigan scrum half Rees Thomas, yet another Welshman and a bargain buy from Swinton just before the Challenge Cup transfer deadline, started the 80-yard tryscoring movement from inside his own 25-yard area. Wigan's huge pack was monopolising the scrums and the tricky number seven swept around the blind side, evading the clutches of Leeds' own half-back star Jeff Stevenson and former Wigan loose forward Harry Street before handing on to Boston on the touchline. As he was faced with threequarters of the length of the field in front of him, few of the Wigan fans ever imagined that he would, seconds later, be putting the ball behind the Leeds line for one of his greatest tries. Yet he did, and he rounded the hapless Quinn, evaded the cover and cruised past the young Leeds flyer Delmos Hodgkinson, who had crossed from the other wing, with all the pace and power of an Inter City train making up lost time for Euston. His tryscoring effort was a classic and one that brought forth the highest of praise from the local scribes.

In the *Yorkshire Evening Post* John Bapty insisted: 'He had threequarters the length of the field to go and he went along the touchline like the master he is. The challengers did not count, and Hodgkinson who crossed from right to left in the Leeds defence could not get within reach of him.'

Eric Stanger saw fit to compare his exhibition of speed and power to the greats of the past: 'What a great player he is. With almost the speed of an Eric Harris and the build and strength of a Lionel Cooper in his stride he is just about unstoppable. His second try, which gave Wigan an interval lead of 6–5, was magnificent. That try will remain in memory when all the other five scored in the game have been forgotten, and there were good ones among them.'

Wigan may have held the upper hand at half time, but the sight of their Great Britain stand off Dave Bolton being stretchered into the dressing rooms was hardly likely to raise morale. There being no substitutes allowed, Wigan would be forced to struggle on with only 12 men in the face of rapier-like thrusts from Jones and Aussie centre Keith McLellan.

David was hobbling about for quite a while in the first half, but there was no way he could continue. Eric Ashton was forced to move up to stand off, and we had to pull Norman Cherrington out of the pack and on to the wing. Terry O'Grady moved into the centre. We knew it would be difficult to hold on to the lead, but our pack kept winning the ball and they held on to it for long stretches, frustrating Leeds.

The unlimited-tackle rule which was then in the rules of play did give a side with a numerical disadvantage a better chance of staving off defeat than the modern six-tackle rule provides. But, with Lewis Jones displaying his full array of skills, it was not long before the home side took the lead. Only a crunching tackle by Boston on Leeds wing Pat Quinn at the corner flag prevented a try, but even Billy 'B' himself could not stop Jones from putting over a neatly taken drop goal and second row Poole from putting youngster Hodgkinson in at the opposite corner for a try.

Tactically, as the game approached its final quarter, Wigan pulled a master stroke by moving second row Cherrington back into the pack and, playing without a full back, added Platt to the threequarter line. Again, under the unlimited-tackle rule, when in possession they had little to fear from the kicking of Leeds and could afford to leave their last line of defence bare. The ploy worked and, in the 63rd minute, after heavy forward pressure on the Leeds 25-yard area, Eric Ashton picked up a ricochet off Leeds scrum half Stevenson and crossed the line for a try. Platt added the conversion to give Wigan an 11–10 lead, and their fans sensed that their 12 heroes might still deny Leeds victory.

It was not to be, as Leeds skipper McLellan scythed his way through the Wigan defence in the 65th minute for what proved to be the match-winning touchdown, though later, with five minutes remaining on the referee's watch, there was still a chance the home side's ambitions could be thwarted.

We were awarded a penalty on the Leeds 25-yard line in front of the posts. A goal would have given us a draw and the chance of a replay back at Central Park. I think we would have won that and perhaps gone to Wembley instead of Leeds. Eric Ashton was in the thick of things at stand off and was, I think, a little out of breath when he went to take the kick. There was tremendous pressure on him. He kicked it straight but, at the last moment, a gust of wind blew the ball just wide of the posts and we had lost.

Headingley's epic encounter and Leeds' win kindled thoughts among their fans of a Wembley visit and, following further wins against Warrington, Halifax and Whitehaven, they were not disappointed. For Billy Boston the memories of a stirring struggle, though lost, remain.

Although we lost the match it was one of the most enjoyable matches I ever played in. The huge crowd made for a remarkable atmosphere, and they were rewarded with a wonderful game of rugby where the result was always in doubt. It was very tough in the middle. I got great satisfaction out of the match and capped it all with two good tries. The game had all that's best in rugby league.

LEEDS Dunn; Hodgkinson, McLellan, Jones, Quinn; Lendill, Stevenson; Anderson, Prior, Hopper, Poole, Robinson, Street.

WIGAN Platt; Boston, Ashcroft, Ashton, O'Grady; Bolton, Thomas; Barton, Mather, McTigue, Cherrington, Bretherton, Collier.

Scorers Leeds   *Tries* Jones, Hodgkinson, McLellan. *Goals* Jones (2).
Wigan   *Tries* Boston (2), Ashton. *Goals* Platt.

Referee R.L. Thomas (Oldham).

Frano Botica

St Helens 8 Wigan 13
Challenge Cup Final, Wembley
27 April 1991

Born 3 August 1963. Though initially not recommended for signing by Wigan's Aussie master coach John Monie, when he joined him at Central Park in May 1990, ex-All Black union half-back star Frano Botica became the cornerstone of his coach's quest for trophies. Hindered by New Zealand's long-serving stand off Grant Fox from adding to his seven Test caps in union, this former North Shore points-scoring phenomenon transferred his talents to the rugby league code in Britain and New Zealand and immediately set about rewriting the record books. Having become only the second Kiwi since the Second World War to play Test rugby at both union and league, following in the footsteps of Jimmy Haig in 1947–48, when he represented his country against both France and Australia in five Tests in 1991, Botica has since concentrated his attentions on the scene in Britain. And with amazing success. The club's achievement in winning four trophies in the 1992–93 season – the Championship, the Challenge Cup, the Regal Trophy and the Lancashire Cup – were, to a considerable extent, due to the shy Kiwi's prolific points-scoring talents. Having equalled the all-time record of goals in a major final, with ten goals in the Premiership final of 1992, the following season he proceeded to shatter the fastest-ever 1000-points record, achieving the total in March 1993 after playing in only 93 matches and smashed ex-Springbok full back Fred Griffiths' goals and points-scoring records in a season at Wigan with 184 goals and 423 points.

Seasoned professionals and fans have little appreciation of the pressures on a convert from the union code. The league star has invariably come up through the ranks, served his apprenticeship in the sport as a 16- or 17-year-old without too much attendant publicity, and succeeded or not after often gradual introductions at first-team level. Not so an international rugby union player, especially one as prominent in the world's sporting press as an All Black. And, despite whatever talents have been displayed in the 15-a-side game, there is no guarantee that the convert's talents will flourish in the professional code. There were to be no such fears surrounding ex-All Black half-back maestro Frano Botica, but, as he admits, even after a season's success the pressure to prove himself on his first trip to Wembley was still uppermost in his mind.

> I was on the world's stage and, coming from rugby union, I had so much to prove. Many ex-union players don't make it, many do. I didn't want to prove a failure; I wanted to succeed. Wembley capped off my first year in rugby league. The season had started off very slowly, but then, to finish with a big finale like the Challenge Cup final, was the dream start to my new career.

In the autumn of 1989 Botica had visited Britain as a member of the New Zealand rugby union squad on tour in Wales and Ireland and, though understudy to Grant Fox, impressed shrewd observers. Indeed, the then 26-year-old's abilities so impressed international referee Fred Howard, a former pupil of mine, in the All Blacks clash with Neath at the Gnoll in Wales that Howard immediately alerted me to his talents. The same speed off the mark, sharp footballing brain and calm approach to the game which helped to see off Neath's challenge were, 18 months later, to be the undoing of Wigan's greatest rivals and one of league's most glamorous sides, St. Helens. A fierce pride in his rugby prowess and the instinct to succeed in his new surroundings saw Botica cultivate, in his first season at Central Park, his greatest asset, and one which was to destroy the hopes of St. Helens and others on numerous occasions, his goalkicking.

> In union I rarely kicked at goal for the All Blacks as Grant Fox was considered to be the first-choice kicker. Whenever he wasn't playing, then John Gallagher and I used to toss up to see who had to take the kicks at goal. Neither of us wanted to kick, and I rarely ever practised at taking goalkicks. When I signed for Wigan, though, I realised that if I was to force my way into such a star-studded backline then I had to offer an asset others couldn't, and that was goalkicking.

With his skills sharpened and honed to suit the faster and more dynamic league code, and with his points-scoring prowess already on its way to eventually shattering records, Frano Botica, although nervous, was ready for the most important match of his league career.

> I'd watched the 1985 cup final on TV back home in New Zealand, when Wigan defeated Hull, and I never thought that I would, six years later, be playing for the club at Wembley. Suddenly I was a part of it, with all my family flying over from New Zealand and friends in London coming to the match. It meant so much to me to do well. I was so nervous beforehand, but just to be a part of a winning team against the

club's fiercest rivals was a fantastic moment for me.

Though Saints rallied strongly in the final quarter, taking a tired Wigan to the limit, the cup holders effectively sealed their rivals' fate in the opening 12 minutes, with Frano Botica, who helped himself to a try and two goals, proving the destroyer-in-chief. Any goalkicker making his first appearance at Wembley realises the value of an early shot at the posts: success can be such a stimulant, such an antidote to the nerves. Botica was to be handed such a chance when his fellow countryman, Saints loose forward Shane Cooper, conceded a penalty after questioning one of Halifax referee Jim Smith's decisions.

> The penalty goal in the opening minutes was awarded wide out, about ten metres in from touch. It was a fair distance, and there was terrific pressure on me to get us off to a good start. I wanted to take the goal attempt to help steady my nerves. As soon as the ball went over the crossbar it was a huge relief and the tension in me just went.

Under the coaching reins of Aussie supremo John Monie, Wigan were accustomed to launching a full-scale attack in the opening minutes of a big match, often hitting the opposition with every weapon in their armoury. Such an onslaught, designed to put players under immense pressure in the vulnerable period of the game, invariably found weaknesses or caused errors in the most professional of sides. Wigan's opening burst in the Silk Cut Challenge Cup final of 1991 provoked one such error and set them on the path to victory.

Wigan stand off Shaun Edwards, using to good effect the breezes that swirl around the vast Wembley arena, hoisted a towering kick in the direction of St. Helens' Australian full back Phil Veivers, and followed up at speed. As the Saints number one, having difficulty positioning himself under the falling ball, rose to catch the ball, there was a clash of heads between himself and Edwards, with the result that the ball spilled loose on to the turf. Quick thinking by powerful centre Kevin Iro, and a speedy pickup and transfer of the ball to wing David Myers, saw the Wigan youngster dive over at the corner for a try. This enforced error earned the eventual winners a 6–0 lead, but it was to be a piece of rugby artistry that was to hand Botica his try and conversion and give Wigan a 12-point lead in just 12 minutes.

From the 1920s and 1930s, when Charlie Seeling and Lance Todd thrilled the fans at Central Park, through the 1940s and 1950s and the era of Brian Nordgren and Cec Mountford, to the 1980s and 1990s, with Wigan skippers Graeme West and Dean Bell prominent, the Kiwi connection has remained strong. More recently, the club has signed ex-All Black winger Va'aiga

Tuigamala. And it was the Kiwi connection, with a dash of the best of British, which swung the game Wigan's way and provided Botica with his moments to remember.

The powerful Dean Bell sliced his way through a gap down the left-hand side of the pitch and immediately caused panic in the Saints ranks. Unable to make the tryline himself, Wigan's strong-running centre looked for support from Great Britain international second row Denis Betts who, like any alert running forward, found himself to the left of Bell and able to take the pass. As fast as Betts is, even he had to concede defeat to the St. Helens cover, and leave Kiwi Botica with the slimmest of chances at the corner.

That blistering burst of speed, first noticed by referee Howard at Neath, left Saints young wing star Alan Hunte floundering on Botica's inside while the speed again, allied to a steely determination, took him under Gary Connolly's despairing last-ditch tackle and over the line for a try. Pleasing for Botica but not for St. Helens youngsters.

When I scored, Alan Hunte thought I had been pushed into touch and he wasn't too happy about it. But I just gave him a little smile. Gary Connolly just missed me as I went over the tryline. I just managed to squeeze inside the corner flag.

The try was even more pleasing for the quiet, unassuming New Zealander for, as the photograph of the incident later revealed, he had proved himself in front of his friends.

The great thing about that try was that when I had the photo blown up I could see all of my mates with whom I used to play union in New Zealand sitting in the seats at the corner. They were there in the photo and that gave me greater pleasure than anything.

With his nerves steadied by the success of his first penalty shot at goal and his spirits buoyed by his first try at Wembley, Frano Botica was hardly likely to miss the conversion to the try no matter from where on the pitch it was to be taken. Striking the ball sweetly with his instep, he swung it around from the touchline and between the posts to the accompaniment of roars of delight from the cherry-and-white bedecked hordes on the terraces.

St. Helens refused to concede defeat and, indeed, Wigan's cheeky scrum half Andy Gregory, possibly anticipating such a reply from Saints, had calmly helped himself to a drop goal in the 47th minute of this pulsating final. Saints' Alan Hunte did redeem himself with a 63rd minute touchdown, and Paul Bishop's touchline conversion and penalty took them to within striking distance of their deadly rivals. But a squandering of possession by St. Helens at crucial stages in the final, hectic, tense minutes, and that Kiwi connection proved the difference between the two sides and sent the Challenge Cup back to Wigan's trophy cabinet for yet another year.

ST. HELENS Veivers; Hunte, Ropati, Loughlin, Quirk; Griffiths, Bishop; Neill, Dwyer, Ward, Harrison, Mann, Cooper. *Subs*: Connolly, Groves.

WIGAN Hampson; Myers, K. Iro, Bell, Botica; Edwards, Gregory; Lucas, Dermott, Platt, Betts, Clarke, Hanley. *Subs*: Goulding, Goodway.

Scorers St. Helens *Tries* Hunte. *Goals* Bishop (2).
Wigan   *Tries* Myers, Botica. *Goals* Botica (2). *Drop Goal* Gregory.

Referee Jim Smith (Halifax).

Phil Clarke

Australia 10 Great Britain 33
Second Test, Princes Park, Melbourne
26 June 1992

Born 16 May 1971. My much-adored predecessor on BBC television, commentator Eddie Waring, used to boast that he could call down any mineshaft around Castleford, Wakefield or Wigan and he could bring up a pack of rugby league forwards. Not any more: rather, he would have to stand outside the gates of a few of our leading educational establishments to seek out his forwards today. A product of Liverpool University, where he gained a BSc in Movement Science, Phil Clarke is more typical of the modern, successful all-running, all-tackling forward. At 6 feet and 15 stones, the son of Colin Clarke, a former Wigan and Great Britain hooker of the 1960s and 1970s, soon showed his mentors that he had the power and pace to grace the international stage and, within two years of leaving the amateur club Wigan St. Patricks, he made his international debut against Papua New Guinea in 1990. Selected for Great Britain's tour of Australia in the summer of 1992, he stepped into the boots of his predecessor in the number 13 role at Wigan, Lions skipper Ellery Hanley, when Hanley failed to recover from a serious hamstring problem and missed out on all three Ashes Tests. Such is Clarke's footballing ability and calm, assured control on a field that he looks destined to be a future captain of his country.

It all began at Newcastle. It all ended in Melbourne. At around 11 o'clock on a warm but wet night in Melbourne, Victoria, Wigan and Great Britain loose forward Phil Clarke sat stunned and staring into space as the team bus pulled out of Princes Park.

On the coach back to the hotel all was quiet, few people were talking. All the players were dwelling on the significance of what had happened. I'll never forget just looking out of the window and up at the sky, not really thinking about anything, just blank in my mind and staring into space. Probably I was shocked at what had happened.

Not only was the 21-year-old Great Britain forward shocked, so was the travelling army of over 8000 fans which accompanied the Lions at every

20

stage of the 1992 tour, so were millions of viewers and listeners back home in Britain who had sat enthralled at the team's stirring deeds, and especially so was the whole of Australia. Great Britain had annihilated the cream of that country's rugby-playing talent and spoiled the celebration party already planned in anticipation of yet another Ashes victory. Great Britain had routed Australia in an historic Test match at Princes Park, Melbourne, by 33–10 amid an atmosphere the likes of which I, as a commentator or as a player, and Phil Clarke have never experienced before.

The atmosphere throughout the match was incredible. You could hardly hear yourself speak for the din all around, and it was the British fans who were making all the noise. Over 8000 of them were dressed in red, white and blue, and they never stopped singing or shouting for us. It really spurred you on and gave a tingle down your spine. There was a marching band which arrived at the stadium all made up of lads from the north of England, and they blew their trumpets and banged their drums all night. It was almost a frightening atmosphere because so many relied on us to do well.

It was at Newcastle, only days before the Kangaroos' fall from grace in Melbourne that after only six minutes of play, Great Britain skipper Ellery Hanley, playing his first game of the tour, slipped out of a tackle, burst past a couple of defenders in midfield and passed to the Warrington half back Kevin Ellis, who was in support alongside. In typical Hanley fashion, the 'Black Pearl', as he is known Down Under, followed the tricky Welshman downfield eager for the return pass. When it came, a low one around his knees, Great Britain's number 13 was forced to stretch forward to catch the ball. He crumpled to the floor, clutched the back of his right thigh and felt for the troublesome hamstring which had been one of the causes to keep him out of the action for the previous five weeks. Ellery Hanley, supposedly the Lions' biggest threat to Australia's continued Ashes dominance, was out of the tour, out of the second Test at Melbourne and out of the papers – much to the relief of the accompanying press corps, who had been forced to listen to and comment on the endless verbal contortions of the management as they explained, daily, just why he had been unable to play since the plane left England on 20 May. Hanley's problems with his stress fracture of the foot, his hamstring trouble, his untimely flirtations with television commentating and his deteriorating relations with the media were over. The Great Britain captain was out of the action for Melbourne, and the heir apparent in the loose forward's jersey, Phil Clarke, was ready to step into the breach.

We had lost Sonny Nickle, Ian Lucas, Andy Gregory and Paul Loughlin through serious injury and all four were out of the tour. When Ellery went down injured there was an immediate feeling that the tour was

21

falling apart and that there was little we could do about it. Every one of the players had been looking forward to Ellery playing again; his presence on the field would have been a huge boost to us. But when he went down injured and we realised that he was out of the tour, then we realised that the second Test at Melbourne was going to be a backs-to-the-wall job.

And yet, after the Lions' Deryck Fox-inspired 22–0 win over the Newcastle Knights, the squad was in high spirits on arrival in Victoria the next day. Ellery Hanley left camp, and coach Mal Reilly reorganised his troops accordingly. Hull's goalkicking wing, Paul Eastwood, was restored to the right wing with Featherstone Rovers powerful young centre Paul Newlove moving into the midfield in place of the injured Paul Loughlin. Wigan's Shaun Edwards was given his chance at scrum half, the position he had favoured as a 16-year-old youngster on entering the game. Perhaps the boldest move on Reilly's part was the inclusion of Wigan's all-action forward Billy McGinty at the expense of his seasoned Test prop Lee Crooks to make up, for the first time in Ashes history, a six pack of forwards all from one club. Their impact on the game was to prove a telling factor, as was the impact of the Australian press who wrote off Great Britain's chances of a win and, in customary 'Pommie-bashing' style, proceeded to savage the reputations of many of the players in the British camp.

Having been beaten in the first Test at Sydney convincingly, all the Aussie press immediately labelled us as 'no hopers' again. They began to criticise us and write off our chances. That had a good effect on us because we wanted to answer them back with a good performance on the field and shut them up with a win. I think only the players in the Lions camp really believed we could win the Melbourne Test. The mood among the lads was very good as we approached the match.

The mood among the lads was even better after just 34 minutes' play as Great Britain led Australia by the amazing score of 22–0 and I was conscious that radio listeners at home in Britain might be turning their volume controls down a little as my voice began to rise a decibel or two. Heady times!

Unlike other pitches in New South Wales or Queensland, where the hot sun seems to bake the grounds, there was a thick covering of grass on the Princes Park pitch and, after a period of heavy rain, the conditions were like those experienced at St. Helens, Leeds or Widnes by the Great Britain players. The British players felt at home, while the Aussies, their ears bombarded by the chants and shouts from the British fans on the terraces, were in hostile country in their own land. The experiment of staging this second Test at the home of Australian Rules Football was not really welcomed by the Aussie players but, with a full house 30,257 crowd, it had proved a huge financial success.

The Wigan six, led by Andy Platt, Denis Betts and Clarke himself, commanded the early stages and set up such a dominance in midfield that, apart from a brief period after half time, they held Australia in a vice-like grip and were able to dictate just where on the pitch the game was to be played. That early territorial dominance and indiscipline from Australia brought the reliable Paul Eastwood two penalty goals and set the supporters in the mood for Phil Clarke's first try of the match.

In a fashion reminiscent of former Aussie loose forward Wayne Pearce's stirring burst and try in the first Test at Hull's Boothferry Park in 1982 which announced to the rugby world that we were to witness a new breed of player, so Clarke, ten years later, announced the same to a disbelieving Australian public. Receiving a pass from Great Britain back Daryl Powell, the tall, athletic number 13 shot forward, created a gap for himself by selling a huge dummy to the harassed Kangaroo defenders and powered between the attempted tackles of 17-stone giant forwards Paul Harragon and Paul Sironen. The tryline beckoned, but not before Wigan's young international experienced a few nervous moments.

The pitch at Princes Park was quite funny really, a difficult one for running. In the middle where there is a cricket square, it was rock hard and very flat, but out wide, where there was plenty of grass, it was very soft, wet and very greasy. The conditions were very slippery underfoot.

When I was about 15 yards from the tryline I thought how careful I must be to make sure I actually touched the ball down properly over the line. I was really frightened by the greasy conditions and dreaded ruining the tryscoring chance. Thankfully, I did get the ball over the tryline and I was mobbed by my team-mates. It was a marvellous feeling.

No doubt a marvellous feeling for father Colin, too, who had himself scored a memorable try at Wembley against the Kangaroo tourists in 1973.

Worse was to come for Australia when Wigan's lively half back Shaun Edwards, revelling in his scrum half role, kicked ahead over the heads of an Australian defence which had, on the outside, come up too fast on the wet, tricky turf. Strong-running centre Paul Newlove beat full back Ettingshausen to the ball for the score and gave Eastwood the opportunity for his fourth goal. Victory seemed assured after 34 minutes, when the slippery conditions underfoot again played into the British hands and skipper Garry Schofield pulled a trick from the top drawer of his repertoire. Again, a chip kick over the heads of a by-now mesmerised Australian defence saw the ball roll tantalisingly in the goal area to the side of the Australian posts. Full back Ettingshausen, unsure of the surface beneath him, raced to cover the slowly

moving ball, lost his footing and missed the ball completely. The eager Great
Britain skipper pounced and suddenly, following Eastwood's fifth successful
goal attempt, the Lions were coasting at 22–0.

Perhaps they were coasting, perhaps they did relax too much, for there
was no denying the strength of the Australian reply immediately after half
time, when crafty Kangaroo coach Bobby Fulton introduced his two
substitutes, play-makers Kevin Walters and Chris Johns. Tries from second
row star Bob Lindner and one from Johns himself, plus a Mal Meninga
conversion, and suddenly, as Phil Clarke insists, Australia were back in the
game.

> After half time the Australians really did hit us with everything. Kevin
> Walters moved the ball around the pitch much quicker than Jackson had
> done, and suddenly there was a little tiredness in one or two of us. We
> really were worried, as they had a superb spell for 20 minutes and pulled
> back to 22–10. Every bounce of the ball suddenly seemed to go their way,
> but the British forwards proved themselves in that 20 minutes.

The front row of Skerrett, Dermott and Platt helped to seal the middle and,
when called upon to help out, covered across field like thoroughbreds. Behind,
the speed men Denis Betts, Billy McGinty and Phil Clarke moved in quickly
with some ferocious tackles to stop Australia's powerful back row stars Bob
Lindner and Bradley Clyde from making the vital breaks down the flanks.
Coach Mal Reilly's gamble of selecting the Wigan six stood the test.

> I think the Wigan pack did the damage in the first half to the Australian
> forwards and then just tackled their hearts out after half time. Playing
> alongside my club colleagues gave me more confidence to try things. We
> knew each other's style of play, and we were all familiar with each other.
> Andy Platt and Martin Dermott never stopped running. It was a great
> effort and one which I think was needed to win the match.

Phil Clarke and company, much to the delight and relief of Britain's ecstatic
fans, had not quite completed their mauling of the Green and Golds. Wing
Martin Offiah sent pacy full back Graham Steadman racing down the touchline
with a short pass where his speed took him past the unfortunate Ettingshausen
and in for a try at the corner. Eastwood's magnificent touchline conversion
acted as the prelude to the Lions' final flourish, a combination between skipper
Schofield and Offiah which resulted in the former Rosslyn Park flyer stretching
his legs and racing over for his side's fifth try.

The celebrations began. The rattles, the bugles, the drums and the cymbals
shattered the ear-drums of the silent Australians glumly making for the exits.
Great Britain coach Mal Reilly, his assistant Phil Larder and tour manager

Maurice Lindsay could hardly contain their ever-widening grins. And nor should they, for the Lions tourists, in adversity, had carved out a win as unlikely as that fabled 'Rorkes Drift' Test back in 1914 when ten true Brits had held the thin red, white and blue line to stave off certain defeat. Great Britain, achieving only their third Test win against Australia in 10 years, had produced a performance which would be the subject of bar-room gossip for years, and a performance whose importance the players were well aware of.

Australia had been so confident of wrapping up the Ashes series they had even planned a celebratory party back at their hotel in the centre of Melbourne. When you have lost consistently to them over a long period you begin to get doubts of yourself at the back of your mind. I was proud to win.

After the match in the dressing room, I was sat next to Joe Lydon who'd played seven or eight times against Australia and had never been once on the winning side. It really struck home to me in the dressing room how important the win was for British rugby, its fans and especially for us, the players. I was really proud that night.

AUSTRALIA Ettingshausen; Wishart, Daley, Meninga, Hancock; Jackson, Langer; Gillespie, S. Walters, Harragon, Sironen, Lindner, Clyde. *Subs*: Mackay, Lazarus, C. Johns, K. Walters.

GREAT BRITAIN Steadman; Eastwood, Newlove, Powell, Offiah; Schofield, Edwards; Skerrett, Dermott, Platt, Betts, McGinty, Clarke. *Subs*: Connolly, Hulme, Lydon, Harrison.

Scorers Australia   *Tries* Lindner, Johns. *Goals* Meninga.
            Great Britain *Tries* Clarke, Schofield, Steadman, Newlove, Offiah.
                          Goals Eastwood (6). *Drop Goals* Schofield.

Referee Dennis Hale (New Zealand).

Bradley Clyde

Canberra 19 Balmain 14
Premiership Grand Final, Sydney Football Stadium
24 September 1989

Born 27 January 1970. Former St. George loose forward John Raper is rightly acknowledged to be the greatest forward ever to wear the Kangaroos' number 13 jersey. As testimony to the prowess of the current occupant of the jersey, Canberra Raiders' Bradley Clyde, is the comparison now made between the two all-action Aussie forwards. And, at the tender age of just 24 years, the powerful Clyde is considered favourably in any estimation of the two players' abilities.

The dynamic, speedy loose forward burst on to the scene in 1988 following a successful career with the New South Wales Under-16s side and amateur outfit Belconnen United. His early career as a centre gave him that extra yard of pace and the superior handling skills which distinguish him from other loose forwards. His performances in the Grand Finals of 1989 and 1991, within a mere three years of making his debut for the Raiders, proved just what an extraordinary talent Canberra had unearthed. His work-rate in defence, his appetite for running with the ball and his ability to pass out of the tackle to a colleague better placed than himself have proved more than an irritant to Great Britain in Ashes Test battles. Sadly for the Lions, Bradley Clyde looks set to be around to torment them for many more years to come.

Bradley Clyde's choice of his most memorable game is one he probably shares with thousands upon thousands of Australian rugby league fans. The 1989 Grand Final, which saw Canberra clinch its first premiership, is generally regarded Down Under as the greatest title decider of all time.

When Canberra were admitted to the then Sydney competition in 1982, rugby league was the second or third most popular sport in the capital, behind rugby union and Australian Rules. A planned city built around an artificial lake, Canberra was created at the beginning of the century as a 'neutral' seat of power half-way between Melbourne and Sydney. It was regarded by most Australians as the sterile inland abode of politicians and public servants.

The Raiders registered eight competition points in their first season, with a team of unfashionable players unwanted by other clubs. As Clyde, who was just 19 in 1989, said:

* * *

I remember going out as a young guy and watching the Canberra Raiders get flogged. Back then, I remember sitting on the bus going home and people were talking about the Canberra Faders because they'd be great for the first 20 and then die in the final 20 minutes.

Under co-coaches Don Furner and Wayne Bennett, however, the Raiders began to stir in 1987 and made a fairy-tale run to the last Grand Final at the Sydney Cricket Ground, where they were beaten 18–8 by big-name Manly. Showing it was no fluke, the 'green machine' qualified for the semi-finals again the following year, under new coach Tim Sheens.

In 1989 the Raiders did even better – but not before being forced into a situation whereby they would have to win nine successive games to take home the Winfield Cup. A mid-season Australian tour of New Zealand had depleted them severely, and they registered three successive losses while Mal Meninga, Gary Belcher, Clyde and Kiwi prop Brent Todd were away.

Teenager Clyde had taken the league world by storm. Selected by New South Wales in only his second year of top-flight rugby, he had won the Australian loose forward's shirt and come back from New Zealand as player of the tour.

The Raiders finished fourth at the end of the regular season, a position from which no team, since the introduction of Grand Finals in 1954, had won the premiership. Ahead of them were first-placed South Sydney, having enjoyed their most successful season in 20 years, Penrith and third-placed Balmain.

Despite their guile, attacking flair (Canberra were easily the season's best attacking team with 97 tries) and courage first to scrape into the semi-finals and then to make the decider, the Raiders were outsiders on the biggest day of the rugby league year. Eight wins in a row was meritorious, but a ninth was considered unlikely.

The week prior to the game, we were given no chance. We were well and truly the underdogs, and I think that really gave us an inspiration.

A lot of the press wrote us off because we had a pretty inexperienced side. Some of the players in the team were Laurie Daley, myself, Matthew Wood, Paul Martin . . . we were guys who were new to this big-time football stuff.

But we kind of took it on the chin. Our forwards particularly were given a pretty hard time because (they said) we weren't a dominant forward pack.

I don't think the people around respected our forward pack enough, and that's why I think we got to the Grand Final. Players like Gary Coyne and Dean Lance were doing the job for us and doing it well.

27

* * *

Canberra's comparative isolation, some 180 miles south-west of Sydney, threw up still more hurdles in Grand Final week.

> We had to leave town on Thursday before the Sunday game because the Grand Final breakfast was held in Sydney first thing Friday morning, around 7.30, so there was no use us going back to Canberra and then returning on the Saturday or the Sunday morning.
> We stayed up there from Thursday night. It really disrupted our preparation, but we had to do that in 1990 and also in 1991, so we've sort of got used to it now.

Balmain, with tough experienced forwards like Steve Roach, Paul Sironen and Ben Elias, were expected to intimidate the 'baby' Raiders, but it was the underdogs who played the more committed, organised rugby from the kickoff, in front of a capacity 40,500 crowd.

Referee Bill Harrigan penalised the Tigers three times in the opening minutes, with Canberra skipper Mal Meninga missing an early penalty shot after Kiwi Gary Freeman was spotted swinging an arm at the Test stalwart. Widnes centre Andy Currier, guesting for the Sydney team, opened the scoring after seven minutes with a penalty goal, Canberra winger John Ferguson having been found guilty of holding down a tackled player.

At the 13-minute mark, a loose pass from Todd was gleefully scooped up, one-handed, by Balmain's former Wallaby winger James Grant. He had a clear run to the line, scoring near the corner to give his side a 6–0 lead. Clyde recalls the opening exchanges:

> Well, everyone I've ever spoken to [about that period] thought that we were achieving what we went out there to do. That was to get on top of the Balmain Tigers in the first 20 minutes. We felt as though we were doing that, but the scoreboard didn't say so. Then Paul Sironen went over and scored a good try and luck certainly wasn't going our way.

Canberra had registered two points in the 27th minute through a Meninga penalty goal, but Sironen's touchdown – which all but silenced the Canberra section of the crowd – was another imbued with plenty of luck.

A minute from half time, Roach put Currier into the clear, and the British Test star kicked infield as the cover defence hauled him in. A horrible bounce meant the ball completely evaded Belcher, and Grant combined with Currier to send Sironen storming over the tryline. With Currier's conversion it was 12–2 at the break – a deficit which appeared to have the Winfield Cup already on its way to Leichhardt.

* * *

One thing I distinctly remember was the feeling in the dressing room at half time. I remember it so clearly; everyone sat down and said, 'We'll win this, we can still win this'. We were 12–2 down and we all felt as though we could win it.

A team being down 12–2 in a Grand Final has got to show some character, and I sort of felt something in the dressing room. I don't know what it was, but there was a bit of hope, I suppose.

The game had already been dramatic, but after half time it began to take the shape of an epic. Balmain forward Bruce McGuire was contentiously penalised for obstruction with 26 minutes remaining, and Raiders half back Ricky Stuart soon after passed out wide to Ferguson, who darted back infield and unloaded to Gary Belcher, who scored a converted touchdown.

With their lead cut to 12–8, it was at this stage that Balmain had a series of golden opportunities to win their first Premiership in 20 years. Skipper Wayne Pearce dropped the ball with Tim Brasher unmarked outside him. Coach Warren Ryan replaced Roach, a decision which remains controversial to this day. At 14–8, after a Currier penalty, Elias first had his drop goal attempt charged down, and then another shot rebounded off the crossbar. The width of the post helped determine the outcome.

I didn't remember it at the time because I was concentrating too much on the game and different things going on around, but watching the video I think the turning point was the ankle tap on Michael Neil by Mal Meninga. If they had scored, it would have been 'shut the gate'. But we worked the ball out of our own 22 then and got the ball down the other end to score a try.

Ryan came up with another substitute gamble when he hauled off Sironen with five minutes remaining, sending out controversial utility Michael Pobjie. With only 90 seconds to go and the crowd at fever pitch, a kick from Canberra stand off Chris O'Sullivan bounced off Garry Jack into the arms of a half-lame Laurie Daley. A looping pass to Ferguson allowed him to skirt inside Neil and touch down triumphantly.

At that stage I still wasn't quite sure of the score! When John scored the try, I sort of wasn't over the moon. I think all the other guys were aware of the score, but I still wasn't quite sure. I remember the players punching the air, and it was only then that I looked up at the scoreboard.

Meninga converted. Full time: Balmain 14, Canberra 14.

I remember distinctly, also, going into extra time, all of our guys just felt so strong. I know I felt *really* strong and really hungry when we went into extra time, and I remember looking over at the Balmain boys and they were defeated then.

As the game moved into extra time, Meninga missed with a penalty attempt, and Ricky Stuart was almost successful with a 45-yard drop goal shot. Six minutes into the first of two ten-minute overtime periods, Balmain's Test full back Garry Jack knocked on. From the ensuing scrum win, O'Sullivan piloted a drop goal between the posts and – after 86 minutes – Canberra had the lead for the first time.

When Sully put it over, I think that gave us a sort of mental edge. Everyone was just dead tired, but they kept themselves going, and when you get to that situation – one point in front – you might as well be 20 points in front because of the fatigue factor.

Ryan put Wigan prodigy Shaun Edwards into the game for the final ten minutes in a desperate attempt to post a try, but nerve-racking breaks by Pearce and Brasher were swiftly cut off by the determined Raiders. In the 97th action-packed minute of the 1989 Grand Final, unknown Queenslander Steve Jackson supported Meninga in what looked to be a regulation 'hit-up' close to the Balmain tryline.

I remember I was probably 15 metres behind him, and he took the ball and I saw him beat one tackle and I thought, 'I'll set myself for the next ruck', because I gave him no chance. Then I saw him stick that arm out and stick the ball over the line and . . . jeez, I was happy! I was just tickled pink.

The Raiders players and supporters erupted. They had won their first title, they had become the first team ever to win from fourth, they had become the first team from outside Sydney to take the prize and they had completed the most remarkable comeback in Grand Final history.

Clyde, the youngest-ever Grand Final player, says the celebrations 'started straight away'.

We flew home to a reception that was just unbelievable. There were people everywhere at the airport, there was champagne everywhere . . . I've never been a really big drinker, but I really hooked into it that night. The morning after, we had a car-cade and I'll always remember that, because the Canberra people lined the streets and we rode in various prestige vintage cars. They took us to a civic reception.

Having made their mark on the Winfield Cup competition, celebrating

Canberra players proceeded to make an albeit accidental mark on the cup itself. Really a statuette, the trophy features all-time great Arthur Summons and Norm Provan in an embrace following the 1963 Grand Final.

> We were loading the Winfield Cup on to one of the old vintage cars and one of the guys dropped it. Old Arthur Summons only had one arm there for a little while!

Aside from being the most dramatic Grand Final of all time, it had been probably the most significant. Along with vindicating the league's expansionary policy, it was put forward that Canberra now 'had a soul'. The 250,000-population city was now known for more than just taxes and parliamentary bickering.

> Canberra was seen by most of the Australian public as a government sort of a town and a town where politicians hang out. But now it's got something else. I know a lot of people and a lot of the true Canberrans, they're happy that the Raiders are a successful rugby league team because it gives them a bit of ammunition when people from other places knock the place. The people, everyone you speak to, pretty well follow the same team and they become very loyal, and if you're not talking about the Canberra Raiders on a Monday morning when you go into work, then you're a no one.

If Penrith, more than an hour from Sydney, is to be regarded as a satellite town rather than a suburb, then the cup has never returned to the city since the Raiders' epic win. And with North Queensland, Auckland, Perth and a second Brisbane team joining the league in 1995, the prospect of more hit-and-run 'raids' on Grand Final day is greater than ever.

> I feel you've got to take the game to the people and the New South Wales Rugby League has done the right thing by including the new teams coming in in 1995 because it's doing exactly that – taking the game to the people and creating more interest in the game, and more people are going to be touched by the game.

Reflecting on the reasons for Balmain's loss after taking such control of the Grand Final in the first half, Clyde says the Tigers were perhaps victims of their own niggling tactics.

> When we played Balmain in 1989, I remember we were playing blokes like 'Blocker' Roach and Paul Sironen and those guys had been around for a long time. They weren't going to risk giving away a penalty or anything like that, but at the same time . . . there was always a bit of roughing up

31

tactics from Balmain whenever I played them. It doesn't happen now, but back in 1989 and 1990 I always felt that.

They probably tried to rough us up and put us off our game, obviously. For some of the players who were in the Balmain team, it was just a part of their nature of play. They played the game aggressively and, I'd say now, obviously a bit too aggressively. I think they probably put themselves off the game. They could have been actually concentrating on their own performance a little bit more instead of worrying about the other stuff.

And what of his own performance on the final Sunday of September 1989?

I remember going into the game thinking, 'I really want to have a great game'. Not just a good game, I really wanted to play well. I thought I played OK. I worked pretty hard all day. I don't believe I played my best game all year, though. The gaps didn't really open up for me or anything like that. I was involved in a couple of breaks, but I just got in there and worked hard and tried to gain as many yards as I could when I did have the ball.

A panel of some of Australian rugby's greatest-ever players disagreed with Clyde's modest assessment. They awarded the 19-year-old dynamo the Clive Churchill Medal as player of the match.

CANBERRA Belcher; Wood, Meninga, Daley, Ferguson; O'Sullivan, Stuart; Todd, S. Walters, Lazarus, Coyne, Lance, Clyde. *Subs*: Martin, K. Walters, Jackson.

BALMAIN Jack; Grant, Brasher, Currier, O'Brien; Neil, Freeman; Roach, Elias, Edmed, Sironen, McGuire, Pearce. *Subs*: Hardwick, Pobjie, Edwards.

Scorers   Canberra   *Tries* Belcher, Ferguson, Jackson. *Goals* Meninga (3).
                          Drop Goals O'Sullivan.
             Balmain   *Tries* Grant, Sironen. *Goals* Currier (3).

Referee Bill Harrigan.

32

Shane Cooper

St. Helens 16 Widnes 14
Challenge Cup Semi-Final, Central Park, Wigan
11 March 1989

Born 26 May 1960. Since making his debut for St. Helens in October 1977, Kiwi Shane Cooper, whether at loose forward or at half back, has directed Saints' attack and marshalled their defence with the calm authority of an outstanding skipper. Though hardly blessed with speed, the former Mangere East, Auckland, and New Zealand Test star revealed such ball-handling skills, such a fine co-ordination between hand and eye and such a shrewd rugby brain that, within 12 months of his arrival at Knowsley Road, the quiet but confident ball artist had captured both team and personal honours. In January 1988 he helped Saints win the John Player Trophy final with a narrow 15–14 defeat of Leeds and, a month later, illustrated his ability to ghost through the narrowest of gaps with a club record-equalling six tries in a match for St. Helens against Hull. A tourist to Great Britain with the Kiwis in 1985 and a member of New Zealand's World Cup final squad against Australia in 1987, Cooper has never been blessed with a powerful physique, standing 5 feet 10 inches and weighing a mere 13½ stones, but, for the past ten seasons, he has proved himself to be one of the most stylish footballers to grace the 13-a-side code.

Outstanding matchwinning tries, long-range goals kicked in the face of a gale, or last-ditch cover tackles usually spring to mind when players reflect on the highlights of their careers. Matches won when their team was the underdog or a challenge achieved against crippling odds are frequently cited by players as reasons for cherishing games and performances of the past. Occasionally, as with St. Helens' Kiwi skipper Shane Cooper, a game lingers long in the memory purely for what it leads to or for what pleasure and satisfaction it brings to one's family. Such a game was Saints' Challenge Cup semi-final clash with hot favourites Widnes in March 1989. For, amid the wild celebrations in the St. Helens dressing room, skipper Cooper was able to appreciate the intense satisfaction the result gave him and acknowledge his pride in his family 12,000 miles away in New Zealand.

At the final whistle, sitting in the dressing room, the actual match meant very little to me, but there was the sheer joy of reaching Wembley for the first time. For the only time in my life I felt homesick after the match for my family back home in Auckland. I had more than a touch of sadness, but I was overjoyed as well. I felt really emotional for my family and friends back home, a feeling of having done it all for them.

Superb wins in the earlier rounds over strongly fancied Yorkshire sides, Leeds and Castleford, had alerted the bookmakers to Widnes's impressive form and the Cheshire side were immediately installed as favourites to land the Challenge Cup. St. Helens, by contrast, had struggled in the opening ties to dispose of lowly opposition Swinton and Barrow, and few expected them to trouble the Chemics too much before a 17,119 crowd at Central Park. Further woe hit the Saints prior to kickoff when their overseas imports, Australian Test stars Paul Vautin and Michael O'Connor, were refused permission by Manly to return from Down Under and take part in the match. In a reshuffled side, Shane Cooper was switched from half back to loose forward, a position in which, in recent seasons, he has excelled.

We suffered a huge blow when Paul Vautin and Michael O'Connor were not allowed to join us for the semi-final. We had to reshuffle the side and, as we didn't have any great depth in our squad, we were a little shorthanded. Widnes were so strong that their coach, Doug Laughton, could afford to leave their record Welsh union capture Jonathan Davies in the grandstand and keep Kurt Sorensen on the substitutes' bench. We really were up against it.

Favourites, however, often have a habit of coming unstuck and, as happened in the 19th minute of this pulsating battle, when the gods above look unfavourably on their subjects down below there is little that can be done to avoid the eventual outcome. Widnes fans, forgetful of St. Helens' sharp, attacking play and eye for a chance, have long insisted that fate or referee John Holdsworth cost them a trip to Wembley and gave Alex Murphy's men the spoils. The controversial dismissal of Widnes loose forward Richie Eyres by the Kippax whistler following a trip on Saints half-back star Neil Holding certainly proved a turning point in the match and cost Widnes any hope of toppling Saints. But an early try from Saints' Cumbrian wing Les Quirk had already illustrated that Saints' expansive style of running and handling might, in the end, prove disastrous for the favourites. And, as Cooper points out, 12 men often have a habit of refusing to lie down.

The dismissal of Richie Eyres was a big blow to Widnes, but I never felt any more confident at having an extra man. Twelve men often raise their performance and can cause upsets, especially in a cup tie when everything is at stake and everyone is trying to play the game of their life.

For 58 minutes Widnes did indeed defy the odds and, with just three minutes of the match remaining, thanks to tries from Darren Wright and David Hulme, and three goals from powerful centre Andy Currier in reply to touchdowns from Les Quirk and scrum half Darren Bloor, plus two Paul Loughlin goals, led by 14–12. Indeed, it was St. Helens' defence which was under constant attack, and it was rugby's most prolific tryscorer Martin Offiah who was testing its resolve and threatening to kill off any threat to Widnes's return to Wembley.

> Widnes attacked strongly in the second half, despite the loss of Eyres, and I can remember having to move across the field to tackle Offiah twice – a feat I rarely ever achieved. But perhaps the tackle of the match was that of Gary Connolly on Offiah when he stopped him in full flight for the corner with a tremendous cover tackle. That one tackle, late in the game, kept us in the match and somehow proved the turning point for us.

With Shane Cooper leading from the front, darting forward to the heart of the Widnes defence and displaying his full repertoire of passing skills, Saints moved ominously upfield. Widnes fans looked hopefully to their watches, only to see three minutes remaining to full time. And suddenly Saints struck with a piece of rugby that characterises the club's attacking attitude and open style of play, so long admired by their rivals. Hooker Paul Groves, neglecting all calls for the ball, strode away on his own from the acting half-back position and, throwing a huge dummy at the Widnes cover, raced through a gap. His long pass to wing Quirk allowed the Saints flyer to scamper over at the left-hand corner for a try, and Cooper's dream of a Wembley appearance was a reality. But not before the longest couple of minutes in his rugby life was played out in full.

> Throughout the match I never thought at any stage that we had won it. At no time did I ever feel safe, but I always thought that, when we went behind, if we got a break we could do it. The final couple of minutes were the longest and most nerve-racking of my life. Following the try we didn't do well from the kickoff. The ball was passed back hurriedly to me, and suddenly we were back on our heels and under pressure. But we held on to win. It was the most emotional and draining game I've ever played in.

Two-try Les Quirk proved the Saints hero in the Sunday newspapers' sporting columns the next day, but the quiet man Cooper had held the side together whenever a defiant 12-man Widnes sensed victory. His shrewd distribution under pressure and, in his role of defensive sweeper, his cover tackles, especially those on Offiah, had cut out Widnes's most promising attacks. The cool Kiwi had every reason to think of his family back home in New Zealand after this tense derby cup battle. Both he, and they watching on television, could reflect on a job well done.

ST. HELENS Connolly; Tanner, Veivers, Loughlin, Quirk; Holding, Bloor; Burke, Groves, Forber, Haggerty, Harrison, Cooper. *Subs*: Bailey, Jones.

WIDNES Tait; Thackray, Currier, Wright, Offiah; D. Hulme, P. Hulme; Grima, McKenzie, Pyke, M. O'Neill, Koloto, Eyres. *Subs*: Dowd, Sorensen.

Scorers St. Helens *Tries* Quirk (2), Bloor. *Goals* Loughlin (2).
Widnes *Tries* Wright, D. Hulme. *Goals* Currier (3).

Referee John Holdsworth (Kippax).

Lee Crooks

Hull 18 Widnes 9

Challenge Cup Final Replay, Elland Road, Leeds
19 May 1982

Born 18 September 1963. Young prodigies who, like Lee Crooks, have achieved every honour the game can offer them by the age of 19, often have a habit of burning themselves out by their mid-20s. Not so with this genial prop forward who, though captain of Great Britain Colts tour to Australia in 1987 within 12 months of joining Hull as a 17-year-old, a Challenge Cup final medal winner the same year and the youngest-ever forward at 19 years and 42 days to pack down in a Test match against Australia, has continued to give stalwart service to Castleford in recent seasons. Campaigns with Hull and Leeds in the 1980s and especially his then world record transfer move for £172,500 to Headingley bear testimony to Crooks' reputation as a pack leader, as do his summer stints Down Under with top Sydney league clubs Western Suburbs and Balmain. Having toured overseas with Great Britain in 1984 and 1988 and then been discarded for the trip to Papua New Guinea and New Zealand in 1990, Crooks, under the shrewd guidance of Castleford's Aussie coach Darryl Van de Velde, following his £150,000 move to Wheldon Road from Leeds, recaptured his best form and returned to the international fold for the 1992 Lions tour.

Eighteen-year-old Hull pack star Lee Crooks hardly shared my feelings at the 14–14 draw in the 1982 Challenge Cup final clash between Hull and Widnes. For weeks, in preparation for my first-ever BBC television commentary of a Challenge Cup final, I had noted all the records surrounding whichever team won, had complete biographies of the winning captains, and had an endless store of trivia in my mind ready to accompany the customary lap of honour by the eventual winners. A draw, with no presentation of the cup, and no lap of honour by the winners, deflated all my plans for the finale to *Grandstand*'s presentation. But the draw proved a blessing for Hull's teenage substitute, Lee Crooks, and launched him on the path to a glittering career.

On the Wednesday following the Wembley final, the area around Elland Road, home of Leeds United soccer club, was a mass of black and white as Hull and Widnes fans, clad in the same colours, arrived for only the third replay in the history of the Challenge Cup final. The M62 was congested with traffic, both east and west, as 41,171 lucky fans fought their way inside the stadium, with many thousands locked outside. The atmosphere for a teenager in his first season with Hull was electric.

> In the Wembley final I came on the field very late into the match as a substitute, and although the Wembley final was a great occasion I didn't really have time to absorb it. I was sat on the bench for a long time and I didn't really think I would ever get a chance. When I did come on, I was just plunged into the action straightaway with no chance to think of the significance or the importance of the occasion.
>   At Elland Road it was different. I had been selected to play from the start, and as we approached the stadium in the coach my knees started knocking. The atmosphere was electric. I was very nervous, far more than I had been at Wembley.

Widnes, visitors to Wembley five times in the previous seven seasons, and winners on three occasions, were worthy favourites to win the replay. The bookmakers, well aware of Chemics matchwinners Mick Burke, Lance Todd winner Eddie Cunningham and Mick Adams, considered that the lads from Humberside had been lucky to force a replay and would be made to concede defeat in Leeds. Not so Lee Crooks and his colleagues.

> The build-up to the replay was so big that it got to all of the players. Everybody had written us off. They said we would be too slow in the pack to hold Widnes because we had three props among our six forwards in Charlie Stone, Trevor Skerrett and Keith Tindall. They did have some great players, but we did dominate the midfield and our coach, Arthur Bunting, made some shrewd changes.

James Leuluai, the classy New Zealand Maori centre, returned to the midfield as partner to the ageing but experienced Clive Sullivan on the wing, and crafty scrum half Tony Dean was restored to the number seven jersey. In the pack Keith Tindall and hooker Tony Duke came into the front row, and ex-Ainsthorpe Youth Club protégé Lee Crooks was given his chance in the second row of a set of six forwards which, though lacking in pace, lacked nothing in skill and experience.

The Hull pack dominated the match and created sufficient space and secured such possession to allow their gifted backs, David Topliss, James Leuluai, Gary Kemble and former Great Britain skipper Clive Sullivan, to flourish. Scrum half Tony Dean, with his short defence-splitting passes and his busy approach in midfield, proved the dynamo behind the Hull six, prodding them ever forward and always on-hand to keep the movement going when either

Charlie Stone, Steve Norton or Lee Crooks were stopped. It was he who provided the pass for one of the finest tries ever executed in a Cup final, a magnificent scissors movement between Leuluai, Topliss and full back Kemble which resulted in the first of two tries for stand off Topliss.

The pass from Dean to Topliss proved so swift from the base of the scrum that the Hull stand off was able to pass to Kiwi international Leuluai and run around him for the return pass before the Widnes centres had time to move in defence. A surging run on to the ball from full back by Gary Kemble provided Topliss with the space he needed to use his undoubted speed and score a classic try.

The try from David Topliss in the first half was such a superb effort that it raised everybody's spirits. It was a perfectly executed scissors movement with Gary Kemble doing a good job from full back of dragging their full back and stand off infield and giving Dave Topliss oceans of room in which to score. Our pack was on top, and I knew then that we could win the match if we kept our heads up front.

David Topliss himself was confident that the 18-year-old Crooks and his pack colleagues would have little difficulty in doing just that:

From early season training I could see that Lee was destined for great things. As a rugby league player he was so mature for one so young. You get a feeling with a player, and I knew early on that Lee would be something special. He had an old head on young shoulders and seemed to know just what to do, and he was never afraid of doing it – as he proved in the match when he later scored from the acting half-back position.

We got on top of Widnes because Lee and the pack dominated the game up front and gave the backs behind such a good platform from which to work.

Widnes, who, in the 1970s and the early 1980s, were known as the 'Cup Kings' for their frequent visits to Wembley, were, however, well aware of the demands of cup rugby. Thanks to a try on the wing from Stuart Wright and three Mick Burke goals, they had kept themselves well in the game, though trailing, with seven minutes remaining, by 13–9. Crooks, casting aside his nerves, had added two goals to Topliss's first-half try, and Kemble, and Topliss again, had kept the momentum going for Hull with further touchdowns. But still the vast army of supporters from Humberside could not count on their first Challenge Cup final victory since 1914. Watches were checked, injury time was added on, but with seven minutes left to play and with just four points difference between the two sides there was a distinctly nervous feeling among the Hull fans. At that time, in the 73rd minute, teenager Crooks announced his arrival at the Boulevard, and sent at least 20,000 Hull fans in the crowd delirious with delight. He scored the match-clinching try and gave Hull the Challenge Cup for only the second time in the club's history.

> Our forwards had driven the ball towards the Widnes posts at the top end of the Elland Road ground. There was a huge noise at that end as most of our supporters were massed on the terraces behind the posts. I can remember moving in to the acting half-back position behind Charlie Stone, who was playing the ball. I took a gamble and just ran away from the acting half-back position. The gap opened up before me, I ran, and then just dived over the tryline beneath the posts. It was a tremendous feeling to run under the posts and put the ball down for a try in front of thousands of Hull fans.

The conversion was still to come, but with the match now almost beyond doubt in Hull's favour the 18-year-old Crooks relished the opportunity to bring his points tally to nine in the match with a well-taken goal. A resounding thud of the ball from the 16-stone, 6 feet 1 inch teenager and, at 18–9, Hull had won the cup. Amid the celebrations and the pandemonium that broke loose on the pitch as the Hull players prepared to receive their medals, a poignant moment touched Crooks more than anything else during or after the match.

> To play well and score a try and three goals was a great thrill so early in my career, but an even greater thrill was that the first person to come and congratulate me was Clive Sullivan. It was perhaps fitting that the oldest man on the field, Clive, should congratulate the youngest. He had been a hero of mine as a kid, and the moment will always stick in my mind.

Many teenagers hit the headlines only to see their true ability fail to live up to the early adulation of a particularly outstanding performance. Many lack the application to set alongside their undoubted skills, and many simply cannot face the weekly grind of training and the stresses that total dedication to a sport can bring.

As he proved in this replay thriller, even from a very early age Hull's teenage forward had a huge appetite for rugby, an even bigger appetite for the physical confrontation of the game, and a tactical awareness second to none. His fierce driving runs at the heart of the Widnes forwards continually gave Hull the momentum for launching an attack, while his enthusiasm for tackling upset the plans of the Widnes pack. Above all, his tactical kicking to touch and his sleight of hand passing to a better-placed colleague revealed the class and timing that were to make him an international forward for the past 12 years. His performance at Elland Road more than justified the confidence David Topliss had in him when his dynamic early season form looked to be slipping away. As Topliss said:

> After the first two months of the season, Lee began to struggle a little and he lost some of his form. Just before we were due to play against Leeds, our coach Arthur Bunting pulled me to one side in training and asked me if I thought that we might be pushing him too hard too early.
>
> I persuaded Arthur to keep playing him in the first team and, against Leeds, he had a blinder and never looked back. I knew he had it in him to pull it out when we were up against it or when the pressure was on the team. He did that at Elland Road.

Lee Crooks, to his benefit, enjoys his rugby and the atmosphere that often goes with the big occasions. As one who has accompanied Lee Down Under on Lions tours I can vouch for the fact that he can relax off the field with the best, a feature of his career begun after the Elland Road triumph and one that has allowed him to be one of the world's leading forwards for the past 12 years.

> After the win we had a big drink in Leeds. It was a real old-fashioned celebration, and we stayed in Leeds all night. We were a team that really liked to enjoy ourselves and we did just that.

And so did the grateful Hull fans.

HULL Kemble; Sullivan, Leuluai, Evans, Prendiville; Topliss, Dean; Tindall, Duke, Stone, Skerrett, Crooks, Norton. *Subs*: Day, Crane.

WIDNES Burke; Wright, O'Loughlin, Cunningham, Basnett; Hughes, Gregory; M. O'Neill, Elwell, Lockwood, L. Gorley, Prescott, Adams. *Subs*: A. Myler, F. Whitfield.

Scorers Hull — *Tries* Kemble, Topliss (2), Crooks. *Goals* Crooks (3).
  Widnes — *Tries* Wright. *Goals* Burke (3).

Referee Fred Lindop (Wakefield).

Paul Cullen

Sheffield Eagles 8 Warrington 12
Tattersfield Stadium, Doncaster
7 January 1990

Born 4 March 1963. Under the current contract system operating in rugby league, few players are awarded a testimonial for ten seasons' play with one club and even fewer players reach the end of their careers having seen service with just one team. The tendency is for the best players to seek ever more lucrative two- and three-year contracts or for clubs to cut their losses and sell when a player is failing to produce the goods. Paul Cullen is that rarity who has seen 13 unbroken seasons at Wilderspool with Warrington. Whether as centre or, in recent years, loose forward, he has served the club well and, despite achieving only representative honours with Lancashire, he has regularly outshone many of the star names around him.

Signed in 1980 by Warrington as a 10½-stone stand off from local amateurs Crossfield Recs, Cullen quickly made a reputation for himself as a fierce tackler and a shrewd footballer. Sadly, for all his success with Warrington, his progress as a centre was hindered by a serious spate of injuries to his ankles and his knees, injuries that caused him to think seriously about his playing future. The switch from the backs to the forwards in 1990 and his increase in bulk to 15½ stones gave him a new lease of life and helped him become one of the most respected back row forwards in the game.

Rugby league can be a brutal game. Few sports are so demanding on the player's body where, especially in the forwards, the bumps and bruises can inflict such damage on bones, muscles and ligaments. Thirty or forty bone-crunching tackles made in a match, a dozen or so powerful bursts down the middle of the pitch, and endless driving of the ball out of defence against a wall of tacklers can leave a player grateful for the warmth and soothing effects of the after-match bath. But, even worse, despite the advances in surgery and physiotherapy, such is the effect of the impact of this high-speed collision sport that many players are forced out of the game and into retirement early in their careers. Warrington's lively centre Paul Cullen faced such a fate when he realised that a series of injuries pointed to the end of his career.

Such were Cullen's difficulties in training and such was his loss of pace

42

that, at the turn of the New Year in 1990, the then 26-year-old Warrington centre faced a bleak future.

> A series of injuries to my ankle ligaments and operations on the cruciate ligaments in my left knee cut down my pace and hindered my sprint training. The pain in my knee was so bad that I couldn't put in all the sprint schedules in training that I needed. I was never the fastest of players, and all the pace that I had was all manufactured on the sprint track.
>
> I knew that, in the centre, I couldn't compete with the speed of the likes of Joe Lydon, Dean Bell and Jonathan Davies, and people were already hinting that my days were numbered. I wasn't enjoying my role and I thought I would drift down the divisions and fade out of the game within a couple of seasons.

That the former Crossfield Recs amateur player didn't fade away and is still very much a regular in the Warrington team today was due to his inner strength and his conscious decision to switch roles. Taking his inspiration from former Great Britain skipper Ellery Hanley and, preparing the way for his new role by building up his body weight from around 12 to over 15 stones, he switched to the forwards and wore the number 13 jersey.

> I made a conscious decision to reorganise my training and my weight training programme, pile on bulk weight, and switch from playing in the centres to the back row of the pack. I knew that my days as a threequarter were over and that I would never get any faster.
>
> Ellery Hanley had made the change at Wigan when he moved from stand off to loose forward with amazing success. He was my example. He was my inspiration for the move and, whenever I played against him, I watched him very carefully.

Paul Cullen's belief in himself carried him through his new training schedules and his rigorous weight-training programme, but always, at the back of his mind, lay the thought that in one match in the future he would have to put his plans to the test. And he knew that when and wherever he came to that test he would soon know the wisdom of his decision.

Players, looking back on the most memorable match of their life, not only cast their minds over the events of the 80 minutes' play but reflect on the atmosphere surrounding their performance. The memories of the motor coach edging its way through the adoring supporters as it nears the ground, the singing of 'Abide with Me' at Wembley Stadium, the sight of the Union Jack fluttering in the breeze at the Sydney Football Stadium or the smells from the hip-flasks at a fierce St. Helens v. Wigan Boxing Day derby clash enhance the imagination. It was not so for Paul Cullen at the tiny, dilapidated

Tattersfield ground in Doncaster where Warrington faced Sheffield Eagles in a championship clash. But the day proved to be the most momentous in his career.

As the Warrington players stepped across the small bridge that spans the stream at the side of the Tattersfield ground, they shielded their faces from the driving rain that swept towards them. The fans, in ones and twos, tightly wrapped in overcoats and scarves, made their way into the antiquated stadium and into one of the two small covered areas that ran alongside both touchlines. The intense cold and the rain, which had set in early that Sunday in Doncaster, had restricted the crowd at kickoff to just 1298 hardy souls. The pitch revealed few blades of grass, only vast areas of mud, ankle-deep, and broken only by the occasional pools of standing water. The picture was a daunting one, and the scene uninviting for a player about to test the strength of his ankles and knee after major surgery and attempting to cope with a new playing position. The conditions underfoot were designed to create knee damage, not instil confidence in a knee that had been repaired and reconstructed. For Paul Cullen, it was to prove the biggest test of his career.

The match was an uninspiring one, with little real relevance in the rugby league world. It is probably a match already forgotten by everyone, but for me it was to prove so important to my future. I was very nervous and a little downcast at the conditions.

This was my first match as a loose forward, and I played with my left knee heavily strapped to prevent the previous cruciate ligament injury. It was ankle-deep in mud, and the rain was lashing down throughout the match, with the result that there wasn't much movement of the ball. It was a battle royal in the forwards. We were forever tackling. I put in 54 tackles and broke the club's record for a tackle count for an individual.

The hours spent lifting weights to strengthen his ankles and knee and to increase his upper body strength stood the Wire's loose forward in good stead as he was forced to face the power of the Sheffield Eagles pack. And a big pack it was too! The 16-stone frame of Gary Van Bellen occasionally blocked Paul Cullen's path, and the power of Great Britain and Aussie pack stars Sonny Nickle and Bruce McGuire was felt in the tackle. The cover tackles on Eagles' outstanding backs, tryscoring centre Daryl Powell and two-goal Mark Aston, had to be made. The punishing runs from his own line out of defence had to be done; no longer could he take a breather in the centre and watch his forwards carry out the hard, bruising work in midfield. He was one of them now and, in one unforgettable moment, Paul Cullen knew it.

My most memorable moment in the match was not a try, a pass or a run but a tackle which was made on me! After about 20 minutes I ran on to a short ball from our scrum half, Martin Crompton. I took a couple of steps forward when the 'Balmain Tiger', Eagles Aussie Test second row Bruce McGuire, hit me one inch below my chin and knocked me through the air five yards backwards.

It was then that I realised how much work I still needed to do on the weights. It was then that I knew how I had to build up my strength to suit the new position.

Though he failed to get his name on the scoresheet, as Warrington, thanks to a try and two goals from Rocky Turner and one try from Tony Thorniley, managed to beat Sheffield not too convincingly, Paul Cullen's strengths did suit the forwards. Noted for his strong tackling in the centres, the Wires number 13 relished his new role and, though still lacking in stature, lost little in comparison to pack colleagues Mike Gregory and Neil Harmon alongside him in the back row. He rarely missed a tackle and, despite the atrocious conditions, found the extra energy needed to drive down the middle at the opposition. His assets as a centre aided his conversion as he brought a good pair of hands, a shrewd footballing brain and an extra yard of pace to the pack. His enthusiasm for the rough and tumble of the game disconcerted one or two of the Eagles forwards, while his instincts as a running back helped him to run into the right positions whenever a Martin Crompton or Gary Mercer break needed support. He played the role of the hard-grafting forward and, perhaps because of rather than in spite of the conditions, he succeeded. At least he thought so as he sat pondering over the 80 minutes' play on his way home over the Pennines in the team bus.

Sitting in the bus on the way home, I thought to myself that I could play in the pack. This one match had given me the confidence to continue the experiment, prepare myself for a new role and change my position permanently. I had enjoyed the close physical contact in the middle of the field and I knew that, although I was too slow to progress as a centre, I had that extra yard of pace to benefit a loose forward – I knew I could do it.

Paul Cullen's experiences against Sheffield Eagles were to change his whole outlook on the game and to help extend his career beyond that which he had forecast for himself six months earlier. His enjoyment of and appetite for rugby quickly returned and, though in January 1990 he could not foresee the rule changes lying ahead in the future, his switch of position was further enhanced when the distance between the players at the play-the-ball was increased, two years later, from the then five metres to ten metres. The greater space between the teams provided more opportunities for a lighter but faster forward, and Paul Cullen took advantage of the situation.

* * *

The new ten-metre rule has actually assisted my positional change because now there is a need for greater mobility in the forwards. I could never have played in the pack when there was the five-metre rule in operation or under the unlimited-tackle count. Then a top forward had to be around 6 feet 3 inches and weigh 16½ stones. The game has changed and altered dramatically during my career, and I either had to adapt to the changes or fade away.

Many an opposition forward who, over the past four seasons, has felt the full force of a typical Paul Cullen tackle will testify that the former Warrington centre star has not faded away. Rather, the reverse: his career has blossomed, and the promise shown on that rainy, windswept Sunday in January 1990 has been fulfilled.

SHEFFIELD EAGLES Mycoe; Nelson, Dickinson, Powell, Gamson; Hardy, Aston; Broadbent, Cook, Van Bellen, Grimoldby, Nickle, McGuire. *Subs*: Farrell, Kellett.

WARRINGTON Lyon; Drummond, Mercer, Thorniley, Forster; Turner, Crompton; Burke, Mann, Molloy, Harmon, Gregory, Cullen. *Subs*: Darbyshire, Richards.

Scorers Sheffield Eagles *Tries* Powell. *Goals* Aston (2).
              Warrington   *Tries* Turner, Thorniley. *Goals* Turner (2).

Referee Alex Bowman (Whitehaven).

Jonathan Davies

Leeds 4 Widnes 39
Challenge Cup Semi-Final, Wigan
13 March 1993

Born 24 October 1962. Jonathan Davies made his debut in rugby league as a substitute in Widnes's 50–8 defeat of Salford just a week after his much-publicised £150,000 transfer of allegiance from the union code on 5 January 1989. The former Wales rugby union skipper, capped 23 times for his country, had risen from his humble home town club of Trimsaran via Neath and Llanelli, where, in just 121 appearances for the two clubs, he had amassed over 669 points, to become perhaps union's most eagerly sought-after player. Though slight in stature, weighing only 12 stones 7 pounds and being 5 feet 8 inches in height, his capture by the then Widnes coach Doug Laughton was to prove a coup for the 13-a-side game.

Following a period of readjustment to the different pace and intensity of league and after a strenuous course of weight training, the Welsh wizard soon set about creating yet more records in his newly chosen profession.

In the 1990–91 season Jonathan equalled Andy Currier's individual match points-scoring record for Widnes with 34 points against Whitehaven, and he completed his memorable season by achieving a club record 342 points. Sadly for Widnes, cash problems determined that their Welsh scoring machine was forced to move on to near neighbours Warrington at the beginning of the 1993–94 season, where he continues to torment the opposition. At international level, having won a place on Great Britain's tour of Papua New Guinea and New Zealand in the summer of 1990, he played a prominent part in both Test series, grabbing 36 points and achieving the distinction of scoring in all five Tests. And, with the restoration of a Welsh national team in 1991, he had the honour of adding the captaincy of the league team to that of the union side. A constant threat to even the tightest of opposition defences, the former Gwendraeth Grammar School pupil proved the success of his switch of codes when, in the summer of 1991, he displayed outstanding form for Canterbury Bankstown in the tough Australian Winfield Cup, scoring 100 points in just 14 appearances for the Bulldogs. Truly a gifted footballer in either code.

Though Jonathan Davies is one of rugby league's most prolific points-scorers and rarely out of the leading goalkickers' charts, he was not too proud to request help before one of the most important games in his career, the Challenge Cup semi-final against Leeds at Central Park, Wigan, in March 1993. Nor was he too proud to take advice from the very man who, in the eventual Wembley showdown, would prove one of the biggest dangers to Widnes winning the cup for an eighth occasion, ex-All Black and Wigan scoring ace Frano Botica.

Realising the importance of goalkicks to the outcome of the battle with Leeds, eventually recording five successful shots out of seven attempts, the Welshman telephoned for the assistance of the Kiwi, and Davies's private pre-match practice session was arranged for the Thursday prior to the semi-final clash.

> I wanted to feel confident taking the goalkicks at Central Park, and Frano Botica was a good friend of mine from my union-playing days, so I decided to ask him to help me and he agreed. We met at Central Park on the Thursday and he gave me a few tips about the wind currents at Central Park. He watched me take some kicks from the touchline and they went over the bar. I felt confident after the session, and knew that I would be on form with my kicks on the Saturday. The three goals which I managed to kick from the touchline proved killer blows to Leeds' morale and boosted us. I was really grateful to Frano for his help and advice.

Jonathan Davies's secret session at Central Park proved a winner for Widnes and helped him achieve the ambition of his rugby-playing career. I well remember the occasion when he first visited Wembley Stadium in 1989 to help with BBC television's broadcast of the Challenge Cup final and asked me to walk with him on the pitch on the morning of the match. His eyes lit up and there was a light spring in his step as he captured the significance of the occasion. He confessed his ambition to return as a player and quizzed me as to the atmosphere and feelings experienced by a player. My words only added to his determination one day to be part of Challenge Cup history.

> Even though, as a union player, I'd played in many famous stadiums all over the world, I had always had an admiration for Wembley. I always used to watch the rugby league cup final and wonder what it would be like to take part in one at Wembley. On that Saturday in March 1993 I knew that I had lost two semi-finals with Widnes and that this could be my last chance. I was determined to grasp it.

The irony that, given greater persuasion by Wakefield Trinity or a sudden expected swoop from Leeds just hours before the Challenge Cup transfer signing deadline, he might not even have been a Widnes player did not go unnoticed when he lined up for the kickoff against the Yorkshiremen.

48

* * *

I actually had talks with Wakefield Trinity just before the cup signing deadline over the possibility of joining them. And it was rumoured that Leeds were also interested in signing me as, owing to the financial crisis at Widnes, it seemed that they would have little option but to sell me. But the players stuck together and battled through the cash crisis. The problems actually helped our spirits.

The match was to prove a media-man's dream, containing all the ingredients necessary to whet the appetites of even the most reluctant of spectators. Both teams contained some of the biggest names in rugby, collected by both clubs at a cost of well over a couple of million pounds. Home-grown talent abounded in both sides, with internationals Andy Currier, Bobby Goulding and Kurt Sorensen and Leeds' own Garry Schofield, Andy Gregory and Ellery Hanley proving big attractions. Alongside these seasoned professionals, from the world of rugby union Widnes had added at great cost John Devereux and powerful Tongan second row Emosi Koloto, while Leeds paraded ex-union stars in Scotland's Alan Tait, England's Jim Fallon and ex-All Black Craig Innes. Yet Jonathan Davies outshone them all.

Further spice was added to the occasion in that the man who had scoured the country to stock the Widnes side and had nurtured as youngsters many of their now-mature stars was none other than the Leeds coach, Doug Laughton. Would he receive his comeuppance for daring to cross the Pennines and desert Naughton Park? Davies himself was at the centre of one of the more spicy ingredients, the battle at stand off where the Great Britain captain Garry Schofield was in direct confrontation with the Welsh captain. A mouth-watering prospect for the fans, though Davies himself didn't see it that way.

Doug Laughton had played me at stand off a year earlier but had moved me to centre and full back. I like playing at stand off; the position really satisfies me in league. I was out to prove a point that I could play at number six, but the press built up the duel and the head-to-head clash between myself and Garry Schofield. I have never been one to bother about personal battles. That aspect of the match didn't bother me. If Garry had played a blinder and we had won, then I would have been more than satisfied.

As events turned out, Widnes not only won, romping home with seven tries from wing David Myers (2), John Devereux, Stuart Spruce, Andy Currier and two from Davies himself, but the mercurial Welshman added five goals to score 18 points himself and carve out a personal triumph. In concert with former Leeds half back, the fiery youngster Bobby Goulding, the Widnes halves overwhelmed the Leeds duo Schofield and the veteran Andy Gregory to such an effect that it soon became one-way traffic towards the Yorkshiremen's tryline. And the deadly accuracy and length of the tactical kicking achieved by both Goulding and Davies allowed Leeds little respite from their own half.

> Bobby was the perfect foil at scrum half because he was so enthusiastic and so strong that Leeds had to watch him closely. That and his long passes allowed me plenty of room in which to work and, as our forwards began to get on top of the Leeds six in the middle, plenty of gaps appeared.

There are few people better equipped than Davies to exploit those gaps, such is his speed off the mark, his instinctive thinking and his bold approach to attacking rugby.

Having signed the former Welsh rugby union captain and spent many hours in the valleys in his attempts to persuade him to travel north, Leeds boss Doug Laughton knew only too well the qualities the little man possessed, qualities that could destroy his hopes of returning Leeds to Wembley for the first time in 15 years. One blistering burst of speed and virtuoso display in the tight opening 40 minutes should have produced Davies's first try and have provided him, eventually, with a hat trick of touchdowns. Only desperate, scrambling last-ditch defence prevented the try, but the action gave Mr Laughton a taste of what was to come.

Moving quickly into the acting half-back position some 20 yards from the Leeds tryline and approximately eight yards infield from the left touchline, the Widnes number six spotted his chance down the blindside. As if shot from a gun, he burst away, taking the still-retreating defence completely by surprise and, but for Leeds full back and former Widnes favourite Alan Tait's last-ditch tackle on the tryline, would have scored. But that electric pace was to return to haunt his opponents. In Andy Currier and Darren Wright, Widnes had centres who liked to run direct at the opposition, rather in the style of wingmen playing in midfield. Both are tall, powerful and quick, and when, as they did in this semi-final, they make breaks then a speedy half back in support can create havoc. Jonathan Davies did just that.

With Widnes leading 17–4 in the 57th minute, he crushed any hopes of Leeds resistance when he raced in support of a midfield break and, in running in an arc from the left-hand side of the field, he outpaced everyone over 40 yards for a try at the foot of the posts. His wide, toothy grin and his punching of the air with his arm were sure indicators of his joy at being on the way to Wembley. Six minutes from the final whistle he produced his *pièce de résistance*, a try carved out of the confidence to dash for the line himself, when lesser mortals would have merely moved the ball to the wing, and allowed his Welsh colleague John Devereux to take his chance at the corner.

A speedy handling movement across the field from left to right, sparked by the lively Goulding, provided just that extra yard of space that is all great players need to torment the opposition. For Leeds the powerful Craig Innes, no mean tackler and with no shortage of pace, had moved into the tackle just a yard too slowly. In an instant Davies was dancing off his left foot, a sudden jab of the foot to the ground launching him to the outside of Innes. His uncanny acceleration around and away from the despairing Kiwi saw him through the gap and scampering the 20 yards to the in-goal area with apparent ease. A masterly solo effort.

When I went for the line from acting half back in the first half I thought I had scored. I picked up the ball, just looked up, saw that Leeds were not in position, and so I just had a go. My second try was my best effort because I knew I had to take Craig Innes on the outside and beat him for speed to the line. Once I got him inside me, then I always had the advantage in pace on him. I probably should have passed the ball, but I like to have a go for a try, and you don't score them unless you do try things yourself.

Two penalty goals from centre Simon Irving were all that Leeds could muster as Doug Laughton's side were humiliated by a brand of rugby which delighted the many millions watching on television. The Leeds coach could only troop disconsolately from the pitch with the knowledge that the man he introduced to rugby league had helped to send his Wembley hopes crashing around him. The delighted ex-union convert was on his way to those famous twin towers in London.

I can't explain the emotion inside me when the referee blew the final whistle. Having lost in two semi-finals, the win was all the sweeter. It was all the sweeter because my season had been a difficult one. I had missed the Lions tour in the summer with a groin strain, and it cost me my chance of a place in the World Cup final. Leeds had been the clear favourites, while Widnes had been racked with all sorts of rumours on account of the club's financial crisis. The joy of knowing that I was going to play at Wembley was indescribable.

It was a great match, so good for the image of the game and appreciated by millions on TV.

Sadly for Widnes, and despite Davies's points-scoring heroics at Central Park, the Cheshire club fell victim to the Challenge Cup kings, Wigan, their sixth victim in a record six years.

LEEDS Tait; Fallon, Irving, Innes, Fawcett; Schofield, Gregory; Molloy, Lowes, O'Neill, Dixon, Mercer, Hanley. *Subs*: Holroyd, Anderson.

* * *

WIDNES Spruce; Devereux, Currier, Wright, Myers; Davies, Goulding; Sorensen, P. Hulme, Howard, Koloto, Eyres, D. Hulme. *Subs*: McCurrie, Holliday.

Scorers Leeds   *Goals* Irving (2).
          Widnes   *Tries* Myers (2), Davies (2), Devereux, Currier, Spruce.
                  Goals Davies (5). *Drop Goals* Goulding.

Referee Ian Ollerton (Wigan).

John Devereux

Leeds 40 Widnes 28

Stones Bitter Championship, Headingley, Leeds
8 March 1992

Born 30 March 1966. Rugby league coach Doug Laughton's forays into the world of rugby union have often proved to be inspired. Former Rosslyn Park star Martin Offiah, Scotland's Alan Tait, Tonga's Emosi Koloto and Wales' Jonathan Davies, among others, bear testimony to his shrewd judgement of a player's ability to make a successful switch of codes. Each of Laughton's converts is blessed with attributes that allow him to succeed in the professional game, whether it be speed, size, attacking flair or defensive ability. Rarely, however, does one player possess all of the skills, and when he does, as in former Wales and British Lion union star John Devereux, it is worth the many hours of patient negotiation. Since his arrival at Naughton Park, Widnes, in October 1989, the 15-stone former Bridgend threequarter has proved the value of his £150,000 signing-on fee.

Two tours with Great Britain to Papua New Guinea, New Zealand and Australia in 1990 and 1992, the topping of his club's tryscoring lists in 1991–92 with 35 tries and the landing of many a valuable goal have all come easily to this powerful, long-striding wing or centre threequarter. His high-stepping run, punishing handoff and crunching crash tackle all indicate an awesome strength which placed him in good stead during his summer stint with top Sydney league club Manly in 1993. Indeed, few converts from the 15-a-side code have made the transition to league with such ease, and few have earned such respect from his fellow professionals.

There were smiles all around the Headingley terraces when Leeds gained splendid revenge for their 24–0 drubbing at the hands of Widnes in the Regal Trophy final just two months earlier. A triumphant return for Garry Schofield after a four-match absence suffering from a fractured cheekbone and a sparkling seven-try display by a revitalised Leeds sent Widnes crashing to their heaviest championship defeat of the season. From the first three minutes, the time when powerful Leeds wing John Bentley swept on to ex-All Black union star Craig Innes' final pass to open the scoring, to the 73rd minute, when Aussie prop Cavill Heugh crossed for their seventh and final try, the Yorkshiremen were in almost total control. And yet, in a match that produced

53

many exhilarating moments of fast, flowing rugby, one Widnes player, John Devereux, earned the unanimous praise of the 9799 fans for his efforts to stem the tide and was to produce the most memorable display of his short but glittering league career.

> It might seem strange to choose a game to remember in which we lost so heavily. At the end of the match I can remember trooping off the Headingley pitch really upset and feeling miserable. Yet, looking back, it was one of the best performances of my career.
> I was so pleased with my performance. Everything I tried came off. Whether running, tackling or kicking I couldn't seem to do any wrong.

Leeds, desperate to put a spate of bad results behind them, were at their best throughout the match, with loose forward Ellery Hanley, scrum half Bobby Goulding and Garry Schofield providing a midfield pivot which troubled the visitors constantly and helped set up positions for tries from John Bentley (2), Paul Dixon, David Creasser, Colin Maskill, Cavill Heugh and Schofield himself. The crowd were thrilled by a display of all-action rugby as Leeds swept the ball across the field in a series of bewildering moves helped by some quite breathtaking handling. Only a team as good as Widnes could have contained the rampant home side to even 40 points and, more importantly, have troubled the scoreboard operator with 28 points in reply from their own brand of attacking rugby. The thick, springy green turf and the stylish setting at Headingley invite a spectacular and open style of play and, as Devereux suggests, both he and his team-mates had no qualms about playing there.

> Headingley is my favourite ground in England. There is always a good atmosphere before kickoff. The playing surface is superb, ideal for running and playing an open game. It suits Leeds' style of open play, but at the same time Widnes were renowned for their speed and attacking rugby. With Jonathan Davies, Tony Myler and Andy Currier in our team, we were all looking forward to the game.

Few spectators, with the scoreline at 10–8 in Leeds' favour, could have guessed at the outcome of this exciting championship clash at half time. And yet they had already been furnished with enough evidence to see what a major part Widnes' Welshman would play in the final, hectic 40 minutes. A 12th minute try by Widnes full back Alan Tait, following combined play by Kiwi prop Joe Grima and wing Mark Sarsfield, opened the visitors' account, but it was left to John Devereux to unnerve the home fans. Receiving the ball just inside the Leeds half in the 25th minute, Widnes' strong-running wing narrowed the gap when he burst through a hesitant Leeds defence and evaded at least four defenders on a wide, curving run to the line. A day to remember had begun.

> When I got the ball I managed to break the first line of defence and set off down the middle of the field. I managed to hand off Garry Schofield and was able to beat a couple of defenders in the broken field by running in an arc. Morvin Edwards was at full back, but I managed to brush past him and touch down for my first try.

As if scoring or stopping tries wasn't enough, the Welshman had been handed the job of kicking the goals, a task which, early in the second half, allowed him to level the scores at 10–10 when Leeds full back Edwards was penalised for a tackle on Widnes giant Tongan forward Emosi Koloto. But it was hardly a task Devereux relished.

> I felt more pressure than usual on me during the match because I had been asked to take the kicks at goal. When I played rugby union I used to kick all the time and, at Bridgend, it never bothered me. But I hurt my knee shortly before joining league, and I avoided kicking and backed away from it because of the wear and tear constant kicking would do to the knee.
> I wanted to concentrate on my running and positional play when I joined league and didn't want to be bothered about kicking. Before the Leeds game I hadn't practised for ages and was a little nervous of the outcome.

He need have had no fears, for the reluctant kicker helped himself to four goals to add to his hat trick of tries.

Though Leeds quickly wrested the initiative from Widnes and continued to race away with the match, grabbing three tries in eight minutes midway through the second half, Devereux continued to prove a thorn in their side when he bagged his second try on the hour, evading the clutches of Leeds wing John Bentley as he raced on to a clever pass on the blindside of the scrum. And, when all was lost, in the closing minutes both he and pacy full back Alan Tait brought respectability to the scoreline with further touchdowns.

His third try was possibly the easiest of his hat trick to score, but the manner of its scoring illustrated the sharpness of Devereux and the genius of Widnes stand off Tony Myler. A delicately placed grubber kick through the advancing Leeds defence by the tall, long-striding stand off allowed the big Welshman to roar on to the kindly bounce, pounce, and score. The execution was typical of the Great Britain half back's quick thinking, and one of many tries that John Devereux acknowledges were made for him by the shrewd footballing brain of Tony Myler.

> Tony had the good sense to draw the Leeds cover on to him before kicking

the ball through and to the corner. It was easy for me to cut through and score.

What a great player he was. He could hold up the ball so well when he was held in the tackle and then send out a long, floating pass to me on the wing. That pass was worth half a dozen tries a season to me.

It was exciting playing outside Tony because he always used to fling the ball everywhere and he tried to get the ball to the wings as often as he could.

Though defeated by 40–28, a 20-point haul by the big Welsh wing confirmed him as a leading candidate for the Great Britain tour of Papua New Guinea, Australia and New Zealand at the end of the season. That his eventual selection was gained as a winger rather than as a centre, the position in which he signed from Welsh rugby union, said much for the adaptability of Doug Laughton's £150,000 signing. In rugby league big, powerful wingers of the Billy Boston, Lionel Cooper and Eric Grothe type have always appealed to and excited the fans. The combination of power and speed in a blockbusting run down the touchline never fails to rouse the fans. John Devereux did just that against Leeds, but, even more importantly, in general play and defence he illustrated the qualities a top winger needs in the modern game – qualities that have since earned the former Bridgend and British Lions centre an international jersey on the flanks.

In rugby union I only played the game on the wing. There you can stand around all day and never see the ball. But in league you receive the ball regularly and then you have to make the yardage. There is also a lot more defensive work to do.

When you are in trouble you can't just kick the ball out of touch as you can in union. You have to run it back upfield at the opposition and occasionally help out your forwards like a full back.

There was plenty of work in the Leeds game because they scored 40 points and attacked us constantly. Being a wing in league suits my style of play, and I think I'm big enough for the job.

There were few in the Headingley crowd who, after his thrilling all-round performance, would disagree with John Devereux's own assessment of his role as a winger.

LEEDS Edwards; Gibson, Creasser, Innes, Bentley; Schofield, Goulding; Heugh, Maskill, Wane, Dixon, Divorty, Hanley. *Subs*: Heron, Anderson.

WIDNES Tait; Devereux, Currier, Wright, Sarsfield; T. Myler, D. Hulme; Grima, McKenzie, Faimalo, Smith, Eyres, P. Hulme. *Subs*: Spruce, Koloto.

56

Dean Bell – an inspirational Kiwi tour skipper in 1987. (*Varley Picture Agency*)

The pace and power of
Billy Boston prove too
much for a couple of
desperate defenders.
(*Varley Picture Agency*)

Wigan's prolific points-
scorer Frano Botica sets
off on another attacking
raid. (*Stewart Kendall/
Sportsphoto*)

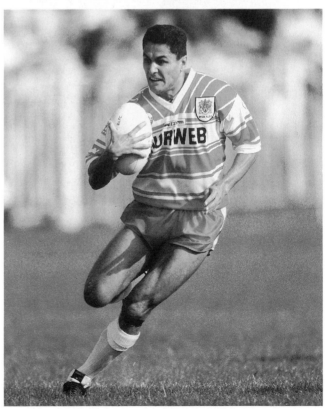

Phil Clarke dives past Australia's Andrew Ettingshausen for the try that sparked Great Britain's 33–10 win in the second Ashes Test at Melbourne, 1992. (*Varley Picture Agency*)

Bradley Clyde looks for an opening and the chance to launch a Canberra Raiders attack. (*Varley Picture Agency*)

Loose forward Shane Cooper, the pivot of Saints' midfield attacks, throws Widnes into confusion during the Challenge Cup semi-final in 1989. (*Varley Picture Agency*)

Teenager Lee Crooks and the experienced David Topliss salute the Hull fans after winning the 1982 Challenge Cup final replay. (*Varley Picture Agency*)

Paul Cullen, now in the number 13 jersey, reveals the determination needed to succeed as a forward. (*Varley Picture Agency*)

Wembley at last! Jonathan Davies celebrates a try during the 1993 Challenge Cup semi-final against Leeds. (*Varley Picture Agency*)

Widnes's powerful Welsh wing John Devereux poised for action. (*David Gadd/ Sportsphoto*)

Paul Eastwood, in determined mood, runs at the heart of Australia's defence in the historic first Ashes Test at Wembley in 1990. Greg Alexander and Allan Langer (left) give chase. (*Colorsport*)

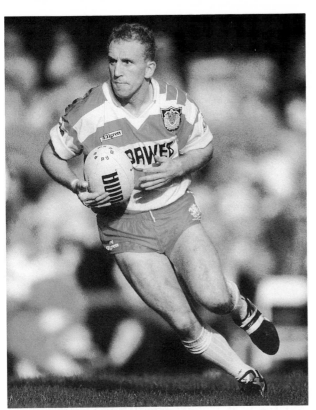

Half back maestro Shaun Edwards takes up the running in midfield. (*Paul McFegan/ Sportsphoto*)

Great Britain scrum half Deryck Fox launches yet another 'bomb' towards Australia's tryline during the 1992 World Cup final. Fox's kicking played an important role in the Lions tactics on the day. (*Colorsport*)

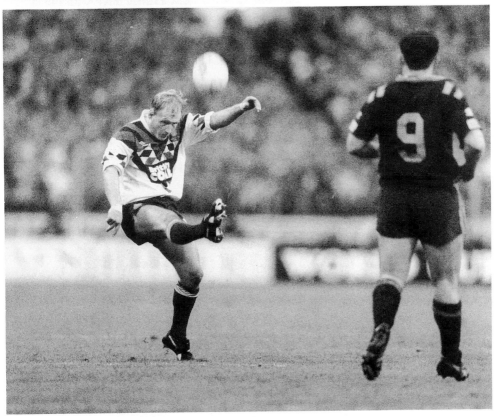

Neil Fox (third from right), having scored a record 20 points in a Challenge Cup final, joins in the celebrations after Wakefield Trinity have won the trophy for the third time. (*Robert Gate Collection*)

Pack giant Jeff Grayshon, stopped by three Kiwi defenders, still seeks to pass the ball to the waiting Ellery Hanley. (*Varley Picture Agency*)

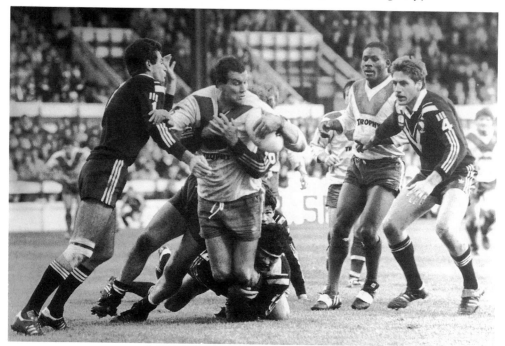

* * *

Scorers Leeds   *Tries* Bentley (2), Dixon, Creasser, Schofield, Maskill, Heugh. *Goals* Goulding (6).

          Widnes   *Tries* Devereux (3), Tait (2). *Goals* Devereux (4).

Referee John Connolly (Wigan).

Paul Eastwood

Great Britain 19 Australia 12
First Test, Wembley
27 October 1990

Born 3 December 1965. The Boulevard, Hull, is renowned more as a breeding ground for tough, no-nonsense forwards than speedy, elusive wingmen. Yet, in former Great Britain captain Clive Sullivan and current wing Paul Eastwood, the Humberside club has produced two prolific points-scorers in a Great Britain jersey. The 28-year-old Eastwood, a former Hullensians rugby union club player, moved quickly into international prominence after a series of good displays in the 1989–90 season, displays that led to his selection for the Lions tour of Papua New Guinea and New Zealand in the summer of 1990. Making his tryscoring debut against Papua New Guinea at Goroka, he amassed over 72 points from 9 tries and 18 goals in just 10 appearances on tour. An outstanding performance in the first Test at Wembley in 1990 heralded a prolific points-scoring spree for Hull with the powerful 5 feet 11 inches and 14 stones 3 pounds flyer topping the club's points-scoring charts with 276 points for the 1990–91 season. A further Lions tour Down Under in 1992 saw Paul Eastwood add to his Test caps against Papua New Guinea, Australia (2) and New Zealand (2).

The successful tour of New Zealand in the summer of 1990 had given youngsters like Hull wing Paul Eastwood a chance to impress in a Great Britain jersey, and coach Mal Reilly did not forget his power and his goalkicking abilities when he came to name his side for the first Ashes Test at Wembley in the following autumn against Australia. After the 2–1 series win in New Zealand, hopes were high that at last Great Britain would dent the aura of invincibility which surrounded the arrival of the Kangaroo tourists in Britain. The Green and Golds had, however, in their opening matches of the tour done little to suggest that they would surrender their reputation easily.

Once again, the visitors had swept through their itinerary in convincing style, dismissing the likes of St. Helens, Wakefield Trinity, Cumbria and even Wigan in contemptuous fashion. Only in the week before the first Test had they been troubled in a hard-earned win at Leeds by 22–10 . There was no reason to suggest that Australia would falter in their run of seven successive Test defeats of the 'auld enemy' in Britain since 1978 as they prepared for

58

their appearance at Wembley. Injuries did, however, play a part in Kangaroo coach Bobby Fulton's eventual lineup, and his pairing at half back of two scrum halves, Allan Langer and Ricky Stuart, did eventually prove an irritation in the customary smooth running of the Australian machine. As Wembley drew near, and a huge publicity campaign in the south was underway to produce a crowd of 54,569 spectators, a record for a Test in Britain, few realised there were any chinks in the Australian armour, least of all Paul Eastwood.

The Australians seemed to be as strong as ever, and their record up to the first Test was very impressive. They had crushed St. Helens and Wigan convincingly, and only Leeds at Headingley had seriously troubled them. The forwards, as usual, were big and strong, and in the backs they had a back line as big as any they have ever brought over. Mal Meninga, Mark McGaw and Michael Hancock were all powerful and hard to stop in the threequarter line. We knew it would be difficult against them, but there was an air of confidence as we approached the big day.

And nerves too!

To many in the Australian camp, Wembley is an arena which conjures up thoughts of heroic and stirring deeds in both football and rugby watched and admired on television 12,000 miles away. Just to stroll around the stadium in the week prior to the match was an unnerving experience to a few of the Kangaroo squad. But that experience, pleasant enough, was nothing to that which greeted Australia ten minutes before kickoff as they lined up in the tunnel to take their place on Wembley's hallowed turf. Rugby league's secret weapon, the Philharmonia Chorus, blasted forth the stirring anthem of 'Land of Hope and Glory'. The words were taken up by the thousands of fans on the terraces, and suddenly, as the words boomed out and chests filled with pride, Great Britain was at war again, against Australia. The effect on the Australians, many already apprehensive of their first appearance at this great stadium, was devastating. Its effect on Great Britain was just what the management wanted.

It was my first time at Wembley, and during the week I had been pretty nervous about playing there in such an important match. I had seen matches at Wembley and always dreamed of playing there. This was it. There had been great pressure on us all during the week, and I felt it especially, having to mark their star winger Michael Hancock. But I never expected anything like the reception as we walked on to the pitch before kickoff. The singing of 'Land of Hope and Glory' made the hair on your neck stand up; there was a great feeling of pride. I don't think the Australians had ever heard or seen anything like it before. Some of them were unnerved

59

by it all; they never expected anything so emotional. The sound was deafening, and I think one or two of them couldn't handle the occasion.

Whether or not the pre-match celebrations did prove too much for the Kangaroos, it was Great Britain who immediately sprang to the attack once the formalities were over and battle commenced. Australia's huge forwards Paul Sironen, Martin Bella and Steve Roach were not smashing through the opposition with ease, as they had done in the earlier club matches. They were being met head-on in the middle of the field, knocked back and dumped to the floor in unceremonious fashion by Eastwood's Hull team-mate, prop Karl Harrison, and Paul Dixon and Roy Powell. Behind, the two scrum halves were having difficulty in building up an easy understanding between themselves and, for once in an Ashes Test match, Great Britain had the control in midfield to enable them to kick for the vital territorial advantage in the early stages. Yet, for all their good work, Great Britain could not translate that advantage into points, having to be content, after 20 minutes of play, with a solitary Paul Eastwood penalty goal.

We were well on top during the first quarter, but we still found it very difficult to score against them, such was the strength of their defence. We began to get a little frustrated, and I had missed two shots at goal. I was very nervous before I put over the first goal. That goal seemed to settle me down and give me confidence.

Though the huge and excited crowd were delighted and roared their approval at the sight of the strong-running Kangaroo forwards being pushed back towards their own tryline, they still had the thought at the back of their minds that Australia would still strike. If one is accustomed to defeat one can rarely forget it. When Australia's skipper, centre Mal Meninga, equalised the scores with a penalty goal, thoughts as to Great Britain's ability to last the pace, doubts as to their fitness began to surface in the minds of many. But, as Eastwood explains, there were few fears among the players on that score.

Many of the team had trained every day on tour in New Zealand, while those who had been injured and unable to tour had had a good rest and were fit and ready for this series. We were as fit as the Australian players and were confident of lasting the pace. We just had to wait for the break.

That break was not long coming in the second half, and it was the irrepressible Ellery Hanley who set up the position for Paul Eastwood's opening try. A delicate chip kick from the Great Britain loose forward had Australia's defence back-pedalling and unable to stop Hanley from accepting the favourable bounce and racing to within a yard from the line. Quick thinking by centre

Daryl Powell transferred the ball from the acting half-back position to Eastwood on the right wing, who used his pace, and especially his strength, to dive under the despairing tackles of Hancock and forward John Cartwright to score at the corner.

> It was a piece of quick thinking which got the ball out to me in the corner, and I knew that I would have to burrow down under the tackles to be sure of getting the ball down over the tryline. The Aussies went over the top of me and I was able to slide underneath with the ball.

England led by 6–2, but not for long, as the sheer size of the Australians told in one majestic run and defence-splitting break from centre Mark McGaw down the right-hand touchline. He passed to the awesome shape of Meninga, who powered over for the equalising try unopposed. Again, fears of the traditional British collapse and worries as to a possible Australian triumph resurfaced in the minds of the disbelievers, but it was not to be, as Great Britain once again wrested control from the masters.

An Ellery Hanley high kick caught Aussie full back Gary Belcher unawares and allowed wing Martin Offiah to pounce on the ricochet from the hapless full back and score at the foot of the posts. Eastwood's second conversion and Garry Schofield's neatly taken drop goal eased the tension and the score to 13–6 in Great Britain's favour. Yet still Australia refused to lie down and, in the manner of Count Dracula, whose hand frighteningly appears from inside the coffin although the stake has been driven through his heart, returned in the final hectic quarter to haunt Great Britain. The Cronulla powerhouse McGaw again beat a path down the right flank, displaying his strength and scattering off attempted tacklers before touching down for Australia's second try. Meninga added the conversion, and suddenly there was only one point difference between the two sides.

> We always knew that, whatever the score, Australia would never give up. Their players are used to winning and don't know what it's like to be defeated. It was a nervous time when they closed to within one point of us, but our forwards seemed to get a second wind and kept them out of our 25-yard area with some strong tackles.

Little did Paul Eastwood know that he would be the one finally to kill off Australia's hopes of victory.

Great Britain coach Mal Reilly had done his homework on Australia's defensive line which, at times, moved up too quickly and did not have a player acting in a sweeper role behind. As Ellery Hanley had shown, a chip kick over the advancing green and gold line could cause havoc, and half back Garry Schofield did just that with his perfectly placed kick and catch. His pass found Daryl Powell running in a broken field and with only Australia's Andrew Ettingshausen confronting him. A perfectly timed pass to Eastwood allowed the Hull wing man to run in at the corner for his second try. Red, white and blue flags waved in the breeze, colourful bob-caps and jockey hats flew through the air and klaxon horns sounded in celebration and anticipation of an historic victory, Great Britain's first win over Australia in this country for 12 years. That anticipation was turned into reality when, minutes later, Paul Eastwood, the hero of the hour, collected his 14th point of the match with a vital penalty goal.

> I knew that the kick could probably be my last of the match. It was a crucial kick, and I was aware that if I put the ball over the crossbar then we would win. The kick was on the wrong side of the pitch for me, but as soon as I kicked the ball I knew it would go over the bar. I was so confident and so relieved that I ran back about ten yards before it actually did go between the posts. There was no way the Australians could come back when we opened a seven-point lead. All the tension suddenly vanished.

Great Britain had defeated Australia in Sydney in the third Test of the Lions tour in the summer of 1988 but, with the Ashes already in Australia's firm grip, the cynics had questioned the significance of the win. Not so with this first Test triumph at Wembley, for Great Britain had outplayed their opponents and shattered Kangaroo coach Bobby Fulton's confident plans to such an extent that he was forced to go back to the drawing-board before resuming battle at Old Trafford, Manchester.

The Wembley success had captivated the public's imagination via television, and the names of Eastwood, Hanley, Schofield and Offiah were on everyone's lips. The success deserved to be celebrated in style, and where better than the haunt of the famous, Stringfellows night-club in the West End.

> It was beyond my wildest dreams to play at Wembley, win and score 14 points against Australia. It didn't really sink in for a while, but when it did we really enjoyed ourselves. We had a big night out in London at Stringfellows. It cost us a few bob, but it was worth it.

GREAT BRITAIN Hampson; Eastwood, D. Powell, Gibson, Offiah; Schofield, Gregory; Harrison, Jackson, Dixon, Betts, R. Powell, Hanley. *Subs*: Edwards, Ward, Hulme, Fairbank.

AUSTRALIA Belcher; Ettingshausen, Meninga, McGaw, Hancock; Stuart, Langer; Roach, K. Walters, Bella, Sironen, Cartwright, Lindner. *Subs*: Alexander, Hasler, Shearer, Lazarus.

* * *

Scorers Great Britain *Tries* Eastwood (2), Offiah. *Goals* Eastwood (3).
Drop Goals Schofield.

Australia   *Tries* Meninga, McGaw. *Goals* Meninga (2).

Referee Alain Sablayrolles (France).

Shaun Edwards

Swinton 0 Wigan 78

Second Round Lancashire Cup, Gigg Lane, Bury
29 September 1992

Born 17 October 1966. To be signed for a world record schoolboy fee of £35,000 on the morning of your 17th birthday by the legendary Alex Murphy before the cameras of BBC television's *Breakfast Show* could have proved a handicap to any youngster setting out on a rugby league career. Within two years, Wigan's exciting half-back star, Shaun Edwards, had become the youngest ever to play at Wembley in a Challenge Cup final, had won his first international cap at full back against France and was on his way to being voted the young player of the year in three consecutive seasons. His relentless, single-minded drive for success still continues to shatter all records and establishes him as a rugby league freak.

The son of former Warrington and Lancashire scrum half Jackie Edwards, and a former England Schools league and union international, Shaun has already won more medals than anyone in Wigan's history, and twice toured Down Under with the Lions in 1988 and 1992, though sadly he was invalided home from Papua New Guinea on his first venture abroad. Though small in stature, being only 5 feet 9 inches in height and 12 stones 6 pounds in weight, his ability to play at full back, centre, scrum half and stand off in an international jersey amply illustrates his ability and versatility, while the granting of a testimonial benefit season at the age of 26 years after over 300 games in Wigan colours is ample evidence of his durability. As is his appearance in an amazing 36 successive Challenge Cup round wins and seven Challenge Cup finals between 1988 and 1994, during which he scored 19 tries.

Bradford Northern and former Great Britain coach Peter Fox is just one who speaks highly of Shaun Edwards' uncanny habit of scoring tries. Insists the outspoken Northern boss, 'He possesses not only all the skills of the game but a unique quality so few have ever possessed, that is to be in the right place at the right time. He turns up inside wingers, outside centres, either side of whichever forward makes the break, and nine times out of ten he will have been instrumental in conjuring up the opening in the first place.' Edwards' ability to change the direction of a game or snatch victory with an astute piece of support play is indeed an art, developed by so few in the history of the game.

In the 1960s there were two such exponents of the art, Harold Poynton of Wakefield Trinity and Alan Hardisty of Castleford. Both moved about the field with such stealth and possessed such an uncanny instinct for positional play that both, like a hawk on its prey, could swoop on the ball and be over for a try before the opposition had time to realise the threat. So successful an artist was Harold Poynton that once, when I was playing for St. Helens against him, he struck with such speed and timing that we continued the movement upfield without the ball. Harold meanwhile was touching the ball down beneath the posts for a try. The Wigan and Great Britain half back star is blessed with the same instinct that propelled both Hardisty and Poynton to the top of their profession 30 years ago.

Support play and scoring tries is all about knowing where to be in fifteen yards and five seconds' time. Other players can be faster than me, but if you know how to cut the field down and run at the right angles then you can arrive at where you want to be before anyone else. It is all about awareness and concentration. There is a way of doing it, but I'm not about to give away the secret yet.

Edwards does admit, however, that his prolific tryscoring in recent seasons and his ten-try feat against Swinton in the second round of the Lancashire Cup have much to do with former Wigan skipper Ellery Hanley's presence, and especially his absence. When Hanley, at his peak adjudged the world's greatest league player, held sway at Central Park registering 50 or 60 tries in a season, his ability impressed Wigan's half back and taught him a trick or two.

I studied Ellery a lot and picked up tips from the way he played. I learned so much from him in the way he knew where to run in support of players who had made a break.

But he also insists that, since Hanley's departure to Leeds, his topping of the league's tryscoring lists in 1991–92 with 40 tries and his 46-try tally in the 1992–93 season has more than a little to do with the fact that the Great Britain loose forward is no longer in Wigan colours.

It's very unusual for a scrum half to score such a large number of tries. When I moved to scrum half I thought the move would restrict my tryscoring chances, but with Ellery Hanley not playing alongside me I have had a lot more chances to score. In the past, when a Wigan player made a break it was Ellery who was usually the first to race alongside him. I would frequently be on the other side of the player, and I only got half of the passes and the tries. Now I tend to get them all.

Indeed he does, as most Swinton fans would readily agree.

With due respect to Swinton, to be drawn against the Lions in the second round of the Lancashire Cup is hardly the stuff that stirs a player's imagination, especially when the fixture takes place at Gigg Lane, home of Bury Football Club on a cold, wet, mid-week evening. On a Tuesday evening players are still nursing the bumps and bruises from the tough championship clash on the previous Sunday and anticipating the match to come at the weekend. Such matches are often looked upon as a chore by many professional players, and such was the attitude of Shaun Edwards when he boarded the coach outside Central Park to travel to the match.

It was a very ordinary match, and there was little about it that would get you keyed up for it. I had a slight hand injury and I was not going to play; I was going to pull out of the team. I was going to save myself for a big game at the weekend and rest my hand. But then I decided to play, and how glad I was that I did. I don't think I'll ever get the chance to score ten tries again.

I thought I would never in my lifetime see or hear of another player scoring ten tries in a match after being present at Martin Offiah's record-breaking effort at Central Park against Leeds just five months previously. But the 26-year-old Edwards proved me wrong.

Despite the inclusion of teenage wing wizard Jason Robinson in the unlikely role of loose forward, and the placing on the substitutes' bench of Great Britain forwards Andy Platt and Phil Clarke, Wigan were far too strong for Second Division side Swinton. Few in the crowd, however, expected a scoreline of 78–0, a ten-try haul for Shaun Edwards and an eleven-goal tally from ex-All Black union star Frano Botica, Edwards' partner at half back. But, as Edwards insists, the Wigan pack held complete ascendancy in midfield and were forcing Swinton into mistakes with the force of their tackling. Such conditions are manna from heaven for a world-class half back.

Our forwards were making plenty of breaks in the middle and were just too strong for the Swinton six. They set up the launching-pad for all our attacks and gave us all the ball we needed to score. Conditions were ideal for a scrum half and it suited me. I scored four tries in the first half and, after half time, the chances just kept coming. Within a very short time I had scored seven tries.

Twice previously in his career the exciting scrum half had scored four tries in a match, but now he was into virgin territory. Swinton's luckless backs were under intense pressure from the Wigan centres Dean Bell and Andrew Farrar, who continually used their power and strength to sweep down the flanks, and always at their side was the ever-alert and try-hungry Edwards. He was especially alert in that final quarter when the realisation hit him that he was just three tries short of equalling Martin Offiah's Wigan record of ten tries in a match.

> When I touched down for the seventh try I thought to myself, 'Let's go for it'. Most of the tries were very similar in that the opportunity to score usually came from someone else's break. I just kept supporting the players who made the break and I just kept scoring until there was one try remaining for the tenth.

While Edwards was racing into the record books, Martin Offiah, Sam Panapa, Jason Robinson and captain Dean Bell also helped themselves to tries, and stand off Frano Botica was more than grateful to his half-back partner for providing him with the opportunity to move on his way to 11 goals. Edwards was especially grateful, however, to his Kiwi skipper Bell, who unselfishly handed him his record-equalling tenth try. The sight of the Wigan captain scything through a gap in the opposition defences, 30 or 40 yards from the tryline, is usually the signal for the Wigan fans to pencil in a try alongside his name in the programme. Though in the latter stages of his illustrious career there are few more deadly finishers in the game than the former New Zealand Test player, yet, instead of lengthening his stride and stretching out for the try, skipper Bell unselfishly chose to allow his team-mate to score the try.

> For most of the tries I had to work, but I was very fortunate to be allowed to score my last one. Dean Bell could easily have scored himself. He was about 40 yards out and could have made it to the tryline, but he just turned towards me and handed me the ball. I shall always be grateful to him.

The second round of the Lancashire Cup may have had little to commend itself to the spectators at the kickoff, but Shaun Edwards and his team-mates ensured that it would be one match to remember for many years to come. The local boy who had signed for his home town club as a 17-year-old for a £35,000 fee had added his name to those illustrious wingers, Huddersfield and Australian Test star Lionel Cooper and Wigan's own Martin Offiah, who have scored ten tries in a match. It was a rare feat, but unique for a scrum half.

SWINTON Wilkinson; Leyland, Daintith, Kennett, Ratu; Hibberd, Kay; Parr, Garner, Barrow, Pickavance, Whitfield, Allen. *Subs*: Errington, Skeech.

* * *

WIGAN Hampson; Lydon, Bell, Farrar, Offiah; Botica, Edwards; Skerrett, Crompton, McGinty, Betts, Panapa, Robinson. *Subs*: Clarke, Platt.

Scorers Wigan   *Tries* Edwards (10), Bell, Offiah, Panapa, Robinson. *Goals* Botica (11).

Referee Stuart Cummings (Widnes).

Deryck Fox

Great Britain 6 Australia 10
World Cup Final, Wembley
24 October 1992

Born 17 September 1964. Having served his club and country for the best part of a decade with unswerving loyalty, Deryck Fox, on his return home from the Lions tour of Australasia in the summer of 1992, insisted he had to move clubs if his international career was to prosper. A club record £140,000 fee finally took him from Featherstone Rovers to Bradford Northern in September and, in October, his ambition was realised. After winning nine Test caps between 1985 and 1986, the former St. John Fisher amateur from Dewsbury made his first start in an international match for six years in the World Cup clash with Australia at Wembley in October 1992, fully justifying his recall. The tiny 5 feet 5 inches scrum half's endless array of passing and kicking skills has brought out the best in many a Featherstone or Bradford forward, while his shrewd captaincy has inspired teams in his charge, not least Great Britain in their mid-week matches Down Under. A veteran of the 1990 Great Britain tour to Papua New Guinea and New Zealand, Deryck Fox played in nine matches on the 1992 visit Down Under, skippering the mid-week Lions side to an unbeaten run but sadly missing out on deserved selection for the second Test against New Zealand owing to a leg injury.

For Deryck Fox, selection for the 1992 World Cup final began five months previously when he flew out with the Great Britain squad on their nine-week tour of Australasia. Ahead of him in the selection stakes for the number seven jersey lay either of the Wigan duo Andy Gregory and Shaun Edwards, while Warrington's Welshman, former Bridgend union half back Kevin Ellis, was also pressing his claims. The tiny Featherstone scrum half, however, initially was forced to start his run for honours from way behind the field when, to the surprise of many, he did not appear in Great Britain coach Mal Reilly's original selections for the tour.

There was no concealing the bitter disappointment at his original exclusion from the tour party, but that setback made him even more determined to prove himself. Bobby Goulding had been chosen ahead of him, but when Goulding was suspended Fox was drafted in to be in the tour party that flew out to Papua New Guinea. He clearly had a great deal to do to persuade Mal

69

Reilly that he was the man for the scrum half role.

> When I wasn't selected in the squad I was absolutely devastated. I had worked so hard with my fitness and with my game throughout the season, and I had been selected in every previous international squad throughout the year. It was such a huge disappointment for me, I thought that all my chances to return to international rugby had gone.

Deryck Fox's recall to the squad and his desperation to prove a point put him back in contention for the coveted number seven Great Britain jersey.

Though a dead leg, received just four days before the second Test against New Zealand, cost him the place he had striven so hard for, his captaincy and inspiration of the Lions unbeaten mid-week side in the previous eight weeks was firmly implanted in coach Mal Reilly's mind. Fox's battling performances and tactical appreciation in the tough clashes with Australia's Newcastle Knights and the Gold Coast Seagulls, and with leading provinces Auckland and Canterbury in New Zealand, proved highlights of the tour.

> Once I'd put the disappointment of not being originally selected for the tour behind me, everything worked out well for me. In fact, it was a roaring success even though I didn't get the chance to play in the Test matches. I had the satisfaction of captaining the mid-week side on an unbeaten run, and we built up a marvellous team spirit. That stood me in good stead for selection for the World Cup.

Deryck Fox, however, knew that something else was needed – a move to another club. After seasons spent guiding the unfashionable Featherstone Rovers club, Fox cast aside the opportunity to have a lucrative testimonial benefit and chose to put himself in the front line with a £140,000 move to Bradford Northern, a record pay-out by his former coach and namesake, Peter Fox, who was now directing affairs at Odsal. His ambitious plans were fulfilled when he was paired with his one-time rival for the number seven jersey, Shaun Edwards, at half back, against Australia's best in Brad Fittler and little 'Alfie' Langer.

> The tour had helped me to prove a point and had put me back in the public's eye. I knew that I had to leave Featherstone if I was to compete regularly in the top flight. My transfer to Bradford Northern came just at the right time and helped to force my way into the Great Britain team again. We hit good form at Bradford right away, and I caught Mal Reilly's eye.
>
> My ambition had been to return to international rugby, and my selection for the World Cup final gave me the satisfaction of doing just that. My

70

return to Test rugby after a battle, and my performance, even though we lost, made it the highlight of my career.

Despite a magnificent winning display in the second Ashes Test in Melbourne in the summer, the Lions had still conceded their tenth Ashes series, and the visiting Kangaroos, as reigning world champions, still had the aura of invincibility around them. In the previous 38 years a Scotsman, Dave Valentine, an Englishman, Eric Ashton, and a Welshman, Clive Sullivan, in 1954, 1960 and 1972, had skippered Great Britain to success in the World Cup campaigns; now it was the turn of a Yorkshireman, Garry Schofield, to see if he could wrest the trophy out of Australian captain Mal Meninga's firm grasp.

In their three warm-up games before the Wembley showdown, Australia had hardly broken sweat, convincingly defeating Huddersfield, Sheffield Eagles and Cumbria. But shrewd Great Britain boss Mal Reilly had learned that, if he were to be successful, he had to employ a strong kicking game against Australia, seek to contain them in their half, keep them on the turn and not allow their giant forwards to pressurise Great Britain near their own tryline. Giant forwards Mark Sargent, Paul Sironen and Glenn Lazarus had to be contained. Similarly, he realised that if the 16-stone Kangaroos skipper Mal Meninga was to make any of his blockbusting defence-splitting runs, then he was going to be forced to make them from within his own 20-metre area. Deryck Fox, one of the best tactical kickers in the British game and one of the cleverest distributors of a ball, was chosen specifically to do the job.

When a team plays against Australia, their defenders are so strong physically and they move up so quickly in midfield that it really is very difficult to pierce their defence. Any gaps that do appear always seem to shut tight within a split second, and they have so much pace in the back row in players like Bob Lindner and Bradley Clyde that they can cover any breaks out wide as well.

Deryck Fox's instructions were clear.

I had to look after 'Alfie' Langer around the scrums and especially at the play-the-ball area, where he is so dangerous. But our aim was to pin Australia back near their line, turn them around and make them play in their own half. We hoped that if we could hold them there then we might be able to seize on any mistakes and attack from close quarters.

There was no doubt in the mind of Bradford Northern coach Peter Fox that his club record buy was indeed the man for the job. Having been at the helm at both Featherstone Rovers and Bradford and observed his tactical

71

appreciation in the loose and around the scrum, he felt Great Britain coach Mal Reilly had chosen well. Insisted Peter Fox:

Deryck is the type of player who creates play for others around him rather than for himself. His commitment to his rugby is one hundred per cent, and he had set his mind on a return to the Great Britain team. There was no better tactician available for the World Cup final than Deryck, and against Australia you always need players with courage. Deryck has that in abundance. He may be small, but he will attempt things and create room for other players when bigger men would hold back.

Coach Mal Reilly's plans worked save for one crucial mistake in defence – a mistake that was to keep the crown on Kangaroo captain Mal Meninga's head.

Great Britain fielded possibly their strongest side available, with tough tacklers Andy Platt, Phil Clarke and Martin Dermott drafted in to blunt any attacking edge Australia might have. Loose forward Ellery Hanley had recovered from injuries which had seen him start just one match on the previous summer's Lions tour, and, in midfield, centres Garry Schofield and St. Helens youngster Gary Connolly were both capable of playing a defensive, containing role should Great Britain's kicking ploys succeed. Indeed, for the opening 40 minutes of this tense, taut World Cup final, apart from the occasional flurry of action from Langer and Fittler, Great Britain held Australia in a vice-like grip and were well worthy of their 6–4 half-time lead.

The two packs, like stags locking antlers, had cancelled each other out in the charges, and what scoring chances had come either side's way came only via kicks at goal. Deryck Fox's long, touchfinding kicks, the occasional high punt and an adventurous chip kick had kept Australia back-pedalling and given him the territorial advantage needed when penalty chances came along. He was awarded three such chances in the opening 33 minutes by New Zealand referee Dennis Hale and he accepted all three, especially the first in the third minute to give his side the boost of a 2–0 lead.

I enjoyed goalkicking at Wembley and was ready for any goal chances. My most memorable moment came with that first goal from 40 yards out. The previous week I had been kicking well against Warrington and had kicked one from half-way, and on the Friday before the final I had been kicking them from all angles and distances on the field.

I knew I could kick the penalty goal and that it would be an early boost for everyone. When Garry Schofield asked me if I could manage it, I had no hesitation in having a go for goal.

Meninga replied with two successes from three attempts, and, as the minutes ticked away in that absorbing second half, Great Britain clung to their narrow two-point lead – and, for all the power of Australia, looked capable of holding it until Great Britain substitute John Devereux's fateful slip proved costly.

Aussie centre Steve Renouf, making his Test debut, had proved the sensation of the season Down Under with the Brisbane Broncos, his electrifying bursts and quick thinking helping the Queensland side to a Winfield Cup Premiership. In the 67th minute the luckless Welshman Devereux came infield a fraction too quickly and the Windai-born wonder was away, dashing 20 yards down the left flank and over for the match-clinching try. The unfortunate Devereux walked sadly back to the goal-line, Australian captain Mal Meninga added the conversion and Great Britain's brave effort was over. Australia were crowned world champions for the sixth occasion.

Deryck Fox's return to international action did not provide the fairy-tale ending many had hoped for, but the little scrum half had shared the honours around the scrum with Aussie half-back ace 'Alfie' Langer and had, in general play, done all that could be expected of him. Naturally, there was disappointment at Great Britain's failure, once again, to topple the champions, but for Bradford Northern's scrum half the satisfaction of proving himself once again capable of performing at the highest level was more than ample compensation. The journey via Sydney, Auckland and Bradford was over.

The World Cup final was the end product of the tour and my transfer. Every match on tour Down Under was a build-up to Wembley. I was disappointed to be on the losing side, but I was satisfied at the quality of my own game. I knew, since 1986, that I could still do it at the top level if I was given the chance. At least I proved to myself that I still had the ability to do it at the top. I can always look back on the World Cup final as giving me the chance to prove myself.

GREAT BRITAIN Lydon; Hunte, Connolly, Schofield, Offiah; Edwards, Fox; Ward, Dermott, Platt, Betts, Clarke, Hanley. *Subs*: Devereux, Skerrett, Tait, Eyres.

AUSTRALIA Brasher; Carne, Renouf, Meninga, Hancock; Fittler, Langer; Lazarus, S. Walters, Sargent, Sironen, Lindner, Clyde. *Subs*: Cartwright, Gillespie, Johns, K. Walters.

Scorers Great Britain *Goals* Fox (3).
Australia *Tries* Renouf. *Goals* Meninga (3).

Referee Dennis Hale (New Zealand).

Neil Fox

Hull 5 Wakefield Trinity 38
Challenge Cup Final, Wembley
14 May 1960

Born 4 May 1939. If any player deserved recognition in the Queen's Honours for services to rugby league, then Neil Fox was surely to be found at the head of those meriting reward. One of the few to play first-class rugby league over the age of 40 years, this veteran of 23 seasons and 29 Test caps proved to be not only one of the greatest points-scoring machines in the history of the game but one of the most modest and unassuming characters one could meet. In 19 seasons with his beloved Wakefield Trinity as a powerful player and afterwards with Bradford, Hull Kingston Rovers, York, Bramley and Huddersfield as a centre or ball-playing loose forward, he amassed a world record 6220 points, including 2575 goals, in over 828 appearances.

Even the most optimistic of Wakefield Trinity's scouts could not have envisaged Neil Fox's deeds and his rewriting of the club's record books when, as a 16-year-old, he made his debut at Keighley on 10 April 1956. In the 1961–62 season he smashed the club's goals and points-scoring records in a season with 163 goals and 407 points. His powerful centre play provided opportunities for many a wing outside him, but he was not averse to using his immense bulk and surprising speed for such a big man to record 272 tries himself in a Trinity jersey.

Instances of father and son playing in a Challenge Cup final at Wembley are rare, the Rismans and the Clarkes being just two examples in the past 50 years. Father Gus, with Salford and Workington, and son Bev, of Leeds and Great Britain fame, both achieved cup-winner's medals at Wembley for the Risman family, while hooker Colin Clarke in the 1960s and son and loose forward Phil in the 1990s have helped Wigan to many a Wembley win. Yet perhaps one family from the tiny pit village of Sharlston in Yorkshire, the Foxes, have stamped their name indelibly on Wembley's roll of honour (or notoriety) more than any other in the venue's 65 years' association with rugby league.

The tale of Don Fox, Wakefield Trinity's celebrated yet luckless goalkicker, who, in the 'watersplash' final against Leeds in 1968, had the misfortune to miss what would have been a matchwinning conversion in the dying seconds

74

of the final, is well documented. The disastrous 30 seconds of the Trinity prop's career have been shown on film to sympathetic audiences around the world, with the result that the mis-kick is now part of the folklore of the famous stadium. In the tiny pit village of Featherstone, brother Peter's masterminding of Rovers' 33–14 cup final win over Bradford Northern against all the odds in 1973 was another memorable day, both for the rugby-mad town and the talented Fox family. However, perhaps the family's greatest triumph took place 13 years previously when the youngest of the three Fox boys, Neil, smashed the points-scoring record for a player at Wembley and helped Wakefield Trinity to a 38–5 defeat of Hull, a record for the highest scoreline which still stands today.

Since his first appearance for Trinity, Neil Fox had proved such a prolific points-scorer and influential player in midfield that it was not unexpected when he made his international debut against France at the tender age of 19. And Trinity fans had every reason to expect a glut of points on his Wembley debut against injury-hit Hull. He didn't disappoint them.

Wakefield Trinity were about to enter a golden period in the club's illustrious history with three cup-winning appearances at Wembley in the space of four years. The premier Yorkshire side was sprinkled with some of the greatest names in the game, especially in the pack, where cup finals tend to be won. Skipper Derek 'Rocky' Turner had few peers in the game, and alongside him were seasoned international campaigners Jack Wilkinson and Don Vines, two of the toughest packmen around in the early 1960s. Behind the scrum there was a mixture of size and pace in wing John Etty, classy Springbok centre Alan Skene, cultured half back Harold Poynton and Neil Fox himself, a giant centre tipping the scales at 15 stones. With such attractions it was no surprise that a crowd of 55,935 fans, a figure never since matched, watched them defeat local rivals Featherstone Rovers by 11–2 in the Challenge Cup semi-final. Wembley beckoned for the first time in Neil Fox's career but, though barely 21 years of age, he was ready for it.

The match against Hull was my first trip to Wembley, but I wasn't especially nervous. I had played all season in the Wakefield side and I had already represented Great Britain. That was my most nervous occasion. We had a great side with many world-class stars under a superb captain, who led from the front, in Derek Turner. We went to Wembley as red-hot favourites and we were all very confident of winning. I must say, though, it was more than I could ever have hoped for to score 20 points in the final.

That Trinity were installed as red-hot favourites by the bookmakers had much to do with the form and playing strength of the team throughout the 1959–60 season, but the crippling injury list at Hull in the weeks prior to the Wembley showdown also weighed heavily in Wakefield's favour. The Boulevard, in the week before Wembley, resembled a hospital casualty ward as players queued up for treatment from the overworked doctor and physiotherapist. The Hull pack, the strength of the team, was devastated when the two Drake brothers, Jim and Bill, and Cyril Sykes were forced to pull out with injuries. Such was the length of the injury list on Humberside that, in several changes to the normal team lineup, the 22-year-old Mike Smith achieved the distinction of making his debut for the club at Wembley. What a start to a rugby career! Trinity, in contrast, had just one injury problem, albeit a serious one, with one of their finest players, Harold Poynton. The experienced Ken Rollin more than adequately deputised.

It was no surprise that the unfortunate Hull side, though gallantly led by the outstanding John Whiteley at loose forward, were no match for their opponents and were soon in terrible trouble. The game was just two minutes old when Fox began the march to his record-breaking 20 points with a well-struck penalty goal that gave him the confidence to perform as well as he eventually did.

I had the good fortune to be presented with a goalkicking chance in the opening minutes. If you can put your first shot over the crossbar in those early minutes then it can make such a difference to your confidence. I had never practised, as many do, at Wembley on the Friday because I felt that whatever I did in practice might not match my ambitions on the Saturday. When the ball went through the posts it gave me the confidence to add more.

Two minutes later, it was Neil Fox's old schoolpal Ken Rollin who increased Trinity's lead to 5–0 when he cleverly supported one of loose forward Derek Turner's breaks, kicked over Hull full back Jack Kershaw's head and dived in at the corner to score. Hull, though they did temporarily level the scores with a Stan Cowan try and a Sam Evans conversion, were never in the hunt. The losers held Wakefield to a respectable 7–5 scoreline at half time, Fox adding the second of his seven goals, but in the second half they were routed by the stronger and faster Trinity. The speed and power of Trinity's back division, and especially Fox and Skene in the centre, caused havoc with the slower-moving Hull forwards, who included prop Sam Evans, at 18 stones 7 pounds one of the biggest men ever to play at Wembley. For Trinity, forwards Turner, Vines and Firth made the breaks, and Fox and Skene, who also grabbed two tries, responded.

For my first try I ran the first 20 yards in support, then when I got the ball I had to straighten up and run 60 yards to score behind the posts. The pitch at Wembley has a tiring effect on your legs, and I was pleased to get that try. That try stands out in my memory. For the other try I crashed over at the corner and was delighted to be able to convert it with a goal from the touchline. Sadly, for neutral fans, it became one-way traffic and we were in complete control. We began to score so often in the final 20 minutes that it became a little difficult to concentrate.

Not only Neil Fox enjoyed himself in Trinity colours for, in the final three minutes of the match, Wakefield wing Fred Smith helped himself to a try, and outstanding scrum half Keith Holliday also touched down in the closing seconds of the game to provide record-breaker Fox with his seventh successful goal attempt.

To score 20 points from two tries and seven goals in a Challenge Cup final and not win the vote for the man of the match takes some explaining. Yet Wakefield's gentle giant did not add the Lance Todd Trophy to his coveted cup winner's medal. Instead, the award went to Hull's courageous Welsh hooker Tommy Harris, who defied concussion and two exits from the pitch for treatment to turn in a tremendous tackling display. And rightly so, according to Neil Fox.

Tommy was a very deserving winner of the Lance Todd Trophy. He was everywhere on the field, tackling everybody in a Wakefield jersey, and he made plenty of good breaks from the acting half-back position. Many people thought I should have been awarded the man of the match trophy, but I've watched the video of the match and I really do think that Tommy deserved the award for the effort he put into his game.

Without doubt, whatever the merits of the award, Neil Fox's performance signalled the arrival of one of the greats of the 13-a-side code. The power of his running and tackling, the precision of his passing and his qualities of leadership stamped him out as one of that rare breed of player who sadly grace the game only at irregular intervals. For Huddersfield and Wigan his appearances at Wembley, however, were not irregular, for twice within the next three years he added to his medal collection and collected a further 19 points at their expense. In 1962 against Huddersfield he became the only player to collect three drop goals in a final, while against Wigan in the following year he displayed his uncanny goalkicking accuracy once again with a five-goal haul.

As ex-Springbok ace Alan Skene, Fox's centre partner and scorer of two tries in the 1960 final, told me from his home in Wilderness, South Africa, few players were more at home at Wembley than Neil Fox:

Neil was truly a gentle giant, so strong in the tackle and such a powerful runner on the burst. It was a pleasure to play alongside him at Wembley, for he was totally unconcerned by the occasion. He was a big-match player and seemed to relish the unique atmosphere. We formed a most rewarding partnership and, I think, acted as foils to each other. His impact on the opposition was immense because whether running, passing or kicking they could never take their eyes off him for a moment. If they did, then it was to their cost. A great player.

WAKEFIELD TRINITY Round; Smith, Skene, Fox, Etty; Rollin, Holliday; Wilkinson, Oakes, Vines, Firth, Chamberlain, Turner.

HULL Kershaw; Harrison, Cowan, Halatihi, Johnson; Broadhurst, Finn; Scott, Harris, Evans, Sutton, Smith, Whiteley.

Scorers Wakefield Trinity   *Tries* Fox (2), Rollin, Skene (2), Holliday (2), Smith. *Goals* Fox (7).

               Hull   *Tries* Cowan. *Goals* Evans.

Referee E. Clay (Leeds).

Jeff Grayshon

Great Britain 25 New Zealand 8

Second Test, Central Park, Wigan
2 November 1985

Born 4 March 1949. Though a latecomer to the sport at 20 years of age, Jeff Grayshon emulated the longevity of those immortals, Wales' own Jim Sullivan and Gus Risman, by playing well past his 44th year and into his 24th season. Indeed, the former Dewsbury, Bradford Northern, Leeds, Featherstone Rovers and Batley pack star achieved the dubious distinction of playing for Featherstone against his own son and Bradford prop, Paul, four years ago. Starting his career in the backs, where he developed his slick ball-handling skills, he became the oldest player, at 36 years and eight months, ever to win a Great Britain cap when he played in his last and 13th Test against New Zealand at Elland Road, Leeds, on 9 November 1985. A giant of a man at 6 feet 2 inches and 17 stones, Jeff revealed a fine turn of pace and speed off the mark which left many a midfield defence flat-footed and put him at the centre of many a shock raid. Rated highly by one of Britain's leading coaches, former Great Britain boss Peter Fox, he proved the cornerstone of Fox's pack plans for many years at Bradford and Featherstone, helping the controversial coach to considerable championship and cup successes.

Around 4.30 p.m. on Saturday, 2 November 1985 over four million of BBC television's *Grandstand* viewers witnessed the sight of a huge, fierce, mud-spattered prop forward turn to the cameras and deliver a wide grin of satisfaction. The Great Britain pack star was sending no fond greetings to those of his family watching at home; rather was he having a laugh at the expense of my co-commentator of the Great Britain v. New Zealand Test, Alex Murphy, who, in the week before, had had the gall to ridicule the selection of Jeff Grayshon, the oldest forward ever to play for his country. An outstanding performance from the front row man had made Murphy eat his own words and admit that Grayshon's recall to the Test scene, after a three-year absence, had been more than justified.

When the match was over I couldn't resist turning to one of the cameras and giving a smile in Alex's direction. I think I proved him wrong. During the week in his newspaper columns he had ridiculed my selection, had said that I was too old to play at Test level. He told me to keep taking the pills. Well, I didn't need any pills, and I think I justified our coach Maurice Bamford's decision.

In the modern game, especially since the introduction of the six-tackle rule, the role of the prop forward has changed dramatically and has been heavily influenced by the style of play of the Australians. Today, the props are expected to drive strongly with the ball in midfield, take the ball up to the opposition and seek to put a dent or two in the defences around the play-the-ball area. If they can gain precious yards and take play even further away from their own tryline then so much the better. And, unlike the demands on a prop in the 1950s and 1960s, both the number eight and number ten are expected to perform similar tasks. Not so when internationals Brian McTigue, Brian Edgar, Norman Herbert and Alan Prescott held sway, and the likes of Cliff Watson, Jack Wilkinson, John Henderson and Elwyn Gwyther complemented them with solid, no-nonsense, non-stop tackling performances. The number eight prop forward was invariably a ball player, a big man who could stand up in the tackle and offload the ball with a delicate short pass or a one-handed delivery of the ball to a runner in support. Jeff Grayshon was one such player, a throwback to a different age and a player who, if the conditions and the tactics were right, could direct the progress of a match. Great Britain boss Bamford wanted the then Leeds prop to do just that against New Zealand's powerful pack.

I had played in two and captained Great Britain in one of the Tests in 1982 against Australia, and I thought my international career was over. When Maurice Bamford rang me and asked me to do him a favour and a job by playing in the second Test against New Zealand, I knew he had stuck his neck out for me. The pressure was really on me, but I knew he had the confidence in me to do well.

I had trained hard all season, but I was more nervous than I'd ever been. I knew I'd still got it despite what others said. If your 'ticker' keeps you going, you are OK. It all depends whether you want it or not, and I did.

New Zealand rugby league, in the mid-1980s under the expert eye of coach Graham Lowe, was on its way to one of the most successful periods in the nation's history, and the Kiwis had certainly sent shock waves through the north with their well-deserved 24–22 defeat of Great Britain in the first Test at Headingley, Leeds. Their world-class forwards, the Sorensen brothers Kurt and Dane, and future captains Mark Graham and Hugh McGahan had laid the foundations for the win and looked too powerful for Britain's six. Maurice Bamford knew what he wanted and, when Lee Crooks went down with injury, then Jeff Grayshon was called in to add variety to the attack.

80

Though the first Test had produced some brilliant tries, the results of outstanding attacking rugby, the introduction of Grayshon was intended to give another point of attack, provide another ball player and allow Great Britain's ball-handling, pacy skipper Harry Pinner to move and attack out wider. The policy succeeded.

Harry was able to run and distribute the ball out wide while I could keep close to the play-the-ball. This gave us two points of attack, and I think the success of the plan was that we picked up four tries, all to Garry Schofield, in the backs.

Jeff Grayshon's 'old head' allowed him to dominate the midfield, where his timely ball distribution found willing runners in the speedy Wigan second row duo Andy Goodway and Ian Potter. They tore huge holes in the Kiwi defences and set up the positions for Britain to launch the attacks that led to Garry Schofield's record-equalling four tries in a Kiwi Test. Skipper Harry Pinner particularly enjoyed himself wider out, linking up with Tony Myler and Ellery Hanley to provide yet more points of attack down the flanks. As coach Bamford insisted, his selection was justified and Murphy's outspoken condemnation of it was proved to be totally misguided. Said Bamford: 'We played the first Test 95 per cent from the heart and only 5 per cent from the head. In Test football you have to do more thinking, and in the second Test we did just that.'

The absence of the Kiwis' outstanding second row, Mark Graham, who had suffered an ankle injury in the Headingley clash, proved a bitter blow to the New Zealand coach Graham Lowe. But the introduction of the giant 6 feet 5 inches Graeme West on his Central Park home ground was expected to lessen the damage. New Zealand had one of the toughest and most fierce of Test packs, and such was its strength that Mr Lowe could even leave the man who had frightened the Aussies in Test rugby, Kevin Tamati, on the substitutes' bench for the opening to the series. Grayshon, Watkinson, Fieldhouse, Goodway, Potter and Pinner tamed them.

When Great Britain do well in Test battles they invariably have big men in their front row. Jeff Grayshon certainly is a big man and capable of slugging it out at close quarters with the best of them. He and John Fieldhouse rarely took a backward step in the heated exchanges between the two packs of forwards and kept the momentum of the Lions pack going forward all the time. New Zealand's much-vaunted pack power was not only blunted but they were swept aside and proved no match for the best of British beef. Jeff Grayshon led the charge and his colleagues responded superbly.

Though I played well, the match stands out in my memory more for proving everyone wrong and proving to myself that I could still perform at the top level. I may have been 36, but I think I proved that I wasn't 'over the hill'. Everyone seemed to think that the British forwards would be afraid of the Sorensen brothers. They were two tough forwards, but they didn't frighten me. Our pack worked really hard, everyone played for each other and the spirit was marvellous. We got right on top of them, and that's when Garry Schofield got his tries.

Such had been the humiliation inflicted on the New Zealand Test side in that Test, and on the pack in particular, that coach Graham Lowe rocked his fans Down Under when he made ten changes for the deciding third Test and retained only the two Sorensens, Kurt and Dane, in the pack – a bold move which acknowledged both the tactical supremacy of his opponents and the impact on the outcome of the match by the ageing battler in Great Britain's front row. Sadly for Britain, Jeff Grayshon's inclusion in the third Test a week later was unable to sway the outcome of the match, the result being a 6–6 draw and a tied series. He did, however, have the last laugh on his critics, and Alex Murphy in particular, in the Test that proved a rugby player's life really can begin again at 36 years of age.

Afterwards, a chastened but gracious Alex agreed with him:

I would never knock Jeff's ability, for at his peak he was a great forward, but at 36 years of age I thought he was past his best and said so in my newspaper articles. Jeff read my article and said to himself, 'I'll show him', and he did.

I hold my hands up to him. He proved me wrong and I'm glad he did, for he helped us to beat the Kiwis and eventually tie the Test series. I thought he was past his best and he proved that he wasn't.

GREAT BRITAIN Burke; Drummond, Schofield, Hanley, Lydon; Myler, Fox; Grayshon, Watkinson, Fieldhouse, Goodway, Potter, Pinner. *Subs*: Edwards, Burton.

NEW ZEALAND Kemble; Bell, Leuluai, Prohm, O'Hara; Filipaina, Friend; K. Sorensen, H. Tamati, D. Sorensen, West, Stewart, McGahan. *Subs*: Ah Kuoi, Cowan.

Scorers Great Britain *Tries* Schofield (4). *Goals* Lydon (4). *Drop Goals* Pinner.
New Zealand *Tries* Bell. *Goals* Filipaina (2).

Referee Barry Gomersall (Australia).

Andy Gregory

Halifax 12 Wigan 32
Challenge Cup Final, Wembley
30 April 1988

Born 10 August 1961. Andy Gregory is a product of the famous amateur nursery Wigan St. Patricks and has been the midfield dynamo at Widnes, Warrington, Wigan, Illawarra, Leeds and Salford for the past 14 seasons. Though barely 5 feet 4 inches in height and 13 stones in weight, this tough, resilient scrap metal merchant proved such an inspirational and powerful force behind a pack of forwards at scrum half that his move from Warrington to Wigan in the 1986–87 season smashed the then world transfer record and raised it to over £130,000. Never happier than when he is battling on the world's stage, Gregory gained 26 Great Britain caps and enjoyed three Lions tours Down Under in 1984, 1988 and 1992 in a long and distinguished international career stretching back to his first appearance in a Test jersey in 1981 against France. His record of never having been on the losing side in eight Challenge Cup final appearances at Wembley and being one of only three players to win the Lance Todd man of the match award twice, in 1988 and 1990 against Halifax and Warrington, highlights the durability of this pugnacious little chap.

Fish and chips, steak and kidney pie – the ingredients are synonymous with each other. Take away one and the taste is somehow lacking. Wembley and Andy Gregory are as traditional on rugby league's Challenge Cup final day as the aforementioned delicacies; add a dash or two of the nuggety, strutting scrum half to the Wembley turf and you have the extra spice to whet the appetite of the fans. Eight times, on cup final day, the Great Britain half back has performed his tricks and his antics at the famous arena and never once has he trooped from the field clutching a loser's medal in his hand. Truly a remarkable record, and one which, following his first playing visit in 1981 for Widnes against Hull Kingston Rovers, he hardly anticipated.

I can vaguely remember my first Wembley as an 18-year-old when I scored a try in Widnes's 18–9 win over Hull KR. It took me three days after the event to come back down to earth and for the celebration drinks to wear off. I could remember little about the game itself just three days after, and

83

when my brother asked me what the experience was like I told him that I would have to go back again to find out.

Little did I know then that it would be for another seven cup finals.

Even visionary Widnes coach Doug Laughton must have known a thing or two about his new signing's future ambitions when he persuaded him to leave the Wigan St. Patricks amateur club and join him at Naughton Park. Though Laughton's fee for the 17-year-old prodigy was a small one, the offer of two Challenge Cup final tickets completed the transaction.

I signed for Widnes in 1979 on the Wednesday before they played Wakefield Trinity at Wembley. Doug Laughton, in trying to persuade me to join him at Widnes, offered me a couple of tickets to go down and watch them play. The tickets he gave me were, I think, more than my signing-on fee. But I enjoyed the day and they did the trick.

Andy Gregory's affection for Wembley, however, began as a tiny youngster when, in common with many schoolchildren in the north, he was taken to the famous twin towers on the annual school trip. Such visits to see the stars in action are usually the end-of-season treat after the hard slog of a dark, wet, windy winter spent learning the skills of the game. So it was with the nine-year-old Gregory as he set out on his first trip to Wembley, ironically to watch perhaps the game's greatest-ever scrum half, Alex Murphy, win the very Lance Todd Trophy Gregory himself was to hold aloft 17 years later.

My enthusiasm for rugby and Wembley was first fired at school, at Whelley Middle School in Wigan, by the rugby master Derek Birchall. He used to take us down to the cup final, and it was he who fired my imagination for the place.

I can remember my first trip was Leigh v. Leeds with Alex Murphy playing, and then I went to see Featherstone play Bradford. They were great occasions for the school.

Derek Birchall spent many hours with me at school helping me to practise the skills, and he must take a lot of credit for my success in rugby. He certainly was the one who started me off on the Wembley trail.

As a player, Andy had visited Wembley with Widnes on three occasions prior to his first appearance with Wigan in 1988, when he also won the man of the match award for the first time. He was already accustomed to the stadium's unique atmosphere, the crescendo of noise that reverberates around the terraces, and that daunting, unnerving moment when a player first steps from the tunnel and on to the pitch. The experience can, and has done frequently, shatter the most seasoned campaigner's nerves. Matches have been won and lost in the Wembley tunnel, heroes have been made or destroyed before they ever touched the ball. Wigan's confident number seven was ready for the experience and relished it.

> The atmosphere is at its most wonderful when you line up beside the opposition in the tunnel. It is so dark in there and you can hear so little. You are sheltered from the sounds on the pitch outside even though you are standing barely 20 yards away from it.
>
> But as soon as you walk out, the roar of the crowd is deafening and can knock you back a little. The light is so bright as you come out of the tunnel it's almost like going on to a stage. It's a tremendous feeling and one I've never got sick of experiencing.

A sell-out 94,273 crowd greeted Halifax and Wigan on Saturday, 30 April 1988 with the customary blaring of horns, the waving of banners and the humorous chants of encouragement. The two Kop ends of the famous stadium, then much more colourful before the introduction of seats, were a mass of cherry and white and blue and white as two of the best overseas coaches in the game, Wigan's Kiwi boss Graham Lowe and Halifax coach Chris Anderson, settled themselves on the bench at the side of the pitch. As ever, the scene was set for heroes, and Andy Gregory, the orchestrator of a masterly Wigan performance, was just 80 minutes away from receiving the accolade that proved it.

To play against Andy Gregory must be a most frustrating experience. I well remember my own infuriating experiences in the 1960s trying to come to terms with similar characters like Roger Millward, Harold Poynton or Tommy Bishop as they dodged and darted about in midfield, having sufficient pace and guile always to keep you at arm's length before, with a flick of the hips, they shot away through the gap you had unknowingly created. Fans rarely appreciate that for a lumbering second row it is invariably much easier to deal with a 17-stone giant bearing down on you. Halifax, slower and more ponderous than Wigan, must have experienced similar feelings as the diminutive 5 feet 4 inches Gregory proceeded to display his complete repertoire of tricks.

Short passes launched Wigan's back row trio of Andy Goodway, Ian Potter and Ellery Hanley at the heart of the Halifax defences and, if those defences held back off the manipulator himself, then Gregory had the wit and the pace to burst through the thin blue and white line. If the defence came up too quickly, a long 20- or 30-yard pass would cut out the too hasty tackler and launch centres Kevin Iro or Dean Bell down the flanks. Kicks of varied length, some to touch, some chip kicks, and some delicately placed grubber kicks to the corners for the powerful Tony Iro, tormented the Yorkshiremen and kept them on retreat for most of the game. And the crowd even had sight of a rare event for Gregory at Wembley, a successful conversion of an Ellery Hanley try. He masterminded the whole operation, combining with stand off Shaun Edwards to produce one of the best half-back performances given by any pair at Wembley.

A taste of what was in store for the luckless Halifax came in the 24th minute when one of Gregory's short passes launched the speedy Edwards through a gap in midfield. He didn't score, but his devastating run close to the Halifax tryline allowed the huge Kiwi, Kevin Iro, to crash over from the resulting play-the-ball. Four minutes later Gregory had combined with Bell to launch wing Henderson Gill down the touchline and in for a try at the corner. Halifax, allowing Wigan's mini-maestro too much room in which to weave his magic, were in serious trouble.

Halifax seemed to hang back a little in the middle and gave us plenty of room. Things just seemed to go well for me. I managed to make a few breaks and was able to get them going backwards with a few little chip kicks, some of which I was able to re-gather and keep the movement going. Perhaps my best memory of the action in midfield was being able to put a pass out of the tackle and around the man to help Dean Bell to a try.

There was to be no respite for Halifax, by no means a poor side and containing experienced internationals Aussie full back Graham Eadie and a fine ball-handling back row trio in Les Holliday, Paul Dixon and John Pendlebury. But, making full use of Wigan's talented army of internationals around him, Gregory simply destroyed the opposition. A try he created for wing Tony Iro in the 46th minute revealed his complete control and that perfect timing between the eye and the hand that all great players possess. On receiving the ball, a quick glance to his right told Gregory that former Wigan favourite Colin Whitfield had moved infield off the wing just a fraction too far in anticipation of executing a crash tackle. His long floated pass to Iro, a yard or two outside Whitfield on the right flank, eluded the grasp of the Halifax defender and immediately placed him in rugby's version of no man's land. Whitfield could neither go forward nor move outside; he could only turn and forlornly chase the powerful Kiwi to the tryline.

The split-second timing of the pass and the immediate realisation of the tryscoring opportunity were just two of the reasons why the nation's rugby league press awarded Andy Gregory their votes for the man of the match award, the Lance Todd Trophy. And yet, for all his outstanding contribution to Wigan's convincing 32–12 victory, he still modestly insists it was the team performance, not his, which won the day.

Probably the highlight of my career was winning the Lance Todd Trophy for the first time with my home town club, Wigan. It was probably the finest team performance I've been involved in.

Rugby league is a team game and everybody has his own job to do. It just so happens that the scrum half is the playmaker and that I have the ball in my hands more often that some of my colleagues, so the press tend to concentrate on my contribution. Though medals, records and awards are OK, the main thing is the performance of the team.

Very true words, but there is always one player who kick-starts a team into life, and at Wembley in April 1988 that man was Andy Gregory.

HALIFAX Eadie; Meredith, Anderson, Wilkinson, Whitfield; Grogan, Robinson; James, McCallion, Neller, Holliday, Dixon, Pendlebury. *Subs*: Scott, Fairbank.

WIGAN Lydon; T. Iro, K. Iro, Bell, Gill; Edwards, Gregory; Case, Kiss, Shelford, Goodway, Potter, Hanley. *Subs*: Byrne, Wane.

Scorers Halifax *Tries* Anderson, James. *Goals* Whitfield (2).
　　　　　　 Wigan *Tries* K. Iro (2), T. Iro, Gill, Lydon, Hanley, Bell. *Goals* Gregory, Lydon.

Referee Fred Lindop (Wakefield).

Mike Gregory

Wigan 36 Warrington 14
Challenge Cup Final, Wembley
28 April 1990

Born 20 May 1964. Rugby league can be a cruel sport, especially when, after thrilling television audiences worldwide with an exhilarating 70-yard tryscoring dash against Australia in Great Britain's Ashes win in the third Test in 1988 and captaining the Lions to a Test series win in New Zealand two years later, almost three years of your career are taken from you. Such have been the trials of Warrington and Great Britain skipper Mike Gregory, whose outstanding career has been marred by crippling injuries. Twenty Test caps and the captaincy of his country between 1987 and 1990 are proof of this blond-haired loose forward's rugby prowess, while his battles against injuries, which would have destroyed the spirit of any sportsman, bear testimony to the former Wigan St. Patricks youngster's courage and dedication. A torn cruciate knee ligament in November 1990, cartilage damage to both knees in March and November of 1991 and the tearing of an Achilles tendon in 1993 would have proved sufficient to finish the best of battlers. Not so Mike Gregory, who remained confident throughout his troubles of a permanent return to the sport he loves. Few players can ever have deserved being awarded a testimonial as much as Gregory in 1993–94 season for his ten-year service to Warrington.

When a soccer player climbs into his car after the match on a Saturday afternoon and heads for the leafy suburbs, he leaves his fans on the terraces at Old Trafford, Elland Road or Anfield far behind. The fans are no part of his daily life, and the pressures on the soccer star are consequently fewer. Most rugby league players, being part-time professionals and pursuing another career from Monday to Friday, never escape the fans. They work with them, talk with them and play with them. The pressures for the practitioners of the 13-a-side code are higher, and never higher than when you are playing against your home town team in front of your former schoolmates, friends and family. Warrington and Great Britain loose forward Mike Gregory was under such pressure when he walked out of the tunnel at Wembley to face Wigan in the 1990 Challenge Cup final. But he was also a very proud young man, determined to prove himself to his own.

* * *

It was my first time at Wembley and I think one of my best games. All my friends and family were there from Wigan and I had so much to live up to. I'll never forget leading the boys out of the tunnel, listening to the roar as it rang around the stadium, and adjusting my eyes to the brilliant sunlight. Wigan had been there many times, but I was so proud to be lining up against them. I wasn't nervous. I knew I had a job to do. I was more nervous on the Friday before the match walking around the empty stadium. It was an eerie feeling. I was nervous then.

Like many captains before him, and since, the Wire's skipper was forced to bow the knee, the one that was to give him so much pain and trouble over the next three seasons. Yet, despite suffering a big defeat, Mike Gregory could stand with pride among his family and friends at the post-match drinks reception and reflect on a memorable performance. The losers' dressing room at Wembley is a lonely place. Coaches tend to lean on the wall, huddling themselves into a corner, hushed and silent, reflecting on what might have been. The club chairman can often be seen moving quietly around among his players, patting the occasional one on the back and whispering condolences in ears which are shut to the world. A journalist will step inside, hesitatingly and somewhat sheepishly, not knowing what to say, not knowing what to expect. The players sit dejectedly, their elbows on their knees and their heads in their hands, staring at the floor. A lonely, melancholy place is the losers' dressing room, yet always there will be a Mike Gregory who, amid all the despondency, knows deep down that he played the game of his life. Such was Wembley, 1990.

Wigan, inspired at half back by Great Britain duo Shaun Edwards and Andy Gregory, were in total control from the kickoff. Edwards, despite receiving a fractured cheekbone as early as the ninth minute, had a hand in at least three tries, while Gregory, the Lance Todd Trophy winner, masterminded the forward play and provided the free-running situations that eventually led to a brace of tries each to centre Kevin Iro and pacy wing Mark Preston. Up front, such was the pressure from the Wigan pack that it was inevitable that back rowers Denis Betts and Ellery Hanley should also get their names on the tryscorers' list. With Wigan wing Joe Lydon in fine goalkicking form, landing six attempts, Warrington were on the defensive for most of the match, and Mike Gregory had soon to put family and friends to the back of his mind.

The Warrington team was far better than the way it performed on the day. The biggest disappointment to me was the way Wigan had gone so far away from us by half time. I had to work hard along with our forwards covering tackles out wide and helping to stop the bigger Wigan pack.

Wigan never let up with the pressure, and the Wembley pitch suddenly became a very large place.

Wigan deservedly strolled to their third successive Challenge Cup, but not before Warrington's loose forward showed just why he was chosen to lead Great Britain's tour of Papua New Guinea and New Zealand a few weeks later. In Warrington assistant coach Clive Griffiths' opinion, his loose forward was the ideal man to take the battle back to Wigan:

> As a captain he led by example, and Warrington could not have had a better captain on the day. He is a powerful player and a model professional.
>
> The try he scored after half time gave us a real lift, and the taking of it epitomised his efforts throughout the match. His try proved to Wigan that we were not dead and buried, at least not for another 40 minutes!

Two tries, one to full back David Lyon and one to himself, plus a superb example of covering, proved the highlights of an outstanding captain's performance.

With a half time scoreline of 16–2 in Wigan's favour, many in the crowd settled back for the expected onslaught from the cup holders. The avalanche of points did eventually bury any lingering hopes Wire's fans might have had of a revival, but at least they had the satisfaction of seeing their skipper go down fighting. His opening try at the beginning of the second half was a gem. A couple of forward drives helped to bunch the Wigan defenders around the play-the-ball area before lively half back Paul Bishop switched play from left to right with a perfectly flighted pass. Running on to the ball at full speed, Mike Gregory used every ounce of his 14 stones and a surprising turn of speed to reduce Wigan's defences to tatters.

> The try came off a move which we had worked a few times during the season. When Paul Bishop switched play, I had to be out wide and running from a deep position. When the ball came to me I was able to wrongfoot Wigan's prop Adrian Shelford, who came into the tackle too quickly, and then I sold Andy Gregory a dummy to take me through the line. I was able to get past Steve Hampson at full back with a handoff and score beneath the posts. I don't score many tries, and that try was one I'll savour for a long time to come.

Warrington full back David Lyon had suffered early in the match when he saw his clearance kick charged down by Shaun Edwards and collected on the rebound by Wigan international second row Denis Betts for a try. He was able to make amends in the 75th minute when, following Steve Hampson's knock-on, captain Mike Gregory stormed off on another charging run and, surprising Wigan once again with his speed and swerve, provided the tryscoring pass. The modern loose forward, as opposed to those of yesteryear like Derek Turner, Vince Karalius and John Whiteley, who did most of their best ball work around the rucks, has to be an all-purpose, all-action, dashing runner able to roam out wide and match the backs for speed. Australia's Wayne Pearce and Bradley Clyde and Great Britain's Ellery Hanley and Mike Gregory are such loose forwards and one magnificent piece of coverwork practised by the Warrington number 13, even if ultimately to little avail, amply highlighted the qualities needed by the loose forward of the 1990s.

A sweeping movement from within Wigan's 20-metre area suddenly burst through Warrington's fragile defences and threatened danger down the left flank. Such was the quality of the support work from Ellery Hanley, Kevin Iro and Shaun Edwards, and the pace of flying wing Mark Preston, there was little chance of any of Warrington's cover tacklers halting the tryscoring movement. But that didn't deter Gregory from getting himself within an inch or two of success.

> Wigan's full back Steve Hampson started the movement about 25 yards from his own line. I tracked him until he passed the ball to Kevin Iro, who passed it to Ellery Hanley. I knew I had them covered all the time they were moving upfield, and knew I could crowd them out. When Shaun Edwards received the ball I continued to follow him down the left touchline, and when I got within diving distance of him I managed to take him out with the tackle. But he's such a quick-thinking player, as I hit him in the tackle he managed to flick up the ball to Mark Preston, and there was no way we could stop him scoring. It was a great try, but I was proud of that tackle as I had to cover so much ground and so many players before I finally made it.

According to Wire's assistant coach Clive Griffiths, only his skipper could have trailed back to catch Edwards so quickly:

> In cover defence Mike is so fit and strong that such tackles come second nature to him. If anyone was ever going to catch up with Shaun Edwards then he alone among our players was the one who could easily get back. He is such a fast runner. He tracked the move perfectly, and was really unlucky when he stopped Shaun Edwards, only to see him flick the ball out of the tackle for another Wigan score. But it was still a marvellous tackle and an example to any aspiring youngsters.

The speed and confidence displayed in his tryscoring runs and courageous cover tackling, however, hid a problem that was to return to plague the Warrington captain. For three months prior to the Challenge Cup final Mike

Gregory had suffered a troublesome Achilles tendon strain, an injury particularly damaging to a forward who relied on his kick start and speed off the mark to glide past defenders. Indeed, such was the extent of the damage that he was advised not to tour with the Great Britain squad to New Zealand in the summer following the clash with Wigan. His gamble only partly paid off for, though his performance at Wembley was hardly below par, he did suffer pain and has continued to be troubled ever since.

> In the run-up to Wembley I was suffering from a strained Achilles tendon, and I was advised that any tour in the summer would seriously damage it. I wanted to lead Great Britain in New Zealand, and I wanted to lead Warrington at Wembley. I gambled that I could get through the Wembley final. I did, but I think it proved costly later.

However, as Mike Gregory sat in the Warrington dressing room around 5 p.m. on that fateful Saturday in April, his thoughts were, unselfishly, not for his injury troubles but for the Warrington fans he felt he had let down. He and his side had held such high hopes, and yet they had suffered a humiliating defeat by a magnificent Wigan side. His thoughts and his sentiments nonetheless amply illustrate the pride and the professionalism which have accompanied him throughout his ten action-packed seasons at Wilderspool.

> Sitting in the dressing room after the match was distressing. It was the worst feeling I have ever had in my rugby league career. As captain I felt that I had let all of the Warrington people down. There had been such responsibility on my shoulders and the defeat was hard to take. I knew that we were a much better team than we had shown, and couldn't come to terms for a while with the defeat. I was pleased with my own performance, but I would have preferred to win the cup for the Warrington fans.

WARRINGTON Lyon; Drummond, Mercer, Darbyshire, Forster; Crompton, Bishop; Burke, Mann, Harmon, Jackson, Sanderson, M. Gregory. *Subs*: Thomas, McGinty.

WIGAN Hampson; Lydon, K. Iro, Bell, Preston; Edwards, A. Gregory; Shelford, Dermott, Platt, Betts, Goodway, Hanley. *Subs*: Goulding, Gildart.

Scorers Warrington *Tries* M. Gregory, Lyon. *Goals* Bishop (2), Darbyshire.
Wigan *Tries* Iro (2), Preston (2), Betts, Hanley. *Goals* Lydon (6).

Referee John Holdsworth (Kippax).

David Hobbs

Featherstone Rovers 14 Hull 12
Challenge Cup Final, Wembley
7 May 1983

Born 13 September 1958. The role of the modern prop forward is far different to that of 20 years ago, when David Hobbs first pulled on his jersey for Feathertone Rovers Colts. Today, the emphasis is on taking the ball up from the play-the-ball areas, tackling around the rucks and hitting the gain line at speed. Bradford Northern and former Oldham and Featherstone forward Hobbs has long since adapted his style to the demands of the modern game, yet, in his powerful kicking, his precision passing and his tactical appreciation of a running game, he reminds one of props of yesteryear like Vic Yorke and Harry Bath. A strong man, standing at 6 feet 1 inch and tipping the scales at well over 16 stones, he has never been one to shirk the action and fierce exchanges between the forwards, especially when confronted with the green and gold jersey of Australia or the black and white of New Zealand. His 12 international caps gained between 1984 and 1989 and his successful tour Down Under with Great Britain in 1984 were fitting rewards for a hard-working, intelligent forward.

In recent seasons he has harnessed his deep thinking on the game to coaching Bradford Northern for 19 months between March 1990 and October 1991 and recently has been assistant to Northern's outspoken boss, Peter Fox.

The 'great divide' which split rugby in 1895 effectively separated, for many years in the north of England, the players into two distinct groups. Those hardy souls who were unable to give up a couple of hours on a Saturday afternoon for their sport without receiving 'broken time' payments for their efforts were mostly to be found among the working classes, populating the mills and the mines of Lancashire and Yorkshire. Those who insisted upon the true spirit of amateurism were inevitably drawn from the leisured classes, and it was natural that both sections of society and their two codes of rugby should develop in vastly differing ways.

Few of the leisured classes inhabited the mining villages of Featherstone, Castleford or Wakefield at the turn of the century, where the tough mining communities developed a spirit of their own and a sport, rugby league, which complemented and unified their way of life. Pits and rugby league, the focal points of many northern towns, developed alongside each other as miners came up for air on a Saturday afternoon and were rewarded with a few shillings for expending their breath kicking a football about on a field. The mines produced tough, hard men, skilful with their hands and nimble on their feet, who could entertain their work-mates and at the same time attain a better standard of living for their families. Pride in their work and their play united the community in those harsh early days of the rugby league code.

In Featherstone, in 1983, that spirit still flourished, that bond between the mines and the game still prevailed, and the lads still came up for air on a Saturday (or Sunday) afternoon to play their sport. On Saturday, 7 May they came 'up for t' cup', and the 24-year-old David Hobbs was one of them.

> We were very much a home town club, a minnow in the world of rugby league. Eleven of our fifteen-man squad at Wembley were miners in the pits around the town, and there was a terrific spirit among the players. There was a special bond between the players and the supporters, many of whom worked alongside the players below the ground. We were all lads from a mining community who just wanted to play for each other and win something for the town. All I ever wanted to do as a lad was to play rugby league for Featherstone.

In the 1982–83 season the odds on David Hobbs winning something for Featherstone seemed remote, as Rovers lay deep in the relegation zone of the First Division and, prior to the draw for the first round of the Challenge Cup, were placed at odds of 33–1 to win the cup by the local bookmakers. At the turn of the year a dismal season was in prospect . . . until another Featherstone lad returned to Post Office Road to take advantage of that unique spirit in the tiny Yorkshire town. Allan Agar, who had joined Rovers as a youngster in 1967 and who stayed a couple of seasons, returned only in December of 1982 after a successful playing and coaching career with Dewsbury, Hull KR, Wakefield and Carlisle. A seasoned, experienced professional, he knew what rich seams he could tap into at Featherstone, but, on his return, as he indicates, his mind was very far removed from Wembley in May:

> The team contained players with the talent to play at the highest levels, but their mental attitude was a problem. Convincing them that they could be effective was difficult. In each round of the cup I felt we would win, but I could not say with any honesty that I thought we would win the cup. After all, it was the fight for league points that really occupied my thoughts.

And Wembley hero Hobbs agrees that when the side faced Batley in the opening round of the Challenge Cup trail the players' priority was the fight for survival in Division One.

* * *

It was a battle all season in the First Division. In that season four clubs were due to be relegated, and all year we hovered around the 12th or 13th position in the league. In the end it all depended on Hull beating Barrow to keep us in the First Division. We finished in 12th position and only stayed up on points-scoring difference. Winning the Challenge Cup was far from our minds.

The bookmakers' odds too seemed a fair reflection of the make-up of the two sides as they approached the fateful day.

The glamorous Hull team harboured few of the leisured classes, yet they were a world apart from the struggling Featherstone club. Having captured the Challenge Cup the previous season with a win over Widnes in a replay at Elland Road, and having won the Yorkshire Cup and the First Division Championship in 1982–83, their odds of 4–1 at the start of the campaign to lift the cup again seemed to offer a realistic bet for any punter. Rovers had a leading goalkicker in Steve Quinn, a crafty scrum half in Terry Hudson, an outstanding loose forward in Peter Smith and the skills of Hobbs himself, but the full 13 hardly looked a match for the Hull side, assembled from all over the rugby world at great cost. International forwards Lee Crooks, Kelvin Skerrett and Steve Norton gave the side its solidity, at half back two more internationals, David Topliss and Paul Harkin, gave the team its guile while, behind, the three Kiwi stars, Gary Kemble, James Leuluai and Dane O'Hara, provided the vital ingredients of pace and flair. Featherstone Rovers had illustrated the hidden steel in their side by defeating the mighty St. Helens at Knowsley Road by 11–10 in the third round but, even as they set out for London in the week prior to their great day, there was a relaxed, carefree approach to the final.

We went down south prepared to give it our best shot. Everyone in the press had written us off, and we were just determined to have a good day. I think we went to London hardly caring whether we won or lost; we just wanted to enjoy the occasion.

Our coach Allan Agar was very experienced, though, and he made it a fun week for us. We split into four teams and played games all week. We were completely relaxed by the time we got to Wembley.

Rovers were so relaxed that, within seven minutes of kickoff, they stunned the giants from Humberside with a cheeky try in the very corner of the pitch where they had practised the move on the previous Friday afternoon.

We practised a little blind-side move in the same corner in which we scored. Hull's centre James Leuluai dashed up a little too fast out wide, and our

95

scrum half Terry Hudson sold a couple of dummies inside and then slipped the ball to me on the outside. The gap was there and I just went for the try.

David Hobbs' try and the first of wing Steve Quinn's goals gave Rovers a confidence-boosting lead which, thanks to the solid defence of forwards Peter Smith, Mick Gibbins and Steve Hankins, they held until, in the second half, Hull finally began to assert themselves and show a little of their class. A Lee Crooks obstruction try and conversion, controversially awarded by Widnes referee Robin Whitfield, allowed the league champions to draw level, while a further try in the 54th minute from Hull's speedy centre James Leuluai, plus two further goals from Crooks, edged them into what looked to be a matchwinning 12–5 lead. That it was not to be owes much to that battling and defiant spirit forged beneath the streets of Featherstone.

Hull had plenty of speed and many players capable of racing the length of the field for a try. When we were 12–5 down I realised just how wide the pitch was, but there was a tremendous spirit in the team and no one gave up the hope of winning. Our pack began to get on top and we began to control possession in the middle, which allowed us to stay mostly in Hull's half.

Territorial advantage allowed Rovers the chance to add to their points with two more well-struck goals from the accurate Quinn and a second try from Lance Todd Trophy winner David Hobbs. A neat combination of passes among Rovers' forwards suddenly released David Hobbs in the clear. A burst of speed, hardly expected from such a huge frame, and Rovers' pack star dived over the Hull tryline to touch down. The scores were level.

Drama followed when, for a few seconds, the Featherstone Rovers fans thought Hobbs had again proved the hero with a matchwinning drop goal. An eagle-eyed referee and the hand of a Hull player desperately touching the ball in flight as it moved in the direction of the crossbar, however, dashed the fans' hopes, and no goal was, quite correctly, ruled. Hull could still not halt the inevitable giant-killing act as the Rovers pack, marshalled by Hobbs and prompted by half back Hudson, moved relentlessly forward and frustrated the faster Hull threequarter line. That frustration proved the Humberside club's undoing for, just when a second replay in successive years for Hull seemed inevitable, a foul tackle by Hull prop Charlie Stone on Rovers number 13 Peter Smith gave Featherstone's crack marksman Steve Quinn the chance to take the cup, unexpectedly, back to Post Office Road with just three minutes of the match remaining. He struck the ball true and flighted it perfectly between the posts to provide David Hobbs and his team-mates with the perfect ending.

To win the cup was a dream ending to the story. We were just overjoyed.

I had managed to score two tries and win the Lance Todd Trophy as well. I was absolutely delighted. No one outside Featherstone had ever thought that we could do it. We literally were a bunch of lads 'up for t' cup'! It was a Roy of the Rovers dream.

It was the realisation of a dream, too, for the families who crowded the tiny streets of Featherstone and the miners' welfare clubs in the days following their heroes' triumph to see and hold aloft the coveted Challenge Cup. That same spirit and pride, first kindled in the closing years of the last century, still burned brightly. Sadly, 11 years later, the mines that produced the players and their stirring deeds have gone, but thankfully their spirit still remains at Post Office Road.

FEATHERSTONE ROVERS Barker; Marsden, Quinn, Gilbert, Kellett; Banks, Hudson; Gibbins, Handscombe, Hankins, Hobbs, Slatter, Smith. *Subs*: Lyman, Siddall.

HULL Kemble; O'Hara, Evans, Leuluai, Prendiville; Topliss, Harkin; Skerrett, Bridges, Stone, Rose, Crooks, Norton. *Subs*: Day, Crane.

Scorers Featherstone Rovers   *Tries* Hobbs (2). *Goals* Quinn (4).
              Hull   *Tries* Leuluai, Crooks. *Goals* Crooks (3).

Referee Robin Whitfield (Widnes).

Garry Jack

New South Wales 22 Queensland 16
First State of Origin Match, Lang Park, Brisbane
27 May 1986

Born 14 March 1961. The blond-haired Garry Jack became an all-too-familiar figure to British rugby league fans as, with one rapier-like thrust from full back, he frequently destroyed their hopes with a tryscoring run. A flying tackle at the corner, his arms tightly wrapped around the thighs of a long-striding wing, would bring gasps of appreciation at his timing and courage. Little wonder that the most exciting number one of the 1980s should, in 1987, be awarded the 'Golden Boot' in recognition of being acknowledged as the world's greatest player.

After a couple of seasons with the Illawarra Juniors and Western Suburbs, Garry Jack in 1982 became one of Balmain's most famous sons, remaining loyal to the Tigers for over 11 seasons. International honours soon came his way, and such was his impact on Australian rugby league that the widely acclaimed Jack represented his country in three Ashes Test series with Great Britain in 1984, 1986 and 1988. It was on the Kangaroos tour of Great Britain and France in 1986 that he achieved the distinction of becoming the first full back to score a hat trick of tries in a Test when he collected three touchdowns in Australia's 52–0 win against France at Carcassonne.

His searing runs from the back and his courageous last-ditch tackles on the line were not confined to the green and gold jersey, for British fans had the opportunity to cheer him when he guested for Salford in the winter of 1987–88 and, in recent seasons, for Sheffield Eagles. He made his first move into coaching when he accepted a return to the Willows in July 1993 as player-coach with Salford.

When New South Wales full back Garry Jack dropped the ball behind his own tryline, following a testing high kick by an increasingly frantic Queensland side, tough prop Greg Dowling dived on the ball for what many considered to be the matchwinning try. An earlier try from Brisbane Broncos' giant centre Gene Miles, Dowling's opportunist try and four goals from Aussie skipper Mal Meninga had eased Queensland ahead by 16–12, and the experts on television, broadcasting the length and breadth of Australia, were of one opinion that New South Wales were finished. The 33,000 crowd packed into

Lang Park anticipating New South Wales' humiliation expected to roar their favourites home to a convincing win. But it was not to be, as the 'Blues' of New South Wales regrouped, summoned up last reserves of energy and spirit, and hit back with a win which was to set in motion the first 3–0 series whitewash in the State of Origin competition's history. As a defiant Garry Jack insisted:

> With 20 minutes remaining, we looked to be down and out, but our skipper, Wayne Pearce, led the fightback and we were soon in the lead again and on our way to a famous victory. We were the first team to win all three State of Origin matches and that was some performance because two of the matches were played at Lang Park in Brisbane. To come away with even one win from there is always very difficult.

With 20 minutes remaining in the first State of Origin match of the 1986 series, Queensland sensed victory as the master himself, Kangaroos' half-back star Wally Lewis, moved in for the kill. Lewis was at the peak of his form, spraying passes out far and wide around the pitch and able to break the tightest marking with the occasional burst down the middle. He was surrounded by a formidable pair of centres in the mighty Meninga and his 15 stone co-centre Miles and blessed with sheer pace on the wing in Dale Shearer. In the pack, Bob Lindner, Greg Dowling and Bryan Niebling were forcing the pace and testing the Blues full back.

> Dale Shearer got a quick ball on the wing and suddenly raced away towards our line. I raced alongside and managed to track him and get the angle on him as he approached our 20-metre line. I nailed him on the touchline, but it was a close-run thing. If he had scored, then we would have been beaten.

Shearer didn't score, and Queensland, despite their 16–12 lead, didn't win. For New South Wales, Garry Jack tackled heroically, and skipper Wayne Pearce, the brilliant Brett Kenny at half back and 16-stone second row Noel Cleal led the charges deep into enemy territory to set up the situation for hooker Royce Simmons' match-turning try. The Queensland fans, accustomed to displaying the same blind fanaticism as the ancient Romans when they bayed for the Christians' blood in the Colosseum, expected the thumbs down signal from their king, Wally Lewis. However, with tries from Chris Mortimer, Andrew Farrar, Royce Simmons and Jack himself, plus three goals from former Wallaby rugby union centre star Michael O'Connor, New South Wales had achieved the rare distinction of daring to win at Queensland's traditional rugby home, Lang Park.

Only those who have experienced Lang Park on State of Origin night can fully appreciate the unique atmosphere and partisan support which are generated in the stadium. High-powered floodlighting, firecrackers, rockets, dancing girls, marching bands and a full-house crowd can be intimidating to any player sitting under the clubhouse grandstand and waiting to come out of the dressing rooms. Those of a nervous disposition have been known to crack before leaving their seats, while even the boldest and the bravest await what is in store with more than a little trepidation. Since its inception, the State of Origin series has presented a tough obstacle for any player, however experienced.

There is always terrific pressure on any player in a State of Origin match, and often selection for the Australian team can depend upon a good performance. It is always most difficult to play at Lang Park; the crowd and the noise can have an intimidating effect on a player. Some players rise to the situation, but some find that they just can't handle the pressure.

By 1980, some 72 years after the first inter-state match between New South Wales and Queensland, the Australian Board of Control could kindle little interest in the contest, such was the one-sided nature of the matches in favour of New South Wales. The contest was ailing and little appreciated by the public of either state until New South Wales and Queensland bosses Kevin Humphreys and Ron McAuliffe hit on the idea of selecting players for the two states by birth or where they had played their first senior rugby league. Instantly, one of the great and toughest sporting challenges was born. Record television ratings and gate receipts were the outcome, and State of Origin fever swept the country, even going into the homes of Aussie Rules Football in Victoria and Western Australia. It is no accident that, since the rise of State of Origin rugby, Australia has dominated the sport worldwide and produced some of the finest players able to handle the heat of intense competition, none better than the two stand offs in rivalry at Lang Park on 27 May 1986, Queensland's Wally Lewis and New South Wales' Brett Kenny.

Both gifted half backs were at the top of their form but, as both sought to put one over the other, Garry Jack, from his vantage point behind, considers that team-mate Kenny proved himself the greater of the two amazingly talented players.

This match and the next two matches in the series confirmed my opinion of the greatest stand off in the world at the time. Brett Kenny was obviously helped by the fact that he had Peter Sterling as his scrum half, but Wally Lewis was at his peak in 1986. Wally was such a strong player and such an inspirational force behind a team, there was little he couldn't do. But Brett Kenny had such incredible vision on a field and such an array of natural skills. He was a superb ball player and one who could ghost through a defence without the opposition laying a finger on him. Brett Kenny was the difference between the two sides in the series of 1986.

Whatever the impact made by New South Wales halves Peter Sterling and Brett Kenny in particular, the unassuming Blues number one set the win in motion with an impressive display of tackling in the crucial opening 20 minutes and with a much-welcomed first try. As hard and as often as New South Wales back row trio Wayne Pearce, Noel Cleal and Steve Folkes swept up Queensland's Wally Lewis-inspired raids, the Blues had the need for the sure tackling of the tigerish Jack as the last line of defence. And they had the need for his pace and eye for a gap on attack when he opened the scoring for the visitors.

> Steve Folkes moved forward and managed to slip me a pass out of the tackle. I saw my chance and decided to go for it. I hit the ball just right and shot clear. I managed to cut inside Queensland full back Colin Scott for the first try of the match. To score a try before such a noisy crowd was a great feeling.

It was an even greater feeling when New South Wales referee Kevin Roberts blew his whistle for full time with the scoreboard revealing a 22–16 triumph for the Blues.

Scorelines of 24–20 and 18–16 in New South Wales' favour in the next two State of Origin matches reveal just how close was the contest of 1986, while the total of 22 tries in the three-match series reveals what a feast of football was laid before the 95,000 fans who attended the three matches. Sadly, today, as the State of Origin series assumes even larger proportions in the Australian sporting calendar, many critics feel that the quality running and skilful passing displayed in the early years of the contests are now becoming rare and that brute strength and power rule. Perhaps spurred on by a crowd atmosphere and support that have, at times, become a little unhealthy, the 'big hits' have become the order of the day, with forwards and backs alike hitting each other with a ferocity that would test the Richter scale. Though the excitement and the intensity remain, perhaps a little of the subtlety and class of a Wally Lewis, a Brett Kenny, a Peter Sterling or a Garry Jack have disappeared.

Critics may carp at recent developments on the field, but there is little doubt that the tension, the power and the pace of the action generated in a normal State of Origin series proved the perfect training ground for Garry Jack. His apprenticeship in a blue New South Wales jersey provided him with the credentials and the character to don the green and gold jersey of his country and face the most hostile of challenges for so long.

NEW SOUTH WALES Jack; Morris, Mortimer, O'Connor, Farrar; Kenny,

Sterling; Roach, Simmons, Tunks, Folkes, Cleal, Pearce. *Subs*: Lamb, Gillespie.

QUEENSLAND Scott; Shearer, Meninga, Miles, Close; Lewis, Murray; Dowling, Conescu, Brown, Niebling, Jones, Lindner. *Subs*: Jackson, French.

Scorers New South Wales   *Tries* Jack, Mortimer, Farrar, Simmons. *Goals* O'Connor (3).

Queensland   *Tries* Miles, Dowling. *Goals* Meninga (4).

Referee Kevin Roberts (New South Wales).

Lewis Jones

Leeds 25 Warrington 10
Championship Final, Odsal, Bradford
20 May 1961

Born 11 April 1931. Leeds have attracted many ex-Wales rugby union stars to Headingley, but none has proved a greater attraction than the 'golden boy' from Llanelli, Lewis Jones. The £6000 fee which tempted Wales' gifted midfield back to trek north at the age of 21 was repaid many times over as this rugby genius proceeded to shatter club and international points-scoring records immediately he arrived in 1952. His incredible pace off the mark, his penchant for the unexpected and his celebrated 'hitch kick' of a sidestep wrought havoc with opposition defences and, aided by his goalkicking, helped him to amass over 3372 points in a 12-season career in Britain. His 13 goals against Blackpool in 1957 and his 31 points against Bradford Northern in 1956 are still individual match points-scoring records for Leeds, while his ten goals for Great Britain in the second Test against Australia in 1954 are a record in Ashes clashes. His staggering 496 points, including 194 goals and 36 tries, in the 1956–57 season are a record and a peak to which many of our most prolific points-scorers today still aspire.

Though only 5 feet 10 inches and 12 stones 10 pounds at the height of his career, Lewis Jones glided through the tough game of rugby league, relying on and beating opponents by brain rather than brawn. His skills were enjoyed by many Down Under when, on his retirement from the British scene, he joined Wentworthville in the Sydney Metropolitan League as their player-coach. Having registered over 278 points on Great Britain's tour of Australia in 1954, a record which, in these days of shorter tours, is likely to stand forever, this was no gamble by the Sydney club, for he was soon to lead them to a string of premiership triumphs.

Leeds, the Yorkshire glamour club whose blue and amber jerseys have been worn by such all-time greats as Eric Harris, Vic Hey, Arthur Clues, Jim Brough and Lewis Jones himself, had, by the opening of the 1960–61 season, won the Challenge Cup on seven occasions. In contrast, five times the men from Headingley had reached the Championship final and yet each time they had lost. On Saturday, 20 May 1961, an ecstatic Leeds captain raised the Championship Trophy over his head to the accompaniment of roars of approval from his fans massed around the packed terraces of the famous Odsal bowl. For Lewis Jones it was, naturally, the greatest moment of his illustrious rugby league career.

> To be the first Leeds captain to lift the Championship Trophy was the highlight of my career and gave me more pleasure than anything. In the 1950s and 1960s I think most players, and perhaps even the clubs themselves, considered a good run in the Challenge Cup more attractive and more lucrative, but for me the Championship has always been the more important. A few good matches and plenty of luck can take a side to Wembley, but you need more than that to win a League Championship. The Championship is the true test of a side.

In recent seasons the advent of three and then two divisions, coupled with the introduction of considerable amounts of prize money, has led to a greater emphasis on the First Division title from the players and supporters alike. Each league match is played with the intensity of a cup round as the title race builds up to a thrilling end-of-season climax. As Lewis Jones states, the team that maintains its form throughout all 30 league matches is the rightful winner of the Championship Trophy and the prize cheque on offer. It was not always so, especially in Lewis Jones' playing days, when all the clubs were grouped in one league of 30 clubs and not all clubs played each other. Indeed, it seems astounding that in the season in which Lewis Jones brought home the cup to Headingley, Leeds, the premier Yorkshire side, did not play three of the most powerful clubs in the game – St. Helens, Wigan and Warrington – in their allocation of league fixtures. Hence the introduction of a top four club play-off at the end of the season to determine the true league champions. The Leeds defeat of the league's fourth-placed club St. Helens and the Warrington defeat of third-placed Swinton ensured that the top two sides did meet in the play-off final, the fact that they hadn't already met that season adding spice to the occasion. Warrington had by far the more glamorous combination, while Leeds, according to their skipper, were more of a homespun side but with a tremendous team spirit.

> Warrington had terrific backs with Eric Fraser at full back, Jim Challinor in the centre and the amazing Brian Bevan on the wing. In the pack they had plenty of pace and experience in the likes of Laurie Gilfedder and Danny Naughton. In contrast, apart from Ken Thornett and Wilf Rosenberg from Australia and South Africa we had a team of lads who were good players but were far from being big names. Vince Hattee and Derek Hallas in the centre were good footballers but hardly household names. But we had a wonderful team spirit and a set of players whose styles blended together to form a strong side.

* * *

And, with two players like Ken Thornett and Lewis Jones in the side, Leeds had the very men to star with a style of rugby in the 1960s which was not as regimented as much of today's offerings. When my own club, St. Helens, won four trophies in 1965–66, our coach, Joe Coan, more a fitness expert than a rugby tactician, allowed the players very much a free rein in training, often allowing them to take the sessions themselves and indulge in impromptu moves and ploys. With stars as talented as Great Britain internationals Alex Murphy, Tommy Bishop, Cliff Watson, John Mantle and John Warlow, plus Springbok wing flyers Tom Van Vollenhoven and Len Killeen, he could afford the luxury of allowing them to play as they pleased. The Leeds training sessions, prior to the championship final, were somewhat similar, with the players being given the freedom to express themselves as they wanted. Such a policy and style of play suited the club's Welsh genius at stand off, who invariably bamboozled other teams by doing his own thing, a practice which he admits he would find difficult to do today.

Our coach, Dai Prosser, developed a great rapport between himself and the team and he frequently told us that there was no need for him to tell us how to play. So he told us to play how we wanted. In those days players had more licence to do things themselves, and that suited my approach to rugby. I liked to attack and try the unorthodox, which sometimes resulted in a mistake. Today, if a player makes a mistake the coach jots it down against him on a marker board and consequently the player is loath to try things which are adventurous. The game today is too stereotyped and predictable. There is far too much emphasis on the game plan and too much attention paid to Australian and even American influences. There is one big difference, though: in 1961 we were offered £36 winning money to beat Warrington. I think they are offered a little more to win today.

The Warrington fiery pack, contrary to expectations, failed to contain the Leeds six, thus giving the Yorkshire side's halves, Welsh duo Colin Evans and Lewis Jones, the running chances they relished. Warrington half backs Jackie Edwards, father of Wigan's Shaun, and Bobby Greenough worked hard to contain them, but the Welshmen moved the ball around at great pace and, with Jones' long passes helping to put full back Ken Thornett in the gaps, it was no surprise that Leeds rattled up five tries from Derek Hallas (2), Jack Fairbank, Colin Evans and Jones himself. Minimising the impact of his own try and five goals, Lewis Jones is especially full of praise for his team-mates, rugged prop Jack Fairbank and Aussie Test star Ken Thornett.

We had it remarkably easy throughout the game, much easier than we expected, for Warrington failed to play to their normal form. Our pack was well led by Jack Fairbank, who had an outstanding match, always in the thick of things. Ken Thornett was strong in defence and always ready to link up with Derek Hallas or myself in midfield. I am always loath to judge or comment upon players from different eras but, without hesitation, I can say that Ken was the finest full back I have ever seen play in any era. He was the greatest whether on attack or defence.

Warrington's international centre, Jim Challinor, using the great Brian Bevan as his foil, helped himself to two tries and fully justified Jones' assertion that in Challinor and Bevan the Wire had one of the most dangerous attacking wing threequarter partnerships in the game. But it was the excitement of Jones' attacking play, his bold approach to the match and his willingness to try the unexpected, whatever the consequences, that kept Leeds moving forward. From first to last he was in the action.

A loose ball allowed Leeds' mercurial Welshman to stamp himself on the match with a typical darting run down the wing where, on finding ex-Springbok flyer Wilf Rosenberg, then a colleague of mine at Leeds University, he launched him on a thrilling touchline raid. The pattern of cut and thrust was set by Lewis but, in those early stages, he does admit that he thought he had blown Leeds' chances of victory.

I think the attacking tone of the game was set in the opening minutes, when I collected a stray pass and sent Wilf Rosenberg on his way down the touchline. His run set us in an attacking mood straight away, but I thought I'd blown it for Leeds in the early stages. Colin Evans threw a long, low pass out in my direction; it was round my ankles and possibly few expected me to catch the ball. I'd taken other such passes in the past, but whether from the pressure or not I dropped it. I dropped the ball with the tryline wide open and only three yards in front of me.

As the eventual scoreline of 25–10 in Leeds' favour tells, however, the mistake hardly proved as costly as Jones envisaged, and he did have the satisfaction of scoring his side's fifth and final try just five minutes from the end of the match.

The try that I scored was hardly one of my best, for I was handed it on a plate. I just had to run under the posts when I received the ball. But the try did crown my day and was one of the most rewarding of my life. The atmosphere around the terraces at Odsal was electric as the Leeds fans sensed that at last the Championship Trophy was ours for the first time. Very few games stick in my mind, but this one I can remember quite clearly, for being the first person to lift the trophy for Leeds gave me more enjoyment than any other match.

* * *

For Warrington, their inability to shackle Lewis Jones, Ken Thornett, Derek Hallas and Colin Evans had proved costly, especially for their manager, former New Zealand Test half back, Cec Mountford, whose last match in charge it proved to be. For Leeds, prompted by the unique talents of their former Welsh union star, it was to prove the start of an exciting decade which saw the club collect two further Championship Trophies and a Challenge Cup. Lewis Jones played alongside greater players and amassed far more tries and goals in a Leeds jersey, but he has never more enjoyed 80 minutes' rugby and its result.

> We were not the greatest of teams, but we did have a winning spirit and a perfect blend of players. It was a privilege and an experience to play for the Other Nationalities teams alongside all-time greats like Brian Bevan, Dave Valentine, Harry Bath and Arthur Clues, but even that couldn't match the thrill of winning the title. Only my first-ever union international for Wales against England at Twickenham would come anywhere near to this Championship decider. The sort of moment that makes rugby worth playing.

LEEDS Thornett; Rosenberg, Hallas, Hattee, Ratcliffe; Jones, Evans; Robinson, Simms, Whitehead, Fairbank, Goodwin, Shaw.

WARRINGTON Fraser; Bevan, Challinor, Pickavance, O'Grady; Greenough, Edwards; Brindle, Harper, Arkwright, Gilfedder, Major, Naughton.

Scorers Leeds   *Tries* Hallas (2), Fairbank, Evans, Jones. *Goals* Jones (5).

          Warrington   *Tries* Challinor (2). *Goals* Gilfedder (2).

Referee R. Gelder (Wilmslow).

Allan Langer

Brisbane Broncos 28 St. George 8
Premiership Grand Final, Sydney Football Stadium
27 September 1992

Born 30 July 1966. That the Broncos' pint-sized scrum half should, within four years of playing his first match in Australia's Winfield Cup competition, be included in the magazine *Rugby League Week*'s list of Australia's hundred all-time great players says much for his impact on the modern game. 'Alfie', as he is affectionately known in Queensland, burst on to the scene in 1987 with his selection to play in the first State of Origin match of that season. Though nervous at the prospect of playing alongside his boyhood heroes Wally Lewis, Gene Miles and Mal Meninga, the then Ipswich Jets half-back star quickly moved on to centre stage himself when, in 1988, he installed himself as the Brisbane Broncos inspiration at half back and eventually the club's captain.

One of the shrewdest distributors of a ball and with an eye for the narrowest of gaps, Allan Langer has established himself as Australia's first-choice scrum half since his first tour of Great Britain in 1990. His speed off the mark and his appetite for work are likely to keep him in the green and gold number seven jersey for many years to come.

The Brisbane Broncos were always going to be a success, from the day Wally Lewis scored three tries in their 44–12 humiliation of big-name Manly at the beginning of their debut 1988 season. There seemed no end to the wealth, power and confidence the high-profile club could muster. But the euphoria of those early days eventually gave way to an acceptance of the Winfield Cup's harsh realities.

Players who could produce memorable performances in State of Origin games and Test matches were not necessarily hardened for the week-to-week grind of top-class rugby. In the Broncos' four formative years, the fact that they had – more often than not – more internationals on their books than any of their competitors counted for little. There were form slumps, injury crises and internal dramas such as the one which led to Lewis's departure at the end of 1990.

And so it was that the Broncos, despite awesome moral and financial support from the entire state of Queensland, took five long, hard years to make the Winfield Cup Grand Final. And with 'Emperor' Lewis gone, it was

108

'Prince' Allan Langer, the 5 feet 5 inches Australian scrum half, who carried the hopes of the Broncos' patient, faithful fans.

He did not let them down.

Brisbane had streaked to the top of the Winfield Cup league table and the minor premiership in 1992, the equivalent of Britain's championship title, by losing only four league games out of 22. After the customary play-off among the top five clubs in the league, their Grand Final opponents were St. George, who had finished second in the league, a distant six competition points, or three wins, behind the Broncos. Wayne Bennett's Brisbane carried their form into the final play-offs, beating Illawarra 22–12 in the major semi-final, and instantly qualified for the decider.

There was little doubt Brisbane deserved to be favourite on the last Sunday in September, but it was believed a couple of factors could work against them. First, they had played just one game in a month leading up to the Grand Final, after their first-place finish had afforded them one weekend off and the win over the Illawarra Steelers gave them another. The Queenslanders could be rusty. Second, it was their first Grand Final – and there was a feeling in Sydney that Brisbane had not 'paid its dues'. Saints, by comparison, had 15 premierships under their belts, including a world-record 11 appearances from 1956 to 1966.

It was very much a case of the old order versus the new, the proud old Sydney club against the upstarts from up north with dreams of grandeur. St. George officials appealed to city and state loyalties in the week leading up to the clash. The battle lines were drawn.

Langer, meanwhile, could scarcely have had a more impressive season. He had helped Australia to a 2–1 Ashes series win over the touring Lions in June and was awarded the Rothmans Medal for the league's best and fairest player in September. His darting runs, organisational skills and kicking game had confounded most defences since February. As Brisbane skipper Langer recalls proudly:

We didn't lose a game from round 15 right through to the Grand Final. We finished minor premiers, we got Illawarra in the semis and – to our minds – we weren't going to lose.

We had already paved the way with our form during the year. We just picked up where we had left off during the home and away games.

With typical modesty, Langer plays down his own influence over the Grand Final. But – as if according to the script of a five-year-long play – the man who most deserved the spotlight in the final scene took it. St. George's delaying tactics and Brisbane's mistakes ensured the first half would be tight. A capacity crowd of 41,560 was on hand, and both teams felt the tension on a warm Sydney afternoon.

After ten minutes, Langer took the ball on the sixth tackle, with no obvious opportunities. Rather than kicking, he passed to second rower Gavin Allen, whose desperation pass back inside bounced off the head of Saints full back Michael Potter – straight back into the diminutive Brisbane number seven's hands.

> With that try I shaped to kick first, but then put Gavin Allen through a bit of a gap and linked around him. He tried to pass to me, the ball bounced off Potter's head and I grabbed it and scored.
>
> Referee Greg McCallum said the try was OK, Terry Matterson kicked the goal and we were leading 6–0. There was a bit of luck in it, I guess, but it was good work from Gavin nonetheless.

St. George, having apparently disposed of a 'safety first' attitude which had permeated their play in previous weeks, hit back just six minutes later. Former Wallaby second row man Scott Gourley passed to centre Michael Beattie, who found Castleford-bound Peter Coyne in support. The clever stand off threw a looping pass out wide, which winger Ricky Walford gratefully accepted to score. Walford missed with his conversion attempt, and the favourites led by just two points at the interval. Despite their well-deserved lead, Brisbane had squandered much possession, and though St. George had been forced to graft hard in defence the game was still there to be won by the Sydney giants. That is until little 'Alfie' Langer struck early in the second half.

Langer said of his 50th minute piece of inspiration:

> The second try I scored was probably the turning point of the game. Willie Carne and Kevin Walters tackled Potter over the sideline after we had kicked the ball into the St. George in-goal and he had tried to run it back. So the referee packed the scrum, we won it and a couple of tackles later I went into the acting half-back position.
>
> I looked to both sides, got the ball out and ran it myself, and I managed to get the ball down [over the tryline] with my right arm, with Tony Priddle still holding on to me. I think that tackle on Potter turned the game in our favour.

Langer had used referee McCallum as a foil, legally, and from that moment on the match turned irrevocably towards the inter-state visitors. Broncos loose forward Terry Matterson added the first of the four goals, which helped him to a club record 156 points for the season, and Brisbane were on their way to a memorable first Grand Final triumph. Four minutes later, second rower Alan Cann was over for the first of his two tries, breaking three tackles on the way.

With 19 minutes remaining, Broncos winger Carne looked certain to be trapped in his own in-goal, only to evade a wall of would-be tacklers and remarkably fight his way into the field of play. From the next ruck two metres out from his own tryline, Langer threw a superb long pass to centre Steve Renouf, who sidestepped Dragons substitute Rex Terp and raced an exhilarating 98 yards to score. At that stage, the Broncos led 22–4. They closed their account when tough pack man Cann beat Saints prop Neil Tierney to touch down. Former Wallaby rugby union pack star Scott Gourley crossed late for the Sydney team in the dying minutes, but, as St. George coach Brian Smith insisted, the Broncos always had the players to attempt the daring:

> The Renouf try was a high-percentage play and I would encourage my team to do it. But the Broncos have players like Allan Langer who can read those things, players who can make the break and players who, like Renouf, can go on and score the try.

Langer was duly named Clive Churchill Medal winner for man of the match, making him the first player to win the Rothmans and the Churchill titles in the same year. In the coming weeks he would lift the World Cup at Wembley before 73,000 people and skipper the first Australian side to win a World Club Challenge game since Eastern Suburbs beat St. Helens 25–2 in 1976. But nothing, the Queensland State of Origin scrum half says, could match the events of 27 September.

> There's no doubt the Grand Final is the favourite game of my career so far. We had five years of ups and downs since joining the competition and throughout that the comradeship was tremendous. All the blokes stuck together, and the feeling after winning the premiership was unbelievable.
>
> There was a lot of hard work which went into that one game. We put in years of hard work, and we finally got the prize. It wasn't just great for us, it was great for all the supporters who had gone to Sydney on the day, and all who had been with us since 1988. It was very emotional.

BRISBANE BRONCOS O'Neill; Hancock, Renouf, Johns, Carne; Kevin Walters, Langer; Lazarus, Kerrod Walters, Allen, Gillmeister, Cann, Matterson. *Subs*: Hohn, Currie, Plath, Gee.

ST. GEORGE Potter; Walford, M. Coyne, Beattie, Herron; P. Coyne, Goldthorpe; Priddle, Collins, Tierney, Barnhill, Gourley, Hardy. *Subs*: Mackay, Smith, Terp, Elliott.

* * *

Scorers Brisbane Broncos   *Tries* Langer (2), Cann (2), Renouf. *Goals* Matterson (4).

St. George   *Tries* Walford, Gourley.

Referee Greg McCallum (Sydney).

Wally Lewis

Great Britain 15 Australia 24
Third Test, Central Park, Wigan
22 November 1986

Born 1 December 1959. Former Queensland rugby league boss Ron McAuliffe once described Wally Lewis as 'the high priest of the spectacular', a description which amply highlighted his appeal to the fans, especially in his native Brisbane and Queensland. 'The King' or 'The Emperor', as he was known throughout his 13 years' playing career with Valleys, Wynnum Manly, Brisbane Broncos and the Gold Coast Seagulls, was blessed with such football skills that his virtuoso performances in midfield appeared to mesmerise the opposition. The powerful half back or centre revelled in his star status and his position as one of Australia's highest-paid sportsmen, yet such were his skills that few could deny his right to the accolades.

In 33 Tests and 31 State of Origin clashes between 1979 and 1991, Australia's skipper invariably revealed that priceless asset which only the greatest of players possess – time to execute his skills. Whether at his favourite Lang Park in Brisbane, the Sydney Cricket Ground or Central Park, Wigan, 'The King' has always directed affairs in his inimitable relaxed manner, spraying passes to the flanks, pressurising the opposition with deep, punishing kicks and, occasionally, deceiving the tightest of defences with a dash for the line that helped him to 20 tries in international football. Such was the aura that surrounded the Aussie captain that it was only to be expected that in 1983–84 he became Britain's first £1000-per-match player with Wakefield Trinity, making just ten appearances for the Belle Vue club and raising attendances from a paltry 1500 to 7000 per week. Strangely, for one so tactically aware and blessed with such rugby knowledge, his short coaching career with the Gold Coast Seagulls failed to match his glittering playing career.

It's no surprise that the great Wally Lewis finds it almost impossible to narrow his most treasured moments down to one 80-minute period. Arguably the player of his generation, Lewis had more unforgettable performances in over a decade in the spotlight than most of his contemporaries had first-team appearances.

When pressed, however, the now full-time Queensland State of Origin coach cites three games that outshine the others. Two are from the Origin series, which many critics believe he was largely responsible for making the phenomenal spectacle it is today.

In Game Two, 1989, Queensland sealed the series with a 16–12 win in Sydney in a match which became inter-state rugby's equivalent of the famous 'Rorkes Drift' Test. The Maroons finished with only 12 men after losing scrum half Allan Langer with a fractured ankle, centre Mal Meninga with a fractured eye socket, second rower Paul Vautin (ankle), winger Michael Hancock (bruised shoulder) and loose forward Bob Lindner (broken leg).

In Game Three, 1991, 'The King's' retirement from Origin football was announced by the Lang Park ground announcer with ten minutes to go, the series level at 1–1 and Queensland leading 14–12. Roared on by an emotional crowd, the Maroons held on, and Lewis closed an era in Aussie rugby league by performing a lap of honour with his family.

But it was the third Ashes Test on the 1986 Kangaroo tour which Lewis says stands above his 32 other Test appearances as the one he cherishes most. And it also featured perhaps his most memorable, and probably best, representative try.

After winning the first two Tests 38–16 and 34–4, Lewis admits many of his team-mates may have gone into the third somewhat complacent.

Great Britain played well early in the first two Tests without really having stretched us. But in the third match they made a few changes to the team and they came back quite well, and really challenged us.

Especially after the way we won the other games. No matter how much concentration we put into the third Test, I remember saying to Don Furner [the Kangaroo coach], 'I can see there's some kind of complacency here. I can see the guys are over-confident.' We put in at training that week a few things designed to get rid of the complacency.

You do a lot of hard work. You tend to bring out the stick a little bit more. In the mid-week match against Bradford Northern, the non-Test team won comfortably and that just added more pressure to the job.

Despite the gloom of two defeats at Old Trafford and Elland Road, an optimistic Great Britain coach, Maurice Bamford, had introduced five new faces for the Ashes clash at Central Park. Widnes powerful wing John Basnett, Wigan centre David Stephenson, scrum half Andy Gregory and forwards Chris Burton and Harry Pinner were expected to inject new life into the somewhat demoralised side. That they did, Aussie skipper Wally Lewis bears ample testimony to, and he and his team-mates were under no illusions in the opening quarter as to the bite in Great Britain's defensive commitment. Though giant Kangaroo centre Gene Miles raced on to a short pass from prop Greg Dowling to score as early as the second minute, Chris Burton, Lee Crooks

114

and Andy Goodway provided stiffer resistance than Australia had expected.

> The guys found out that they were going to be in a bit of trouble as soon as we got into the match. They kicked off to us, Mal Meninga caught the ball. Mal played in the second row in that game. One of their blokes hit Mal, first tackle of the game, right from the kickoff, and nearly knocked his block off! Mal was gone, for a good 15 or 20 minutes he didn't know who he was, where he was or anything. He got hit by a classic high shot and turned straight around and looked at the referee, Monsieur Rascagneres, and he just looked at me as if to say, 'Well? What do you want me to do about it?' and it just got worse and worse from there. They weren't going to let anything stand in the way of showing they were back in the game.
>
> The Poms just gave it everything.

For the first time in the series Australia's half-back duo, scrum half Peter Sterling and stand off Lewis, failed to command the midfield and both were, especially in the opening 40 minutes, given a torrid time by the new Great Britain pairing Tony Myler and Andy Gregory. The British duo were aided on attack by the skilful ball-handling ability of St. Helens loose forward Harry Pinner, who caused headaches for the Australians with his array of short or long defence-splitting passes. Pinner's prompting lay behind many a Great Britain attack while, as Lewis acknowledges, the pugnacious Gregory proved a tough customer around the scrums.

> I've always been a huge fan of Andy Gregory. He's always been the hardest to play against, as far as Pommies I've come up against, in just about any position.
>
> He's easily the best and he took the bit between his teeth that day and he had a real go. He tried everything. And they also played Harry Pinner. He was about the most skilful bloke we came up against on the whole tour, and why he wasn't given a better chance by the national selectors was a bit confusing.

Sadly for Great Britain, for all Gregory's and Pinner's inspiration, full back Joe Lydon's strategic kicking and Garry Schofield's two tries, it was a costly mistake by French referee Julien Rascagneres, which, after 57 minutes, saw them trailing by 18–12. Earlier, there had been more than a hint of a forward pass in centre Gene Miles' opening try for Australia, but when loose forward Bob Lindner touched down for a second try 19 minutes later and wing Michael O'Connor added the second of his four goals, the stage seemed set for yet another Australian stroll to victory. It was not to be.

The 21-year-old Schofield proved just what a contribution he would make to international rugby in later years by helping himself to two tries, the first in the 28th minute as a result of a devastating move in midfield with Myler and Pinner, and the second in the 46th minute courtesy of good support play with centre partner David Stephenson. Two conversions, one from exciting wing Henderson Gill and the other from Joe Lydon, tied the scores at 12 points each, and the 20,169 crowd held their breath in anticipation of a home win. Monsieur Rascagneres intervened.

In the 57th minute Aussie wing Dale Shearer chased his own kick inside the Great Britain 25-yard area, only to be tackled by Widnes's John Basnett. Controversy reigns even today as to whether the kick was too long or whether Shearer, without the attentions of Basnett, would have been able to reach it and score. Whatever the merits of the French referee's controversial decision to award an obstruction try, Australia's skipper has few doubts that luck was on his side.

> We got the first couple of tries. Gene Miles scored a try off a Greg Dowling short ball which even our blokes said was a metre forward. They came back, they got a try after we got to a 12–0 lead which we didn't think was fair, but that made it one-all so we weren't worrying too much. Then they came right back. They got to 12–12 and Dale Shearer got a penalty try awarded. He kicked ahead, and then chased and got tackled. The ball took one bounce and bounced over the dead ball line. I mean, he was never ever going to get to the ball, and it was awarded a penalty try. We were very, very fortunate again there. I think most of our blokes thought that we were doing it pretty lucky. But, you know, you take the luck that's given to you in games like that.

To their credit, Great Britain refused to lie down and, as the game approached the final ten minutes, Australia's powerful forwards, for the first time in the series, were unable to gain ground. Aussie pack stars Greg Dowling, Mal Meninga and Bryan Niebling were hurled back in the tackle, Great Britain's Lydon and Schofield added a penalty goal and a drop goal, and suddenly, with just three points the difference between the two sides, the crowd sensed an upset. Not so, for it was Wally Lewis who was to crown the series for Australia with a breathtaking captain's matchwinning try.

> Despite the score, I was pretty happy. They kept coming back at us, but most of the guys were trying hard and they realised it was a tough game. I just said to Sterlo and Gene Miles and Brett Kenny that we were going to have to try and pull our fingers out a bit because a few of the other guys . . . had got injured and a couple of other blokes were just starting to go off a little bit and not concentrate so well. I just grabbed them. One thing I noticed about the Poms was that they really did have a weakness on the blindside, especially in that particular match. We kept running the ball

down this side of the field. We just kept going there, and we probably came up with three or four breaks. I just kept coming up and having a go and things kept coming off.

The weakness on the blindside, highlighted by the shrewd Aussie skipper, eventually proved Great Britain's undoing. Great players like Wally Lewis take a split second in which to make a decision. Their movements with a ball are often instinctive, while their penchant for the unexpected is much higher than the average player's. It was pure instinct and vision which led to Lewis's memorable touchdown in the 73rd minute, a try which clinched Australia's fourth successive Test series whitewash.

Towards the end of the game I was standing at half back. Royce Simmons shot down the blind – it was only about two metres wide – and one of the opposition chased him infield about five or six metres. I don't know, it's just one of those things that goes through your head very, very quickly. You realise that if that player came in, if he comes that far infield, there's got to be a big gap down the blindside. So I angled back to the blind off Royce and got the ball from a standing start. I ran and there was a winger, John Basnett, marking Shearer. I threw a dummy and he just stuck with Shearer. He was going to come in; he was thinking, 'I'm looking after my man, he's nobody else's'. I probably threw about five or six dummies and he stayed there all the time, and everything worked the right way and then Joe Lydon came across. I managed to get a step on the inside and I was in under the posts and that was it, that was the game.

Any player capable of producing such a brilliant solo effort in the closing minutes of a Test match deserves to be pleased with himself. But to Wally Lewis, voted Australia's man of the series, the final touchdown realised a dream, an unbeaten 13-match tour of Great Britain. In the closing stages of this hectic and tense Test there were moments when even the confident Aussie skipper must have had doubts whether or not his Green and Golds were going to hang on to their unbeaten record. When they did and he scored the try that ensured the tourists' hundred per cent record Wally Lewis was naturally delighted.

At the time I wouldn't have swapped the try for anything at any other time because we were doing it pretty tough and I kept thinking, 'Don't let it come this far, having won every match up until now and then get beaten in the last game'. It made me nice and happy. I know that. In that third Test I thought they threw everything at us. They played an almost perfect game of football. They mixed a lot of discipline, which they hadn't shown in the first games, with a lot of skill and a little bit of the old style – aggression is a nice word for it – that was bordering on breaking the rules, but in Test matches you really don't care if it is in the rules or not, only if it works. They lost because a lot of times they just made the wrong decisions.

GREAT BRITAIN Lydon; Gill, Schofield, Stephenson, Basnett; Myler, Gregory; Ward, Watkinson, Crooks, Burton, Goodway, Pinner. *Subs*: Potter.

AUSTRALIA Jack; Shearer, Kenny, Miles, O'Connor; Lewis, Sterling; Dowling, Simmons, Dunn, Meninga, Niebling, Lindner. *Subs*: Lamb, Davidson.

Scorers Great Britain   *Tries* Schofield (2). *Goals* Lydon (2), Gill. *Drop Goals* Schofield.
Australia   *Tries* Miles, Lindner, Shearer, Lewis. *Goals* O'Connor (4).

Referee Julien Rascagneres (France).

Bob Lindner

Queensland 24 New South Wales 12
Third State of Origin Match, Lang Park, Brisbane
31 May 1993

Born 11 November 1962. During his career Bob Lindner has been forced to undergo two major knee reconstructions and has suffered a broken leg on three occasions, yet such has been his indomitable spirit that the powerful Australian second row has triumphed over all adversity and taken his place among the greats of Kangaroo forward play. Starting his career with Souths and Wynnum Manly in the Brisbane league between 1983 and 1986, Bob Lindner has represented many clubs both in Australia and Great Britain with distinction, notably Castleford, Parramatta, Gold Coast, Western Suburbs, Illawarra Steelers and Oldham. But above all he has been a tower of strength for Queensland and Australia, twice touring Great Britain with the Kangaroos in 1986 and 1990, and being voted the player of the tour at a special presentation after the Elland Road Test match in 1990.

In season 1993–94, the strong-running loose forward, on a lucrative contract with Oldham, did much to save the Lancashire club from the drop to Division Two.

Great players have been wonderfully scattered across rugby league's magnificent 99-year history. They have scored great tries, kicked great goals, played in great matches and left great imprints on the minds of entire generations.

When players achieve a level of excellence by which they transcend their contemporaries and the years, there is little to separate them. They are champions. Sure, people argue whether Murphy was better than Sterling, or Boston than Horder or Graham than Karalius, but no one really cares. All of them were very special, and greatness is absolute. You can't be 'more great'.

But one thing does separate the true geniuses of rugby league, although it would be ridiculous to suggest this factor renders one better than another in the end. Some make great farewells to the game, and fate conspires to stop others from having that last memorable moment.

Australian champions Ray Price and Michael Cronin retired from club rugby in their homeland (Price would later make a comeback with Wakefield Trinity) by performing a victory lap of the Sydney Cricket Ground after

Parramatta's 1986 Premiership win. Yet Ellery Hanley's final appearance for Great Britain consisted of six minutes in a tour match against Newcastle. Andy Gregory played in eight Challenge Cup finals at Wembley, winning seven and drawing one. Wayne Pearce made the Grand Final twice with Balmain, and lost both times.

Fate affects everyone, even our heroes.

Around 9.55 p.m. on the night of 17 May 1993, Bob Lindner trudged off the Sydney Football Stadium convinced he was not destined to be a lead character in anyone's fairy tale.

Lindner, a veteran of 21 Tests and – as of that moment – 24 State of Origin games, had made his last representative appearance at the game's Australian headquarters. He had signed to play out his career with Peter Tunks' Oldham, and had informed current club Illawarra that his first year with them would also be his last. And, after years of being mostly a winner, he was a loser. New South Wales had won the second State of Origin clash 16–12, tying up the series for the second consecutive season. The Steelers had been successful in only four games from eight after going into the winter with high hopes, and despite the best week-to-week form of Lindner's distinguished career. No, this durable 30-year-old Test colossus – who had never played in a Grand Final – was not going to have the sort of exit to write home about.

Queensland gambled in their selection of the team for the third State of Origin match at Brisbane's Lang Park two weeks later, if it is possible to gamble in a no-win situation. Brisbane Broncos full back Julian O'Neill was surprisingly picked at stand off, a position he occasionally occupied with Widnes a few months earlier but to which he was a stranger with his club side. Regular Queensland number six Kevin Walters was again the fall guy, demoted to the substitutes' bench, while 19-year-old Canterbury winger Brett Dallas was to make his debut. Newcastle's Adrian Brunker was the casualty.

Lindner's impending departure for colder climes was a popular topic among the Queensland players-in-camp leading up to the final match, but it was not spoken of in the solemn tones one might expect.

> Everyone knew it was to be my last match, but there wasn't a great deal of serious attention paid to it. We actually had a lot of fun in camp that week. They were all geeing me up, saying, 'This is your last State of Origin breakfast'. Every night was like the Last Supper or something. They mentioned it all the time . . .

Humour is a big part of the Queensland State of Origin tradition; a conductor for the 'family' atmosphere which has created something of a dynasty in Australian rugby league.

At the time, Lindner had no concern for writing himself a career postscript,

120

Andy Gregory proves once more what an elusive character he can be on a rugby pitch. (*Stewart Kendall/ Sportsphoto*)

Steve Hampson fails in his attempt to prevent Mike Gregory from scoring under the posts at Wembley. In the background, Andy Gregory is still picking himself up after being dummied by the Warrington captain. (*Varley Picture Agency*)

David Hobbs goes in at the corner for one of his two tries for Featherstone Rovers in the 1983 Challenge Cup final. (*Varley Picture Agency*)

New South Wales full back Garry Jack punishes Queensland with a tactical kick to touch during a State of Origin clash. (*Varley Picture Agency*)

Leeds' record points-scorer, Lewis Jones, celebrates winning the Championship Trophy in 1961. Prop Don Robinson looks on. (*Robert Gate Collection*)

Allan Langer aims to launch a Broncos raid down the flanks with one of his long defence-splitting passes. (*Varley Picture Agency*)

Wally Lewis orchestrates the Kangaroos attack during the third Ashes Test at Central Park in 1986. (*Colorsport*)

The New South Wales defender feels the full effect of a punishing drive from Queensland loose forward Bob Lindner. (*Varley Picture Agency*)

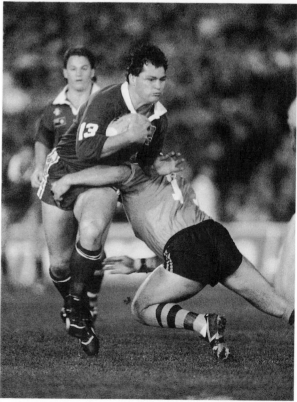

Paul Loughlin puts the full force of his 15-stone frame behind this kick from defence during the third Test at the Sydney Football Stadium in 1988. Forwards Mike Gregory and Ellery Hanley give chase. (*Varley Picture Agency*)

A proud Roger Millward displays the rugby league World Cup trophy. (*Varley Picture Agency*)

It takes two defenders to try to stop Bradford Northern's Keith Mumby. (*Varley Picture Agency*)

Leigh player-coach Alex Murphy hoists aloft the Challenge Cup in 1971. Kevin Ashcroft holds the base of the trophy. (*Robert Gate Collection*)

Paul Newlove attempts to evade the tackle of Castleford prop Lee Crooks. (*Varley Picture Agency*)

No way through Great Britain's defences this time for Kiwi loose forward Tawera Nikau. (*Varley Picture Agency*)

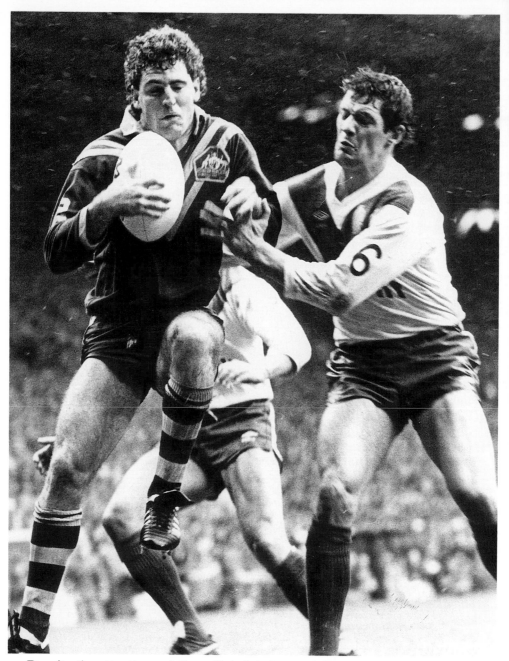

Despite the attentions of Great Britain's Tony Myler, Aussie wing Michael O'Connor manages to hold on to the ball during the 1986 Kangaroo tour. (*Varley Picture Agency*)

or for anyone else writing it for him. The spirit in camp at State of Origin time is far too stirring to let any personal ambitions rise above it. As Lindner said, trying to pin down the Origin mystique:

> To me there was a tradition before I came into the Queensland side that Queenslanders always had great football ability but they never stayed in Queensland. We had been robbed of our best players for years and years. I remember clearly as a kid how they'd play for New South Wales and we'd get flogged.
>
> And when you come into the Queensland camp, you are forever reminded of those years. And since the Origin series was brought in, we've had a bit of success and maintaining that has also become a part of the tradition. The thing they talk about, the family thing which 'Tosser' [Maroons manager Dick Turner] and everyone brought to the team has carried on and is a big part of our success and why Queensland sides have had tremendous spirit over the last decade.
>
> I would hate for them to go out and try to win for the wrong reasons. Everyone just said, 'It's Bob's last game, let's make it a good one'.

But despite his selfless approach to his final appearance in the famous maroon strip, in front of an adoring 31,500 home crowd, it soon became apparent to Bob Lindner that the night was going to be special. Everyone else, bar the 13 New South Wales players, were going to ensure it was.

> Mal [Meninga] ran me out first as leader of the team. The Lang Park crowd was its normal parochial self. The fact we had lost the first two games in the series meant they were pretty quiet to start with, but they really got behind us as we gathered momentum. They were dying for a win. I think they were sick of seeing us getting beaten.

Queensland, stinging from three successive losses, started powerfully. After three minutes, scrum half and captain Allan Langer worked a blindside move with full back Dale Shearer and a dangerous-looking Lindner. Queensland almost scored.

> I was happy about my performance because I could see I was being effective in attack and defence. The first three or four times I touched the ball, it led to fairly long breaks and that was pretty satisfying.

After seven minutes, against the run of play, disaster struck. New South Wales half back Ricky Stuart hoisted a towering 'bomb', which bounced off the head of Queensland winger Willie Carne. As the ball lolled into the in-goal area, Dallas tried to kick it dead. Instead, the ball skewed diagonally across the field, New South Wales winger Andrew Ettingshausen dived on it and, with Rod Wishart's conversion, the Blues were 6–0 ahead.

Debutant Dallas, a youngster from Townsville, was crestfallen. Meninga and Lindner consoled him. 'Bob and Mal and a couple of the other blokes came over to me in the in-goal,' Dallas later told *Rugby League Week*. 'They told me to keep my head up and try to forget about what happened. There was a long way to go and we could still win.'

Dallas duly 'lifted his head' – and lifted it further three minutes' later when the Blues botched a group attempt to diffuse Allan Langer's bomb, and referee Greg McCallum awarded Carne a try with O'Neill converting for 6–6.

I remember that we scored early and we never really looked like losing. We got a great start and the crowd just urged us on.

Origin football's brawling past then came back to haunt it. With places in the Australian touring team to New Zealand up for grabs, a scrum broke up in the 23rd minute with New South Wales hooker Ben Elias slugging it out with bitter rival Steve Walters, while Paul Harragon (New South Wales) and Martin Bella (Queensland) did likewise a few feet away. All four were dispatched to the sin bin, with Queensland receiving the penalty.

O'Neill goaled to give the Maroons an 8–6 lead.

New South Wales had the last say before the break, however, when Harragon topped off his win in the fight by winning in his attempt to reach the tryline in the 36th minute. Accepting a Brad Fittler pass, he plunged over to ground the ball one-handed and give his side a four-point lead at the interval.

Nineteen minutes after the resumption, Shearer played the ball forward, split the Blues defence and passed to Langer. Centre Mark Coyne became involved, returning possession to Shearer, who was tackled deep in New South Wales territory. From the ensuing ruck, Kevin Walters, who replaced O'Neill at half time, fed brother Steve, and the hooker burrowed over for a try.

With Meninga's goal, Queensland led 14–12, and for the next five minutes the match teetered agonisingly in the balance. The Lang Park mob roared itself hoarse as fortunes seesawed, until Lindner was finally cast in that fairy tale he never thought would be written.

With just 17 minutes remaining, substitute Darren Smith darted out of dummy half and caught the Blues back-pedalling. Bob Lindner loomed up, accepted the pass and careered over the top of Stuart and Tim Brasher to touch down triumphantly. Lang Park erupted.

Willie Carne would touch down a second time before a fight between Smith and Paul Sironen would usher in the full time siren. Queensland 24, New South Wales 12.

As Lindner now says:

It turned out to be a very special night, even though we didn't win the series. I scored a try and I won the man of the match award. I just couldn't have asked for any more. It was very special. At the end of the game I did a lap of honour and everything just happened perfectly that night.

I could never imagine I would go out like that, but it's just the way the game developed. I've had a long State of Origin career, and I'm just pleased it ended the way it did. That game gave me some tremendous memories, because of the reasons I've already mentioned and also because it was timely.

Lindner's departure from the international scene was only minutely less spectacular – a series-deciding 16–4 win over New Zealand, again in front of the home Lang Park crowd, a month later. But the Origin series carried more emotional weight, he says.

Again, that was a good series win to go out on, but I've never been involved in a loss at Australian level. I've been lucky enough to be around during a great era which Australia has totally dominated.

At the Maroons' animated post-match function, 'Bobby' was named the players' player of the match, awarded the Wally Lewis Medal for man of the series and was presented with another medal to commemorate his 25th appearance for the Maroons.

And a poem, apparently written by an anonymous supporter, was read to the gathering of family and friends at the team's traditional base, the Travelodge Hotel:

He knew what it was to be proud of his state.
He fought for his honour, he bled for his mate.
The blue-eyed destroyer, the forward advancer,
When hard yards were calling, he was the answer.
Such was his hunger and hard dedication,
The man was a legend, a true inspiration.
Origin history will echo the name
Of the warhorse from Queensland who lived for the game.
It may be his last, so we forward to the lobby.
Let's celebrate, fellas,
We did it for Bobby.

QUEENSLAND Shearer; Dallas, Meninga, Coyne, Carne; O'Neill, Langer; Bella, S. Walters, Hohn, Larson, Gillmeister, Lindner. *Subs*: Kevin Walters, Smith, Jackson, Moore.

* * *

NEW SOUTH WALES Brasher; Wishart, Fittler, Ettingshausen, G. Mackay; Daley, Stuart; Lazarus, Elias, Harragon, Fairleigh, Sironen, B. Mackay. *Subs*: Gillespie, Hill, Gourley, Taylor.

Scorers Queensland   *Tries* Carne (2), S. Walters, Lindner. *Goals* Meninga (2), O'Neill (2).

New South Wales *Tries* Ettingshausen, Harragon. *Goals* Wishart (2).

Referee Greg McCallum (New South Wales).

Paul Loughlin

Australia 12 Great Britain 26
Third Test, Sydney Football Stadium
9 July 1988

Born 28 July 1966. Three times a badly broken right arm has threatened to put an end to giant 6 feet 4 inches and 15 stones Paul Loughlin's career, but he has remained at the heart of the St. Helens attack since he joined the Knowsley Road club as a 16-year-old from his home town U.G.B. amateur side in 1982. Having graduated through Saints' Colts and Alliance sides, Paul made his first team debut in March 1984 against Oldham and quickly became such a prolific points-scoring centre that, against unfortunate Carlisle on 14 September 1986, he amassed a club individual match points record with a haul of 40 points from 16 goals and 2 tries in Saints' staggering 112–0 thrashing. In an effort to combat the sheer physical strength of Australian midfield powerhouses like Gene Miles and Mal Meninga, who helped to groom the stylish Loughlin when with Saints in 1984–85, Great Britain international caps have regularly come this gentle giant's way, including two Lions tours Down Under in 1988 and 1992.

The grass verges surrounding the Lions training pitch at Manly on the eve of the historic third Ashes Test in Sydney resembled a casualty clearing station. Warrington's dynamic loose forward Mike Gregory sat with a pained expression on his face and with an ice-pack on his groin, Widnes's Richie Eyres held a similar pack to his troublesome knee, hooker Bob Beardmore hobbled off the pitch and out of Test contention with a severely bruised hip, and the cornerstone of the Great Britain pack, 17-stone giant prop Kevin Ward, sat precariously on the perimeter fence, unable to take part in the training and suffering from a badly damaged ankle. As I watched, notebook in hand and eager to send home stirring words on Britain's chances of winning their first Test against Australia in ten years, I could not help but reflect that the medieval knight in days of yore had more chance of finding the legendary Holy Grail.

As did Great Britain's 21-year-old centre Paul Loughlin.

Having lost the first two Tests, nobody gave us a chance of winning the third, and on that Friday afternoon I think few of us deep down really thought we could do it. We had so many injuries in the squad that we couldn't even raise 13 players for the final training session. Paul Hulme and Hugh Waddell were happy at being brought into the side for their debuts but, as we walked back to the Pacific Hotel after training, we were a little sad and tired. It really was a backs-to-the-wall job.

Nothing, however, rouses a true Lion than when he is the underdog, ridiculed by a hostile Australian public and humiliated by a cynical Sydney press. John Hogan, rugby league correspondent of *The Australian* newspaper, summed up the feeling of the home press corps when he informed his readers that 'this match is just a sham. The Lions are simply not good enough and will be forced to field a team which is not in the same class as their awesome opponents'.

Such criticism stung the crippled Great Britain team and, as Loughlin insists, proved the spur to one of the greatest upsets in the history of Ashes confrontations.

There was no sympathy for our problems; the Aussies were ridiculing us and laughing at our chances. One newspaper even advised fans not to turn up at the Sydney Football Stadium as we were considered not good enough opposition for them. Only 15,994 spectators actually did turn up, but those that did were in for a big surprise. All the attacks on us only made us more determined to ram them down their throats.

And the lads in the red, white and blue did just that, as the green and golds and the adoring Australian public paid dearly for a confidence which bordered on arrogance. Though I now confess to having compiled every high-scoring statistic and record scores against Great Britain in anticipation of their use in my BBC television commentary that day, to my astonishment, and to the delight of the bugle-blowing Union Jack-waving British fans scattered around the sparsely populated stadium, Great Britain defied the odds to give the long-striding St. Helens centre the most memorable moments of his then short but glittering career.

It was a marvellous feeling. It was my first tour to Australia and I never expected to make the Test team. But injuries and suspension to Steve Hampson gave me my chance to force my way into the team. Australia were expecting to put 50 points on us, but we gave them and their fans the shock of their lives. It was the most satisfying moment of my career because we did something nobody thought we could.

* * *

Shocks began as early as the 16th minute, when a well-rehearsed run-around move between Great Britain prop Kevin Ward and man of the match Andy Gregory allowed the irrepressible Lions half back just sufficient space to lob a high pass in the direction of wing ace Martin Offiah, isolated and lurking dangerously on the touchline. The former Rosslyn Park union star's anticipation and speed off the mark did the trick as he swept infield for the opening try. Four minutes later the elusive Phil Ford, switched to full back and with Paul Loughlin moved to his favourite centre position, sidestepped and ghosted his way through a mesmerised Australian defence to add the second try. Loughlin added the conversion to give the Lions an unexpected 10–0 lead but, such had been the Kangaroos' domination of the 'auld enemy' for the past decade, the excited centre and his colleagues could hardly believe what was happening. There was certainly no feeling that this Test was well and truly won.

> Everything happened so quickly in that opening 20 minutes that nobody had time to think about the next hour. We were surprised at the ease at which we had scored two tries, and everyone was so hyped up that we just had to settle ourselves down and concentrate even harder. Deep down, I think I knew that Australia would strike back, that they would not allow something like this to happen to them.

Strike back they did, for, despite all of Gregory's defence-splitting passes, the powerful runs of props Kevin Ward and Hugh Waddell, and the long, tactical, punishing kicks downfield of Loughlin, Great Britain made no further impression on the Green and Golds' defence up to half time, as the shaken Kangaroos realised their opponents at last meant business. When they did strike, it was Wally Lewis, the arch enemy in so many dramatic Ashes encounters, who made British hearts flutter and miss a beat. Two minutes after the interval, he showed he had lost none of his legendary sidestepping abilities or his strength when he raced through the attempted tackles of hooker Paul Hulme and Hugh Waddell and rounded Phil Ford before crashing over beneath the posts for a superb solo try. Michael O'Connor added the first of his two goals, and Great Britain's euphoria had vanished.

Within six minutes, however, Great Britain's entertaining wing, Henderson Gill, had replied with a further try courtesy of Gregory's perfectly placed chip kick behind Australia's full back Garry Jack. Loughlin added the second of his three goals and, despite giant Aussie prop Sam Backo's opportunist try, Great Britain were on their way to a famous victory, and one in which the St. Helens full back had played a major role and which, according to Great Britain coach Mal Reilly, broke a huge psychological barrier:

* * *

Paul is one of the biggest kickers in the game, and we knew that if he could kick us into position on the Australian half of the pitch then we could contain them. In the first Test, when Paul was doing the kicking, we were on the top, but when Andy Gregory and Garry Schofield took over they didn't have the distance to keep Australia near their line. In the final Test Paul gained huge distances with his kicks and helped set up the platform for the win.

It was a turning point for Great Britain in that we shattered a big psychological barrier. As the players realised they could win the match they oozed with confidence, and since that match our players know that they can beat Australia and have done so a couple of times in convincing fashion. That third Test win has helped many players to approach a Test match against Australia properly.

In the second Test at Brisbane we were perhaps too motivated, too passionate and played too much with our heart and not with our heads. Our teams now know what is needed.

A piece of indiscipline sealed the win. Saints midfield giant, Loughlin, received the ball close to his own tryline and seemed to be hemmed in on the right touchline. His instructions from coach Mal Reilly were to kick the ball as high and as far downfield as possible and seek to contain the Aussies deep in their own half for the remainder of the match. It was not to be.

I was handed the ball near our own tryline and close to the right touchline. I was supposed to just kick the ball downfield to relieve our line, and we had practised such tactics many times in training throughout the tour. But I just caught sight of a couple of green and gold jerseys coming towards me very quickly, too quickly. I sidestepped them, spotted a gap and went for it.

As Loughlin indicates, he raced past the two Australian defenders and powered his huge frame upfield, surprising the partisan Australian fans, by now in a high state of anxiety at the proceedings on the field, with his sustained burst of speed over the next 50 yards. Wigan's powerful, stocky wing, Henderson Gill, cruised alongside and, when launched to the corner by his centre's pass, easily rounded full back Jack to score one of the most memorable tries in the history of the game. Gill's toothy grin and wiggle of the hips after touching the ball down at the corner was captured for millions of viewers worldwide by television and illustrated the sheer joy of winning experienced by this beleaguered Great Britain side.

Great match-clinching tries are often made to look easy and are often meticulously planned, but this 85-yard tryscoring dash down the right touchline came purely from the instinct of an outstanding centre who disobeyed his coach.

> The try should never have been, and I'm sure Malcolm Reilly was upset when I set off running instead of kicking the ball. But everything just opened up for me, and I decided to take the chance. Henderson Gill was on hand, and all I had to do was give him the ball and let him go for the corner. I'll never forget his grin and wiggle of the hips after he had scored. It was a great moment for us all.

Despite Loughlin's defiance of Mal Reilly's instructions, it was also a great moment for the Great Britain coach:

> Paul didn't do what we had planned he should do but, in the heat and tension of a Test match, that is often what illustrates the difference between a good player and a great player. Great players always keep open their options and that is what Paul did.
>   He can seize an opportunity when it comes along. He stopped, thought about the kick, and then, in a split second, realised what was the better thing to do. That's the mark of a great player.

An outrageous dummy by the supremely confident scrum half Andy Gregory and a 50-yard dash to the Australian tryline by his namesake, Great Britain second row Mike, completed the Kangaroos' humiliation and saw the electronic scoreboard display the historic scoreline of Australia 12, Great Britain 26 – truly a memorable day for British rugby which, for ten years, had striven to raise its standards to those of the masters Down Under. And, as Ray Chesterton, a highly respected Sydney journalist disclosed, a result which left Paul Loughlin and his heroic team-mates under no illusions as to its impact on the international scene.

> Tears flowed more freely than champagne in the Great Britain dressing room, with tough rugby league players weeping openly as one of the longest sieges in English sporting history was finally lifted.

AUSTRALIA Jack; Ettingshausen, O'Connor, Jackson, Currie; Lewis, Sterling; Bella, Conescu, Backo, Fullerton-Smith, Vautin, Pearce. *Subs*: Belcher, Lindner.

GREAT BRITAIN Ford; Gill, Stephenson, Loughlin, Offiah; D. Hulme, A. Gregory; Ward, P. Hulme, Waddell, M. Gregory, R. Powell, Hanley. *Subs*: Case, Wright.

* * *

Scorers Australia   *Tries* Lewis, Backo. *Goals* O'Connor (2).
           Great Britain *Tries* Gill (2), Offiah, Ford, M. Gregory. *Goals*
                           Loughlin (3).

Referee Francis Desplas (France).

Roger Millward

Australia 7 Great Britain 28
Second Test, Sydney Cricket Ground
20 June 1970

Born 16 September 1947. A casual observer strolling on to the terraces of a rugby league ground in the 1960s and 1970s and seeing a little man, just 5 feet 4 inches in height and weighing hardly 10 stones, tangling with 16- and 17-stone giants could have been excused for thinking that somehow the tiny mite had wandered into the wrong game. However, a darting run, a majestic sidestep or a glorious kick to touch from the mini-maestro and the spectator would soon have realised that he was watching someone special, Roger 'The Dodger' Millward MBE, in fact. The diminutive Great Britain half-back star who, in amassing a total of 29 Test caps between 1966 and 1978, became one of the few players to play in five Anglo-Australia Ashes series and three World Cup tournaments, compensated for his lack of size with an immense array of footballing skills and with a heart beneath his jersey as big as any prop forward's.

On leaving school, just yards from Wheldon Road, the home of the Castleford club, it was only natural that he should sign professional forms for his home town team, making his debut in their colours against Dewsbury in October 1963. An outstanding half-back combination in Alan Hardisty and Keith Hepworth, however, blocked the youngster's path to the top, and it was no surprise when a £6000 fee took him to Hull Kingston Rovers, where he enjoyed a most rewarding career as both player and coach. Though small in stature, Roger was always the big-occasion player, his proudest moment being his equalling, in the second Test against Australia in 1970, of Leeds' Lewis Jones' 20-point record haul in an Ashes Test.

I well remember one Sunday morning in 1962, leaning on the pitch perimeter wall at St. Helens after a particularly heavy training session and watching a tiny boy, clad in a jersey two sizes too big for him, mesmerising 13 older and bigger opponents with his antics with a ball. I was not alone in my appreciation of the 'Artful Dodger's' skills, for many more, sitting at home in the comfort of their lounges, were also being entertained by him in the televised Colts rugby matches at that time being screened by ITV. Surrounded by youngsters two and three years older than him, and some often three or four stones

131

heavier, he appeared as someone's kid brother who had been allowed to tag along for the day. But when this 14-year-old genius took hold of the ball it was obvious that here was no player who would just 'tag along' with the rest; here was one who would lead the rest a merry dance with an array of skills that rarely come together in one player. Six years later I myself was to enjoy the benefit of his incomparable footballing skills when I accompanied him to Australia and New Zealand with the Great Britain World Cup squad. Within a very short time I came to appreciate just what a dangerous player he could be, and so did Australia, where the name of Roger Millward was rarely out of the headlines whenever the Ashes were at stake.

The most successful Lions tour in history, the visit of the 1970 squad, is often held up as an example to other parties making such trips as the tour party containing the ideal blend of players to win in Australia. Tough, uncompromising front rowers and equally tough but speedy back rowers in the pack, tricky, dodging, darting half backs and powerful, pacy backs, plus a goalkicker or two, would adequately describe the 26-man party that set out in 1970 in the quest for the Ashes. Yet, after their 37–15 mauling in the first week of June, few British supporters were under any illusions that the Lions side was about to mould into a finely tuned fighting machine capable of sweeping through the rest of Australia and New Zealand without losing another of its remaining 18 matches. An outstanding display from Roger Millward in the second Test at the Sydney Cricket Ground inspired the team to great heights and proved the launching-pad for a 2–1 Ashes series win and a 3–0 Test series in New Zealand.

Tour manager Jack Harding and coach, former Great Britain loose forward John Whiteley, travelled from the northern outpost of Darwin down through the Barrier Reef coastline of Queensland with smiles on their faces as the Lions, against not too strong opposition, stormed to five wins in five outings, helping themselves to 165 points. When they arrived at Lang Park, Brisbane, for the first clash with Australia, however, the Great Britain team, selected more on play and reputations back home than in the vastly different conditions of Australia, was devastated. In heated exchanges the slower, more ponderous Lions forwards were no match for the quicker-moving and more inventive Aussies and, behind, there was a hesitancy and lack of fluency in the back play. The result was a demoralising 24 hours and, according to Millward, a drastic rethink on the composition of the team for the crucial second Test in two weeks' time at the famous cricket ground in Sydney.

On the way down from Darwin the matches had been easy, and many of the older players had rarely been tested. The side for the first Test in Brisbane was therefore selected more on past reputations and form back home in England. The team consisted of well-worn regular combinations, and it was found badly wanting in all departments. John Whiteley had a complete change of mind and brought in many fresh faces. It was badly needed.

Hull KR's confident little half back, a substitute for that first Test, was one who was included in coach Whiteley's plans. Millward had rarely kicked goals back home in England, but, such were full back Terry Price's problems in that department, that he was pressed into service, with the result that alongside his 18 tries in just 16 appearances he added 23 goals to make up a century of points for the trip.

Terry Price was having a nightmare with his kicking, adjusting to the hardness of the grounds and the different balls themselves, so I was asked to try my hand at goalkicking. I had never really done any kicking before, but they suddenly seemed to go over the crossbar. The side began to knit together and was in fine shape for our arrival in Sydney.

It is an interesting fact that the 1970 Ashes Test series proved to be the only one played under the four-tackle rule, a rule that produced much frantic football and frenetic handling and was soon changed in favour of the six-tackle rule. Few of us playing the game in 1970 who had served the best part of our careers under the old, unlimited-tackle rule ever really adjusted to the 'touch-and-pass' frenzy which accompanied the four-tackle version and were much happier with the extra two-tackle allowance. Perhaps one or two forwards in the Lions party were more accustomed to their once-traditional stereotyped midfield role under the unlimited-tackle rule but, whatever, heads rolled after Great Britain's Brisbane débâcle.

Australia were rocked when their inspiration of the first Test, Graeme Langlands, who had set a new Ashes goalkicking record with nine successful kicks, was out nursing an injured thigh, but few expected the wholesale changes made to the British lineup. For varying reasons, out went Terry Price, Clive Sullivan, Mick Shoebottom, Alan Hardisty, Dave Chisnall, Peter Flanagan and Dave Robinson and in came Derek Edwards, Alan Smith, Syd Hynes, Dennis Hartley, Tony Fisher, Jimmy Thompson and Roger Millward. Rovers' gifted stand off was to partner his old Castleford team-mate Keith Hepworth, and the pressure was once again on Millward.

I had been in the international side all year previous to the trip Down Under, and Alan Hardisty was only called into the Great Britain tour party late. But once in Australia I was battling for a place against the old Castleford combination of Hardisty and Hepworth. I had battled against them at Castleford when I first signed professional and here I was again. I enjoyed it, though. I've always been a fighter; you have to be when you are so small. The pressure for me to do well at the cricket ground was enormous, but I had played there a couple of times before in the 1968 World Cup and enjoyed its atmosphere.

The impressive, new, all-concrete-and-glass structure of the Sydney Football Stadium now stands on the rise alongside the old, famous Sydney Cricket Ground. The sweep of its terraces and the arching curves of its roof are glowing testimony to the marvels of modern architecture, yet there is something more appealing about the painted wooden railings in front of the dressing rooms at the cricket ground. The sound of studs shaking the timbers beneath the members' enclosure and the dressing rooms, the walk along the wooden balcony at the back of the members' seats and the passage down the flight of wooden steps and through the wicket gate on to the famous turf evoke memories of cricketing heroes Don Bradman and Jack Hobbs, and rugby legends Jim Sullivan and Clive Churchill. The place is steeped in tradition and, for Roger Millward, there could have been no more awe-inspiring arena in which to display his many talents.

I loved playing at the Sydney Cricket Ground. It has an atmosphere and a tradition of its own. When I was a kid I used to look at the tour photos of the great players taken on the cricket ground, photos of Ernest Ward, Gus Risman, Joe Egan and company, and whenever I arrived at the ground I used to think that I was now standing and playing at the very same place. It was a marvellous feeling and one which did so much for me whenever I played there. It was a stadium for doing great deeds.

It was great deeds from Millward himself which quietened a massive 60,962 crowd, the majority of whom had congregated to see the Lions suffer further embarrassment and the Kangaroos take the Ashes. To the amazement of the fans packed on to the once-notorious hill at the cricket ground, Great Britain swept into an 11-2 half-time lead and held such a tight grip on the Green and Gold opposition that the fickle Aussie fans occasionally turned angrily on their own favourites. Roger Millward struck for the first of his two tries as early as the third minute of the game and displayed the opportunism that was to grab him many more tries on the tour.

Our loose forward Mal Reilly made a good break down the middle, and he continued the movement forward with a high kick downfield. The ball bounced badly for the Australian full back, and both Mal and Ron Coote, Australia's second row, missed the bounce of the ball when they chased for it. The ball bounced over their heads, and I was able to gather it and race in for the score.

Great Britain's half-back star added the conversion and, along with five further goals and a drop goal, proceeded to break Australia's hearts with an immaculate hundred per cent goalkicking display. Australia, through prop and skipper John Sattler and speedy second row Ron Coote, did threaten to haul themselves back into the game immediately after half time, but such was the power of the Great Britain pack, the nimbleness and tactical superiority of Millward and Hepworth at half back, and the rock-like defence of skipper Frank Myler and Syd Hynes in the centres that defeat was a foregone conclusion.

> Our pack was in complete control. The front row of Dennis Hartley, Tony Fisher and Cliff Watson was too powerful for them. They were very big men. If you wanted them to play football, then they could, and they were tough. If the Aussies ever fancied a fight, then they could easily oblige them. Behind them we had Doug Laughton, Jimmy Thompson and Mal Reilly, who all had an unbelievably high work rate. They could run and tackle, and in that pack there were no prisoners taken.

To play behind a platform as solid as the one in front of him was paradise for Roger Millward, and he and Hepworth in the final 40 minutes continued to orchestrate the Lions attacks. Great Britain increased their lead when centre Hynes followed Millward's first half example and slotted over another two-point drop goal but, for the first time in the match, he created a little nervousness in the Great Britain camp when he was dismissed three minutes later for kicking out at Australian second row 'Artie' Beetson. The Lions were reduced to 12 fit men as Australian referee Don Lancashire chose to ignore the fact that Syd Hynes had been provoked into the attack following a high tackle to the head by the fiery Aussie forward. Yet, despite a late penalty goal from stand off Phil Hawthorne and a 78th minute try from St. George wing Johnny King, Australia offered little to benefit from their numerical advantage. Perhaps the implementation of the four-tackle rule, which hardly allowed a side the time or the amount of continuous possession to dominate the opposition, came to Great Britain's aid during the final 24 minutes. Their defensive resolve and far greater footballing skills, however, counted for far more in overcoming their disadvantage.

The Lions roared in for three tries in the final quarter, wing John Atkinson grabbing an easy try when Aussie giant Beetson failed to control a loose ball, and hooker Tony Fisher crowning a masterly performance with, for a number nine, a rare 30-yard interception try. Millward, in the 75th minute, added his second try of the match which, along with his seven goals, allowed him to equal Lewis Jones' record 20-point haul in an Ashes Test set back in 1954.

> John Atkinson put a little chip kick over the Australian defence and I managed to race around them, pick up and score. They were very tired,

despite having a man more than us, and we just ran them ragged in the final 20 minutes. John Whiteley's team changes had paid off and, from that moment, there was a wonderful team spirit and camaraderie in the camp.

Written off by the vitriolic Australian press, Great Britain had triumphed against the odds in a match that was to prove the turning point of the most successful tour in the history of Lions trips Down Under. Naturally, as the players waltzed deliriously around the boundary of the cricket field, the atmosphere, to say the least, was euphoric.

It was a marvellous feeling after the match, especially after the team had been so heavily beaten in the first Test. There were fights on the hill among the frustrated Aussie supporters at the end of the match, but we were happy.

There were no cliques in the tour party. If you were having a drink at the bar of the Olympic Hotel where we were staying and anybody came downstairs, he joined you and you went out together. We had the fight and the Aussies hadn't.

Stunned Australian selectors made seven changes for the third and final Test but, for all the seven goals of full back Allan McKean, their team was swept aside by five tries to one in a defeat far more convincing than the 21–17 scoreline suggests. Roger Millward, Mal Reilly, Cliff Watson, skipper Frank Myler and company continued to sweep all before them, becoming only the second touring team to win three Tests and every provincial game in New Zealand. Truly a Lions tour which hinged on those magical moments at the Sydney Cricket Ground.

AUSTRALIA Laird; King, McDonald, Brass, Cootes; Hawthorne, Smith; Wittenberg, Fitzsimmons, Sattler, Coote, Beetson, Weiss.

GREAT BRITAIN Edwards; Smith, Hynes, Myler, Atkinson; Millward, Hepworth; Hartley, Fisher, Watson, Laughton, Thompson, Reilly. *Subs*: Shoebottom.

Scorers Australia   *Tries* King. *Goals* McDonald, Hawthorne.
            Great Britain   *Tries* Millward (2), Atkinson, Fisher. *Goals* Millward (6). *Drop Goals* Hynes, Millward.

Referee Don Lancashire (Australia).

Keith Mumby

Bradford Northern 6 Widnes 0
John Player Trophy Final, Headingley, Leeds
5 January 1980

Born 21 February 1957. Odsal, home of Bradford Northern, can be a cold, wet, forbidding place in January, but to long-serving full back and centre Keith Mumby there was no finer place at which to spend his winters. For 17 seasons between 1973 and 1990, during which time he made 578 appearances for the club and scored over 1820 points, Keith Mumby was a permanent fixture in the side, rarely ever failing to satisfy the most fickle of fans. Tempted by Sheffield Eagles manager Gary Hetherington, he did enjoy a short stay in the steel city, mixing playing with coaching, but he was quick to return to the fold when, in October 1992, his old mentor, controversial coach Peter Fox, arrived at Odsal to take charge once again. Renowned for his strong tackling defence at full back, his ability to link in attack and his sure kicking, the Bradford stalwart had a brief but exciting international career, gaining 11 Test caps in a hectic 24-month period between 1982 and 1984. Sadly, for all his efforts and never-say-die attitude, he was one of the few players to achieve the unwanted distinction of playing and losing in all six Tests against Australia and New Zealand on the Lions tour of 1984.

When new Northern coach Peter Fox arrived at Odsal on 27 April 1977 he soon set to work building a side that would bring trophies back again to Bradford. Nor did he waver from his belief that a strong pack is the prerequisite to success for, without the ball and the protection up front, no backs, however talented, can run and display their skills. Over two seasons he consistently added to the strength of the pack at Odsal, and, on virtually each occasion he recruited, he shattered the club's transfer fee record. A record £10,000 secured perpetual tackler Jimmy Thompson in 1977 and, in the following season, he added former Dewsbury prop Jeff Grayshon at a record £14,000. He paid a record £23,000 for Hull KR tearaway forward Len Casey three months later, and, another three months into the season, captured hooker Keith Bridges from Featherstone Rovers for an even bigger £24,500. Behind the scrum, the wily Fox had attracted a tall, long-striding centre, Derek Parker, from Bramley and a clever tactician in Nigel Stephenson from Dewsbury at half back. By the start of the season in September 1979, Bradford Northern, with Keith

137

Mumby as the rock of defence at the back, were ready for their biggest successes since the glory days of the 1950s.

Under Fox, Bradford Northern lifted the First Division Championship, pipping their great rivals Widnes by just one league point, and beat them in the final of the John Player Trophy in the January of the same season. Keith Mumby well remembers the final showdown with Widnes, not particularly for any great personal performance on his part but, in typically unselfish manner, for the quality of the team's play and the effects on the Bradford club.

At the time of the John Player Trophy final, Widnes had some of the biggest names in the game and were very much the favourites to win, even though we had a fine side and were playing exceptionally well. Whenever we played them, they always seemed to have the knack of beating us. Every time we got to a final or met them in an important match, they always seemed to enjoy the bounce of the ball and have all the luck. They were playing well at the time and everybody expected them to win as usual, but we did them this time. The match will always stand out for me because it was a turning point for Bradford. I was pleased with my own personal performance, but the win and the manner of the win gave us such confidence that we went on to win two championships.

And it was Peter Fox's newly bought pack and Keith Mumby himself that 'did them'.

In Jimmy Thompson, a hero in Great Britain's last Ashes-winning team in 1970, Jeff Grayshon and Len Casey, Northern had three forwards who had been or would be the backbone of Great Britain's pack, and in international hooker Keith Bridges they had a steady ball-winner and a shrewd distributor around the rucks. Gary Van Bellen was a giant of a man capable of resisting the fiercest of midfield challenges, while prop Colin Forsyth proved what a danger he could be to any slack defences when, in April of the 1979–80 season, he became the top-scoring prop of all time by registering the 100th try of his career. They were a formidable six, able to mix it with the best, including Widnes.

Our pack was outstanding, always able to control the game and able to slow it down whenever they wanted. Colin Forsyth was an exceptionally fast prop, always likely to pick up a try, and in Jimmy Thompson we had the best tackler in the game. Jimmy never stopped running throughout the match, and he certainly dented a few reputations.

For Widnes, their latest points-scoring sensation from Waterloo rugby union club, Mike Burke, was on the left wing and Great Britain star Stuart Wright

138

was on the right. Eric Hughes and Reg Bowden were as tough a pair of half backs as any in world rugby, while up front in hooker Keith Elwell, prop Glyn Shaw and loose forward Mick Adams they had a trio of forwards at the top of their form. But Widnes did not have, according to Keith Mumby, the secret weapon, Peter Fox.

The Bradford coach's motivational powers are legendary, while his skill at collecting old players under his wing and coaxing another two or three seasons' play out of them is second to none. Peter Fox too was ready for the clash with Widnes.

> There is nobody in the game better than Peter Fox for inspiring a team. He gets really worked up himself and sets just the right atmosphere in a dressing room for the players. He fires you up and motivates you so much that you think you cannot lose. He did a good job in the few minutes before we went out to meet Widnes. We were ready for any side when we went out.

Despite coach Fox's stirring speech, it was Bradford who, in the early stages, were on the receiving end of a fierce onslaught from Widnes. With halves Hughes and Bowden making good use of the ball and bringing their speedy threequarter line into play, the Northern cover was fully stretched, and it required solid tackles from back rowers Thompson and Casey, and Mumby at full back, to keep out the Chemics. Tempers became a little overcharged as the forwards wrestled for control in midfield, and referee Billy Thompson, heavily involved, as ever, haranguing, cajoling and joking with the players, worked hard to keep matters under control. Widnes attacks floundered on the deadly tackling of the Northern six and, on the rare occasion there was a lapse out wide, Mumby was alert to Wright's and Burke's tryscoring abilities down the flanks.

Indeed, so accurate and tenacious was the Bradford full back's tackling that day, and for the 14 seasons since, that his coach Peter Fox believes that his style of coaching has often been labelled as being defensive because of him. Insists Peter:

> In the final, Keith Mumby's defence was absolutely outstanding. His tackling was so secure and so effective over the years that I became labelled as being a defensively minded coach. We had the best defensive record in the game for four out of the eight seasons I was at Odsal, but the sole reason was because of Keith Mumby, not because of any special planning by myself.
>
> He has been the most solid tackling full back I've ever seen in my life, courageous and honest in every match he played.

A ninth-minute penalty goal from Keith Mumby gave Northern an early 2–0

139

lead, and it was against the run of play when Bradford's pacy midfield back Derek Parker snatched a try in the 25th minute. For all Widnes's creative play and occasional sweeping attacks, the Bradford pack held their opponents in a tight grip in midfield and, once they had eased themselves into a tackling role, were able to handle everything that Widnes could offer. Keith Mumby, sure under the high kicks and content to scoop up any low, raking grubbers to the corners, hovered behind them marshalling the defence or highlighting a gap or a weakness with the occasional shout to a colleague.

The second half developed into a game rather like chess, with Bradford's defence moving easily about the field to contain any Widnes thrusts or ploys and, in the 43rd minute, striking out with a solitary Nigel Stephenson drop goal. Northern's line was never crossed in 80 minutes, and the former Dewsbury half-back star's drop goal proved the killer blow to Widnes hopes, for, having so far proved incapable of scoring once, they would now have to score twice if they were to deprive Bradford of their second John Player Trophy.

> The pack got on top of the Widnes forwards and they set up a stalemate in the middle with the strength of their tackling. Len Casey, the man of the match, and Jimmy Thompson were everywhere on the field tackling, and whenever we broke out in attack they were there too. There was no one star on the day; all the team played for each other. The support work was good, and the longer the game went on the more confident I was that six points would be enough to win the trophy. It was a superb win and did a lot for the players and the club.

The match had followed the pattern of Bradford Northern's previous John Player Trophy win five years earlier when, again against Widnes, they had triumphed by an even smaller score and by an even closer points difference of 3–2.

Sensationally, man of the match Len Casey, within three weeks of Bradford's second John Player Trophy final defeat of the Chemics, was on his way back to Craven Park to rejoin Hull Kingston Rovers for a then world record £38,000 fee, giving Fox a hefty £15,000 profit in just 13 months. Casey's departure, however, failed to halt Bradford's and Keith Mumby's momentum, for a second First Division Championship trophy was added in the following season and Northern's number one became the holder of the most tries scored by a full back at the club when, on Boxing Day 1980, he grabbed the 47th touchdown of his career, beating the record set by ex-Kiwi full back Joe Phillips way back in the early 1950s.

Evergreen full back Keith Mumby, after 20 glorious years at Odsal, was still serving the Bradford club last season, but Bradford boss Peter Fox, now in his second term of office at Odsal, still bemoans what could have been:

* * *

We won two Championships, a Yorkshire Cup, a Premiership and the John Player Trophy, but we could have won everything if the directors had listened to me. After the match I told my directors that if they would buy me two more forwards, Trevor Skerrett and Charlie Stone, then we would win every trophy in the game. I felt that there would be no team within reach of us.

But they ignored my advice and even sold Len Casey back to Hull KR. They made a huge mistake, for we could have really built upon the success of our John Player win and the First Division Championship that season.

BRADFORD NORTHERN Mumby; Barends, D. Redfearn, Parker, Gant; Stephenson, A. Redfearn; Thompson, Bridges, Forsyth, Grayshon, G. Van Bellen, Casey. *Subs*: I. Van Bellen, Ferres.

WIDNES Eckersley; Wright, Aspey, George, Burke; Hughes, Bowden; Hogan, Elwell, Shaw, Gorley, Hull, Adams. *Subs*: Mills.

Scorers Bradford *Tries* Parker. *Goals* Mumby. *Drop Goals* Stephenson.

Referee Billy Thompson (Huddersfield).

Alex Murphy

Leigh 24 Leeds 7
Challenge Cup Final, Wembley
15 May 1971

Born 24 April 1939. Since 1958, when Alex Murphy burst into the headlines and, as an 18-year-old, became a national hero for his Ashes-winning exploits Down Under, the controversial half-back star has proved himself to be one of the game's greatest-ever players or coaches. As a player, his sensational speed and craft around the scrum earned him 27 Test caps for his country and every individual honour with St. Helens, Leigh and Warrington. And, when the mercurial Murphy left his scrum half role at St. Helens in October 1966 to accept a five-year player-coaching appointment at Leigh for the then princely sum of £30 per week, he embarked upon one of the most successful coaching careers in the history of the game.

Already familiar with Wembley as a player for St. Helens in 1961 and 1966, he returned on another six occasions, as player-coach with Leigh and then Warrington, then as coach with Warrington, Wigan and St. Helens (twice). Nor have Alex's travels been confined to just those four clubs, for he has also enjoyed spells in charge at Salford and, lastly, with Huddersfield, his first appointment in Yorkshire, in September 1991. Ever his own man and never afraid to pillory the game's hierarchy from his many newspaper columns, it is probable that his outspoken views have cost him his ambition of coaching Great Britain in a Test series. He did, however, enjoy some success in charge of England in the 1975 World Cup, losing out to the winners Australia by a point in the final league table.

In its 65-year history of hosting the rugby league Challenge Cup finals, Wembley Stadium has proved the setting for many heroic deeds. Widnes, including 12 locally born players, deservedly captured the public's imagination with their unexpected defeat of top of the table St. Helens in 1930 and, in 1952, skipper Gus Risman earned the admiration of all when, as a 41-year-old, he led Workington Town to victory a mere seven years after the formation of the tiny Cumbrian club. When the small pit town of Leigh in south-west Lancashire dared to challenge league's most glamorous city side, Leeds, then eight-times winners of the Challenge Cup, few of their supporters can have bargained for the events that were to pass into history and legend on Saturday,

15 May 1971. But close observers of the rugby league scene, well aware of the name of Leigh's illustrious player-coach, were hardly surprised when the man at the helm, Alex Murphy, inspired his side to the greatest victory in the club's history and provided fans worldwide with an argument that has raged for the past 23 years.

An open-top bus carried Leigh's heroes, a collection of almost unknowns and one of the world's greatest-ever players, around the streets of Leigh on their return from Wembley. They and their delirious supporters had been 'up for t'cup' and they had brought it back to Lancashire with them. For Murphy, Leigh's success against all the odds had proved to be the most momentous occasion in his glittering career.

> To take Leigh to Wembley and beat Leeds was the biggest thrill in my rugby life. Leeds were like the Wigan of today and were priced at 5–1 on to win the Challenge Cup while we, before the first round, were quoted at odds of 66–1 to win it. It was one of the greatest achievements ever by underdogs at Wembley. Nobody gave us a chance, but we had played and beaten them twice in the league that season and I was surprised to see us so unfancied by the bookmakers. It was my greatest achievement in rugby.

Historians had to search back to 1921 to see the name of Leigh recorded on the base of the Challenge Cup, while for their win over Halifax the team had only to journey down the road to the now-defunct Broughton Rangers ground at Salford. Nor did record-keepers 50 years later expect to be troubled too much by Leigh after the 10–4 struggle to beat Huddersfield in the semi-final. They didn't bargain, however, for one Alexander James Murphy who, though slower than when he last visited Wembley with St. Helens in 1961 and 1966, had lost none of the craft and guile that made him the fiercest of competitors. As Murphy's team-mate Kevin Ashcroft insists, there was plenty of life still left in the old master:

> Many people said he was at the end of his career, but he wasn't, far from it. He had a rugby brain second to none and knew exactly what was wanted for success at Wembley. He had built up the team in the previous year and created a real family spirit. He had a great inner feeling for his players, and he inspired many of us to perform above ourselves.

Both Wembley finalists suffered blows to their prospects in mid-week when Leigh prop Dave Chisnall was suspended and scrum half Tommy Canning was ruled unfit. Derek Watts moved into Chisnall's place at number eight in the pack, and the mercurial Murphy restored himself to his old scrum half role with Tony Barrow taking up the stand off position. Leeds were missing two of their international stars, wing Alan Smith and loose forward Ray

143

Batten, and had John Langley and Bill Ramsey deputising. Despite the loss of their Great Britain stars, Leeds were still installed as red-hot favourites. But Murphy, buoyed by the prophecy of a lady spiritualist in Leigh who had confidently predicted him holding aloft the cup, was confident of success, believing that Leeds and their supporters had totally underestimated his team.

I had been to Wembley twice before and knew what was required to win. We had some young lads in the backs, like David Eckersley, Joe Walsh and Stan Dorrington, who were undersold by Leeds. And in the pack Leeds had no better forwards than our own Kevin Ashcroft and Peter Smethurst. We all thought we would win the match and left Leigh in confident mood.

Before the players boarded the coach at Hilton Park on the Thursday morning for their trip to London, their boss, according to Kevin Ashcroft, had one more trick up his sleeve to put them in the right frame of mind for the task ahead.

As we were due to leave on the Thursday morning for Wembley, Alex walked on to the coach with a newspaper in his hand and held it up for all to see. The headlines said that the fans were in for the dullest final ever and that the result was a foregone conclusion. He insisted that everyone read the article and told them that if the story didn't motivate us then nothing would. He fired us up before we even left Leigh.

Alex Murphy's Wembley experience also told him that the first prerequisite for a visit to Wembley was a goalkicker, and he had one in ex-Swansea rugby union star Stuart Ferguson.

Stuart was one of the best kickers in the game at the time. He could always be relied upon to put over three or four goals a match and usually came up trumps in the big matches. I knew he would handle Wembley well and provide us with plenty of points.

Leeds forwards Tony Fisher, Bob Haigh and Bill Ramsey were expected to prove a powerful threat in midfield and, behind, skipper Syd Hynes, Great Britain wing John Atkinson and wily scrum half Barry Seabourne were tipped to give Leigh a tough time. But, for most of the 80 minutes, and certainly for the opening quarter, they were surprisingly thrown on the defensive. Leigh never let up in their efforts, and it was their player-coach who masterminded the operation, displaying his complete repertoire of tactical kicks, shrewd passes and darting runs from the scrum. Hooker Kevin Ashcroft, especially around the play-the-balls, and powerful forwards Jim Fiddler and Paul Grimes followed their captain's lead with some spirited play. It was no surprise that

144

Leigh left the field at half time leading 13–0, thanks to a try from centre Stan Dorrington, three goals from Stuart Ferguson, one from Fiddler and a cheeky 30-yard drop goal from Murphy himself. The fans may have been treated to only one try, but it had been scored by Dorrington after the sweetest of passes from Murphy.

Leeds, in the person of their 19-year-old full back John Holmes, did hit back immediately after the interval with a penalty goal, but with Leigh loose forward Peter Smethurst tackling like a demon and Murphy proving a constant threat to the Yorkshiremen a further drop goal from the skipper and a penalty goal from full back Ferguson in the 56th and 58th minutes gave Leigh an even tighter grip on the trophy. With the scoreline at 17–2 in Leigh's favour, neutrals in the stadium could have been forgiven for any lapses of concentration as the minutes ticked away towards the inevitable result. The 65th minute, however, provided such drama and, for the past 23 years, such controversy that the then BBC television commentator Eddie Waring was moved to record, in his colourful account the unique situation at Wembley 'one captain walking off and one captain being carried off the field'.

Leeds, desperate for points, had mounted an attack down the left-hand side of the pitch, where skipper Syd Hynes was stopped in full flight by opposing captain Alex Murphy. Though the ball was moved away quickly from the tackle, Murphy was left lying spreadeagled on the floor and in considerable discomfort. After a brief consultation with his touch judges, Huddersfield referee Billy Thompson ruled that Hynes had butted Murphy and he had no hesitation in sending off the Leeds captain and according him his unenviable place in history as the first man ever to be dismissed at Wembley. After some two minutes, Alex Murphy was stretchered from the field, substitute Les Chisnall entered the fray, and the arguments began to rage.

Had Alex feigned his injury in an effort to have Syd Hynes dismissed from the match? Such an argument gained considerable support in Leeds, especially when Leigh's maestro recovered sufficiently in time to mount the steps and receive the coveted trophy from the Right Honourable Reggie Maudling MP. In after-match reports, Syd Hynes insisted, 'I tackled Murphy and I thought that was it. He just fell back to the floor. I could not believe I had been given my marching orders'. Alex, however, much to the disgust of irate Yorkshiremen who persist in taking their beliefs to the grave, insists that accounts of his acting ability could not be further from the truth.

The tales of Syd Hynes and myself are now more far fetched than those of Jesse James. The stories get worse as the years go by. I've heard tales of me getting off the stretcher and stories of me winking at Syd as he was walking off. Syd is one of my best friends in rugby, but I must say that he took a chance and got caught.

I was sat in the bath in the dressing room, still dazed, and the Wembley doctor had said that I could take no further part in the game when the message came that the Leigh players wanted me to go up to receive the cup. They had struggled long and hard to win the cup and I wasn't going to disappoint them.

Tempers became frayed long before Alex Murphy reappeared from the trainers' bench to receive the Challenge Cup, as the final quarter was played out with more than a hint of frustration from both sides. Leeds, down to 12 men and now no match for a confident Leigh, were unable to stop outstanding full back David Eckersley from adding a fourth drop goal and then, in the 75th minute, from cutting through a tiring defence for a try. Consolation did come Leeds' way when half back Tony Wainwright, almost on the stroke of full time, was awarded an obstruction try by the alert Billy Thompson. However, the unbelievable had happened: Leigh had won, and the man who just would not lie down, Alex Murphy, was 'up for t'cup' to the cheers of the adoring Leigh supporters and to the occasional boos from the angry Leeds fans.

For the first time in the club's history, tiny Leigh had triumphed at Wembley, and the directors' decision to snatch their captain away from his home town of St. Helens six years previously had succeeded. They, the players and their wives were entitled to their celebrations in a Kensington hotel on the Saturday night, and yet, even amid the festivities, the day of drama had not quite ended.

We all attended a dinner and ball in our Kensington hotel on the night of the cup final and were all enjoying ourselves when suddenly the police came in and asked for Bert Hulme, one of our directors. Bert was a bookmaker, and he had already lost a fortune on the result of the match by giving overgenerous odds to the players and myself. A policeman took him to one side and told him that someone back home in Leigh had broken into his house and stolen his safe. It wasn't Bert's day.

Two drop goals, a trymaking pass from the scrum for colleague Stan Dorrington, the Lance Todd Trophy for an outstanding man of the match display, stretchered from the field, and the first Leigh coach to take home the Challenge Cup for 51 years – it was Alex Murphy's day. It was his 12 team-mates' day, too, and, according to hooker Ashcroft, they owed so much to the maestro.

We didn't have a lot of skill, but we had a lot of endeavour, and he brought the best out of us. He had a terrific effect on players, always got an extra 20 per cent out of us, and always had a kick up the backside for anyone who was slacking. It was an honour to play with him. Controversy has always seemed to be attracted to him, and fans and players either loved him or hated him. But he gave his all for us and Leigh, and I'll never forget that.

LEIGH Eckersley; Ferguson, Dorrington, Collins, Walsh; Barrow, Murphy; Watts, Ashcroft, Fiddler, Grimes, Clarkson, Smethurst. *Subs*: L. Chisnall, Lester.

LEEDS Holmes; Langley, Hynes, Cowan, Atkinson; Wainwright, Seabourne; Burke, Fisher, Barnard, Hick, Haigh, Ramsey. *Subs*: Dyl, Cookson.

Scorers Leigh   *Tries* Dorrington, Eckersley. *Goals* Ferguson (5). *Drop Goals* Fiddler, Murphy (2), Eckersley.

           Leeds   *Tries* Wainwright. *Goals* Holmes (2).

Referee Billy Thompson (Huddersfield).

Paul Newlove

Featherstone Rovers 24 Castleford 16
Post Office Road, Featherstone
17 March 1992

Born 10 August 1971. Amateur rugby league enthusiasts in the Featherstone area needed little persuading that the tall, talented teenager spearheading the Travellers amateur club's attack was destined for higher honours. In Paul Newlove here was one local boy to make good. A move to the professional club at Post Office Road, a season spent maturing in the centre, and by the time he had reached the tender age of 18 years 72 days he had become the youngest-ever player to win a Great Britain Test cap. His entry on to the field against New Zealand as a substitute in October 1989 earned him the honour and began an international career that has since seen him play against every major international rugby league nation and fly with the Great Britain tourists to Australasia in 1992.

The sheer size of Paul Newlove, weighing over 15 stones and standing 6 feet 1 inch tall, is a huge advantage for any young man charging down the flanks and hoping to create space for his winger, but surprising pace for such a big man and an acute positional sense must be added to his extraordinary abilities. Those abilities, which enabled him to amass a world record number of tries for a centre with 52 tries in the 1992–93 season, were recognised by his former Featherstone Rovers coach Peter Fox, and it was no surprise, when he became unsettled at Post Office Road, that he should join his former mentor. Though placed on the transfer list at a world record asking price of £750,000, Rovers' powerful midfield back was quickly attracted to Bradford Northern by their coach Peter Fox. An offer of £150,000 and a willingness to appear before the Transfer Tribunal eventually resulted in Paul Newlove moving to Odsal in July 1993 for a fee of £245,000.

Anyone who, before reaching the age of 22, had scored a try in Great Britain's sensational 33–10 defeat of Australia in the second Ashes Test at Melbourne in 1992 and grabbed a hat trick of tries and the man of the match award in his country's crushing of France in April 1993 would seem to have little reason to look elsewhere when searching for the most memorable match of his short but glittering career. Not so with Bradford Northern's club record buy, Paul Newlove, whose local background and 'home-town boy' approach made him look no further than a Featherstone Rovers v. Castleford derby battle on a cold, damp night in March. Difficult to explain? Not really, according to Rovers' former centre star.

> It was a wonderful experience playing for Great Britain and doing well against Australia and France, but there is no match like a local Featherstone v. Castleford derby, especially when Rovers needed to win to avoid the threat of relegation. The atmosphere for this particular match was something special, and I was fortunate to have a very good game and score a try that helped to turn the match for Featherstone. I don't think I've ever enjoyed a win so much. A win over Castleford for a Rovers player and their fans is worth any other in the season.

Those ex-players, and possibly a good few avid fans, who have experienced 80 minutes' battle in a local derby will easily understand Paul Newlove's enthusiasm for such a seemingly normal run-of-the-mill league championship fixture. In my own playing days in the 1960s and early 1970s on the other side of the Pennines, the St. Helens v. Wigan fixture was, and still is, the premier derby clash of the rugby league code. Passions were aroused among both players and fans alike prior to kickoff as in no other match in the season, and the intensity of commitment on the field was invariably raised a few notches up the temperature scale. The south-west Lancashire clashes have attracted – and still do – the biggest crowds of the season to Central Park or Knowsley Road in anticipation of seeing one side receive their comeuppance. It is tribal warfare in rugby jerseys. Though the crowds at Post Office Road, Featherstone, are far smaller than their counterparts over the hills, there is no depreciation in fervour 'for t' local derby'.

Like the towns of the Old West, Featherstone, to the irregular visitor, appears to have only one road passing through its tiny centre. Put your foot down on the accelerator pedal of the car and you have passed the tiny rugby league ground which nestles at its heart in Post Office Road. But it is the centre for the inhabitants' passions whenever the enemy from down the road, Castleford, appear at its gates. The small, compact stadium, lovingly and sensibly refurbished in recent years, provides for the perfect atmosphere even though the crowd attendance these days is limited to around 10,000. The fans huddle together under the covered stands down the touchlines or squeeze alongside each other on the railings, while a few from the vantage point of their bedroom windows hang out of the tiny terraced houses which line the back of the goalposts at one end. A crowd of 5000 under the bright glare of the floodlights can feel like a 50,000 crowd at Old Trafford or Wembley and can seem to make just as much noise. If a considerable majority of those decked out in the blue and white colours of Featherstone Rovers are your work-mates and some of those in the yellow and black of Castleford are your former school-mates, then the match assumes an extra significance. If a player, at kickoff, doesn't appreciate the importance of such a match then, unlike Paul Newlove, he cannot have lived and worked in the district for the week prior to the showdown.

> More than anything you want to win a local derby match. All my friends, work-mates and former schoolfriends are either Featherstone or Castleford supporters. During the week, it is all part of the build-up to the game that they pull your leg and taunt you about the match. It means so much to them that it comes to mean so much to you as well. I end up putting bets on the result of the match with everybody.
>
> Another great motivator, though, is that somehow Castleford appear to have a more up-market image than Featherstone; they are considered to be a little more classy. Rovers were always considered to be the underdogs and the inferior club, and that made you even more determined to do well and win. You seem to be playing for your friends and your family.

For Featherstone stars Paul Newlove and Deryck Fox and Castleford's Graham Steadman, Mike Ford and Lee Crooks there was another important reason compelling them to give of their best. The selection of the party for the Great Britain tour to Papua New Guinea, Australia and New Zealand was just three weeks away, and Great Britain coach Mal Reilly would be an interested spectator in the packed grandstand.

> I think everyone was conscious that the selection for the Great Britain tour was near. I wanted to play well and impress Mal Reilly. This was the ideal type of match to fire you up to play a good game and catch the eye. The possibility of winning a tour place added a little spice to the match.

Though the 20-year-old Paul Newlove was to prove the vital difference for Featherstone, it was the veteran John Joyner and the vastly experienced prop Lee Crooks who orchestrated events throughout the thrilling 80 minutes for Castleford. The amazingly fit Joyner, 20 seasons in a Castleford jersey and playing in his first full game for over three months, sent out a stream of defence-splitting passes and, using his years of experience, found the gaps through which his seemingly ageless legs frequently carried him. His pack partner, Lee Crooks, was never far away from the hard work in the middle, constantly troubling Rovers with his powerful charges and his punishing kicks to touch. It was no surprise that, with 20 minutes remaining in the match, Castleford, thanks to two tries from John Joyner and Tony Smith and a goal from Lee Crooks in reply to an Owen Simpson length-of-field try and Deryck Fox conversion, led by 10–6. Despite Simpson's breakaway spectacular effort, Rovers had found it difficult to pierce Castleford's strong

150

tackling, though a couple of searing breaks by Newlove were to prove an indicator of things to come.

> Owen Simpson managed to pick up a dropped ball near our line and, with all the Castleford team up in attack, he was able to race away the length of the field to score. But Castleford deserved their lead because they had tackled well and pressured us in the middle. Things looked bad for us until we hit back late in the second half.

It was Newlove himself who hit back, launched Featherstone on the way to three spectacular tries in just 11 minutes and earned himself a place on Great Britain's tour Down Under. In the 61st minute, Rovers' big centre roared on to a well-timed pass just inside the Castleford half and, displaying his fine turn of speed, raced past the tiring Joyner and rounded opposite centre, Aussie Graham Bradley, who had been switched there in the absence of Castleford's injured full back Graham Steadman. He swept down field and beat Castleford's last line of defence, St. John Ellis, with the neatest of sidesteps to score. The Featherstone directors, sitting immediately in front of me in the full grandstand, forgot themselves, some leaping from their seats and punching the air in delight. Castleford's stranglehold had been broken and the floodgates would soon open.

> I got the ball just across the half way line, a yard or two inside Castleford's half, and I knew I had a little space in which to move. Both Joyner and Bradley missed me, and I was left with plenty of room to sidestep St. John Ellis. He did force me out wide, though, making it an awkward kick at goal for Deryck Fox. But he got the conversion and we had the lead at 12–10.

Three minutes later the giant centre was prominent in perhaps the best combined attacking move of the night, a breathtaking piece of high-speed handling which led to a try for young Featherstone wing Ikram Butt.

> I think this was perhaps Featherstone's best try of the match. It all seemed to happen out of nothing and wasn't planned in any way. It started on one side of the field between myself and Owen Simpson. Chris Bibb, our full back, linked up and continued the movement and gave the ball to Ikram, who finished off with a try. It was a terrific handling movement and covered about 60 yards of the field.

In the 72nd minute Newlove's hard-running co-centre Terry Manning provided the pass for the lively Bibb to score. Rovers half back Deryck Fox added a second conversion and, suddenly, within the space of 11 minutes, Rovers had raced into a ten-point lead with only eight minutes remaining. The thrills and the excitement, however, were not over, as the final, long-drawn-out eight minutes contrived to drain every last ounce of passion out of the frantic fans of both sides. Featherstone skipper Deryck Fox takes up the story:

> We really struggled at the back end of the match because we thought we had the game easily won. But Castleford threw everything at us in those final hectic minutes, and we always seemed to be camped in our 20-metre area and doing all the tackling. There was no way we should have relaxed in such a fierce local derby as this because Castleford refused to give up and played some delightful rugby against us. Luckily, we just held on.

The loss of Cas full back Graham Steadman in the tenth minute with rib cartilage damage had severely restricted the visitors' attacking edge and robbed them of his blistering pace from behind. But, with John Joyner enjoying himself in midfield and with prop Lee Crooks continuing to put out a stream of short pressure passes close to the Rovers line, that ten-point lead still looked vulnerable. It was reduced to four points with just four minutes remaining on the timekeepers' watches when Crooks and Grant Anderson produced the opening for Tony Smith to cross for his second try. Crooks' conversion gave the Castleford supporters hope and caused Rovers fans' nerves to fray at the edges. Solid tackling by Newlove and Manning in the centre, a couple of long kicks down field by Deryck Fox and some spirited running from forwards Leo Casey and Ian Smales, however, took the game to Castleford and set up the position for the alert Manning once again to serve wing Simpson for his second and final try in the last seconds of this pulsating match. Featherstone had eased their relegation worries with a win over their long-standing rivals and had satisfied the honour of their fans with a team performance of the highest quality. Yet it had been that dramatic 61st minute burst by Paul Newlove, his punishing tackling and his free running and handling throughout the match which had given Rovers the edge. It was the type of display which tempted Bradford Northern coach Peter Fox later to prise him away from Post Office Road and join his former colleague and skipper, Deryck Fox, at Odsal. Featherstone Rovers' captain of that night has no doubts as to the quality and importance of Paul Newlove's memorable display.

> We relied on Paul to score the long-range tries and he did just that whenever the pressure was on us. The most interesting point in this match was that Castleford's St. John Ellis had told Paul before the kickoff that he was going to follow him all night, that he would never let him get past him and that he would tackle him out of the match. He really had a go at Paul.
> Well, Paul went past him easily when he raced in for his try, and St.

John hardly got near him all night. I think that pleased Paul more than anything.

I've told him many times that if he increased his upper body strength that he would be Great Britain's answer to Australia's Mal Meninga. His legs are very strong and he runs with a very long stride which make him difficult to hold. Against Castleford he was well-nigh unstoppable.

FEATHERSTONE ROVERS Bibb; Butt, Manning, Newlove, Simpson; Pearson, Fox; Casey, Whiteley, Burton, Smales, Rose, Fisher. *Subs*: Sharp, Akaidere.

CASTLEFORD Steadman; Middleton, Ellis, Smith, Nelson; Anderson, Ford; Crooks, Southernwood, England, Bradley, Ketteridge, Joyner. *Subs*: Whitehead, Sampson.

Scorers Featherstone Rovers   *Tries* Simpson (2), Newlove, Butt, Bibb. *Goals* Fox (2).

Castleford   *Tries* Joyner, Smith (2). *Goals* Crooks (2).

Referee David Campbell (St. Helens).

Tawera Nikau

Otahuhu 28 Te Atatu 14
Fox Memorial Final, Carlaw Park, Auckland
September 1990

Born 1 January 1967. Nothing excites a crowd more than a thrilling burst of speed down the flanks, a display of subtle ball-handling skills or a devastating smother tackle. Castleford's athletic loose forward, New Zealand Test star Tawera Nikau, is one player who has the skills to bring a crowd to its feet in eager anticipation whenever he handles the ball. Blessed with exceptional pace, this 6 feet 2 inches and 14 stones 7 pounds lithe forward has emerged in the past couple of seasons as one of the world's greatest forwards. On leaving the Otahuhu club in Auckland, New Zealand's player of the year in 1990 served his apprenticeship in Britain with Ryedale-York and Sheffield Eagles, for whom he scored five tries in just ten appearances, before joining Castleford in 1991. He proved to be one of Castleford coach Darryl Van de Velde's most valuable buys, skippering the Yorkshire club to a County Cup final victory in only his tenth appearance for the club.

Having toured Great Britain and France with the 1989 Kiwis, Castleford's creative loose forward made his Test debut against Great Britain at Palmerston North in June 1990. He looks set to be a worthy ambassador for his country for many years to come.

Carlaw Park in Auckland is one of the most atmospheric of grounds. It may lack the beauty and grace of the futuristic Sydney Football Stadium, and it may lack the crowd capacity and impressive surroundings of our own Wembley Stadium, but it does not lack tradition and charm. Tiny and compact, and nestling almost in the centre of Auckland, Carlaw Park reminds one of the grounds of yesteryear. The open spaces at either end behind the goalposts and the quaint wooden grandstand with its pigeon loft of a press box perched atop the roof give a primitive appeal to the ground. Yet, when full, with over 20,000 spectators packed into the ground, there is no better atmosphere and enthusiastic response from fans anywhere in the world.

The annual Fox Memorial final, the culmination of a play-off by the top four teams in the Auckland league, is one occasion when Carlaw Park looks at its best. The fans, decked out in their club colours, never fail to support the event in large numbers and invariably celebrate in carnival style. Tawera

154

Nikau, the 23-year-old skipper of Otahuhu, certainly appreciated the atmosphere and the significance of the match as he led his team through the wooden wicker railings and out onto the field. Captain in a final for the first time in his short career and conscious of Otahuhu's great traditions in the competition, it is little wonder that he holds the game so dear in his rugby memories.

I think this match stands out above all others because I was not only captain of what proved to be a winning team but it was the first final I had ever played in, and leading out the team at Carlaw Park meant so much to me. We had come through to the final as underdogs against all the odds and that made it all the more enjoyable. It was a very hot day in September, and the big crowd was very noisy and eager for the kickoff.

Few, including possibly Tawera himself, could have expected Otahuhu winning through to the final. Finishing third in the league on 22 points behind Te Atatu (26 points) and leaders Northcote (34 points), they had surprised everyone by reaching the final after wins against Glenora and Northcote in the end-of-season play-offs. Indeed, after losing seven of their last ten league matches, they had qualified for the play offs only by winning their last match of the season to scrape into fourth place ahead of Glenora.

Nobody really fancied us to get through to the final as it took a last-gasp win in the last match of the season to qualify. Against Glenora in the sudden death play-off we had to recover from an 18–9 deficit with a burst of 28 points in the second half to win. By the time we reached the final, though, we were playing as a team and had easily beaten the favourites, Northcote, by 26–8.

Though Tawera Nikau rated his side as underdogs, there was no shortage of talent in the Otahuhu side for, alongside him in the pack, he had New Zealand Test colleague Francis Leota and behind, at half back, Kiwi stand off Dean Clark controlled the midfield. A powerful attacking force in the threequarter line was his Castleford international colleague Richie Blackmore. Te Atatu, traditionally a force in the Auckland league, were led by former Barrow player Ron O'Regan and included two Test stalwarts themselves in Peter Brown and Sam Panapa. Carlaw Park was ready for the clash of the two in-form teams, and there was no prouder captain than Tawera Nikau as he shook hands with Test referee Dennis Hale in the centre of the field. He had realised already one of his great ambitions.

Otahuhu had had two of New Zealand's greatest captains in past finals in Hugh McGahan and Mark Graham. Both were back row forwards

155

and great Test players for their country, and here was I, at loose forward and captain, following in their footsteps. I was so proud to follow such great players, it gave me a great lift and made it a special day for me.

Within minutes, Te Atatu's Terry O'Shea struck a penalty between the posts to give his side an early 2–0 lead and sound a warning that, if Otahuhu were to win their ninth Fox Memorial Trophy, their captain would have to inspire his side as did his famous predecessors. The team's fans need have had no fears for, aided by the clever running of Dean Clark, who collected six goals from six attempts, the Otahuhu captain treated the crowd to an all-action display of ferocious tackling and tricky running in the very mould of his heroes, McGahan and Graham.

Throughout rugby league history, clubs have scoured the transfer market for fast, strong-running back row forwards in their search for the player who can burst free of the tightest defences. A try-creating or tryscoring forward can often be found in the best of teams, and players like Leigh's Mick Martyn and St. Helens' Dick Huddart from former days and Wigan's Denis Betts and Halifax's Michael Jackson today readily spring to mind. Castleford's Tawera Nikau is one such forward, and it was he who ensured Otahuhu's victory with two devastating bursts of speed.

A 21st minute Dean Clark penalty goal followed by a lengthy run from his own 20-metre line and a converted try for Vila Matautia earned Otahuhu an 8–2 half time lead. But it was Nikau's dramatic intervention six minutes into the second half that set them on their way to victory. Surprising a couple of would-be tacklers with his extra pace, Otahuhu's skipper swept past and, using his customary body swerve, threaded his way through a broken field to the Te Atatu line for the type of try that confirms the wisdom of John Monie, coach to the newly formed Auckland warriors, in making him a priority signing.

Te Atatu's player-coach, Ron O'Regan, did respond with a clever move between himself and Carl Magatogia, which resulted in the former galloping 70 metres to score. O'Shea's conversion gave his side hope until Nikau struck again. Modern loose forwards in the style of Great Britain's Ellery Hanley and Australia's Wayne Pearce, though great players, have not been renowned for their close passing work and ball-handling skills around the scrums. The loss of such skills in the modern loose forward is sad, but Tawera Nikau is one who has such skills in abundance and one who positively delights in a creative role at the scrums. His blindside dash and perfectly executed pass to wing Rusty Matua illustrated loose forward play at its best and resulted in a try and a fourth goal for Clark that were to prove, despite Te Atatu skipper Ron O'Regan's courageous fight back, killer blows.

* * *

156

It was a very tough, physical game in the forwards with plenty of heavy tackling on both sides. For a long time the result was in doubt and it was very close. It could have gone either way. There were few gaps in either side's defences, and we had to work for every chance that came our way. I was fortunate that I managed to be able to create two tries with a couple of good runs. I think Rusty Matua's try probably sealed the win despite the never-say-die attitude of Ron O'Regan.

A pass from the tireless O'Regan somehow found its way via pack man Peter Brown to Sam Panapa, who gratefully accepted the try, but any thoughts of a furious finale from Te Atatu were dashed when their increasingly frustrated skipper was sent to the sin bin in the 71st minute for a high tackle on Harvey Mason. Otahuhu's numerical advantage allowed the outstanding Clark to add two goals and create a try for Mark Riley before the delighted Nikau duly lifted the Fox Memorial Trophy above his head in acknowledgement of the congratulations from the crowd.

Speed and guile had proved the difference between the two sides, while Otahuhu's fierce pack, where Mark Faumunia, Dean Noble and Jim Paul had borne the brunt of the work, had inflicted untold damage on their opponents' defence with punishing solo runs. Dean Clark, at half back, had revelled in the control of the six in front of him and gave an immaculate display of goalkicking, but the inspirational Tawera Nikau had led from the front, produced the tryscoring breaks when needed and dashed back in defence when the line was under threat. Testimony to the Kiwi loose forward's all-round skills is the high number of tackles, 29 in all, made by a forward whose forte is his running and ball-handling skills.

His first-ever final win, his emulation of two of Otahuhu and New Zealand all-time great skippers, Hugh McGahan and Mark Graham, and his outstanding matchwinning performance naturally made it a game to remember. Yet he could still pay tribute to a gallant opposition and their outstanding captain.

They, and Ron O'Regan especially, gave everything they had in the opening half hour. We really had to work and tackle, but we withstood it all. Te Atatu are a very good side that never say die in a big match, and they really roared back at us in the second half. It was an honour to follow in Hugh McGahan's and Mark Graham's footsteps, and it was a great thrill to have a hand in two tries in my first final. The perfect day really for any player.

His elevation to New Zealand's player of the year in the same year only added to his memories and helped to crown his season.

* * *

157

OTAHUHU Graham; Matua, Matautia, D. Clark, Blackmore; A. Clark, Riley; Noble, Mason, Leota, Paul, Faumunia, Nikau.

TE ATATU Magatogia; Tangira, Panapa, Bailey, Henare; O'Regan, Taylor; Brown, Huggins, Hall, Stockman, O'Shea, Robards.

Scorers Otahuhu   *Tries* Matautia, Clark, Matua, Riley. *Goals* Clark (6).
Te Atatu   *Tries* Magatogia, Panapa. *Goals* O'Shea (2), Bailey.

Referee Dennis Hale (Auckland).

Michael O'Connor

Queensland 16 New South Wales 20
First State of Origin Match, Lang Park, Brisbane
2 June 1987

Born 30 November 1960. The incidence of rugby union players turning to the professional code in Britain is quite high, and illustrious names like Lewis Jones, Jonathan Davies, Gus Risman and Martin Offiah have enhanced rugby league by their deeds on the field. In Australia the number of converts switching between the two rugby codes has never reached the same levels as in Britain, but Ken Kearney, Trevor Allan, Ray Price and, especially, Michael O'Connor bear testimony to the quality of league's recruits.

It was the challenge which brought the gifted O'Connor into league with St. George in 1983, and his 401 points in just 78 matches for the Sydney club were early indications that he was to meet the challenge with ease. A further five-season spell with Manly and an off-season stay with St. Helens in 1989–90 only added to his reputation as an elegant centre, quick in attack and resolute in defence. His electrifying speed, his sidestep and his handling ability stamped him as a player of the highest class, one destined to join the few who have represented their country at both union and league.

A Kangaroo tourist to Great Britain and France in 1986, Michael O'Connor represented his country in 17 Tests between 1985 and 1990, scoring 17 tries and 61 goals. Though at his happiest when playing in the centre, he was frequently used by Australia as a wing, where, against Papua New Guinea in 1988, he scored a record 30 points. His unpredictability and his original thinking have turned many a game for Manly and Australia, earning the highest praise from his club and national coach, Bobby Fulton: 'He can do unbelievable things. Unlike any other player at top level he just takes things in his stride.'

State of Origin rugby league elicits a passion among the game's Australian followers which we outsiders find hard to fathom. Surely such matches, notwithstanding inter-state rivalry, are mainly selection trials for the Test team? Surely the degree of competitiveness, or rivalry and – let's face it – hate could not compare with that of a full-blooded Ashes Test.

In fact, State of Origin games have surpassed Tests in the eyes of many of rugby league's faithful Down Under. The three-pronged annual 'war' is the

159

most-watched event on television in New South Wales and Queensland, while blockbuster movies, historic newscasts and Olympic opening ceremonies just don't stand a chance in competition. Born in 1981, the series can now justifiably rank alongside the surf lifesaver, lager and vegemite as a true blue – or maroon – Australian cultural icon.

But after the 1986 series, there were earnest calls from New South Wales critics for the concept to be scaled down. The Blues, in a Kangaroo tour year, had scored the first-ever 3–0 series whitewash, and prophets of doom predicted a return to the bad old days pre-Origin, when Queensland won only one game throughout the 1970s.

So Wayne Pearce's Blues entered Origin I, 1987, at Lang Park with very little to gain and much to lose. There was talk of a dynasty about.

There is nothing, in inter-state football, like beating Queensland at Lang Park. Throughout your time in Brisbane you are constantly reminded of how much everyone in the street, in the hotel, everywhere, wants you to lose.

We'd won 3–0 the year before and we were confident we could win another series. I can't recall too much from immediately before the game – the nerves stop you from thinking straight.

State of Origin football is probably the best there is because you have the elite players playing to the maximum of their potential. That happens very rarely. It is the best possible players performing at their top level.

It is that much quicker than a club match, and there is just tremendous interest. You hear about the game everywhere; you go into it with the weight of the world on your shoulders. Even people barely interested in sport want their state to win the Origin series.

It was on this particular June night in 1987 that 'super-coach'-turned-television commentator Jack Gibson dropped one of his most memorable droll lines. Surveying a lubricated Lang Park crowd – several members of which had already been arrested by kickoff time – he remarked, 'They'd boo Santa Claus, this mob'.

The pride of Queensland had been deeply dented the year before, so closely is the state's self-image tied to the fortunes of its football team. It was the year before the Brisbane Broncos arrived on the scene, and the Maroons had only three chances every year to lift Queensland on the national stage.

For sheer excitement, tension and exhilaration there was nothing in my career to beat that first match in 1987. The teams were full of absolutely great players. We had Kenny, Sterling, Pearce, and Queensland – of course – had Lewis, Miles, Langer, Dowling and the rest. And my try, just before half time, was probably the most important of my career.

* * *

Never a dirty player, or one to employ illegal tactics, O'Connor had a score to settle on this steamy Brisbane night. Wally Lewis, the fabled 'king' of Origin football and of Lang Park, had recently released the first of three autobiographies in which former Australian coach Terry Fearnley was quoted as being critical of O'Connor.

'Can't play . . . no heart . . . lucky he can kick goals or he wouldn't be here,' were among Fearnley's alleged comments about O'Connor. Lewis's book was discussed by the Australian Rugby League Board, and there was speculation he would be stripped of the national captaincy over it. ARL chairman Ken Arthurson took the somewhat extreme pre-match measure of warning both camps against violence.

And so it was that one of the first incidents of Origin I, 1987, was a scuffle between O'Connor and Lewis; after O'Connor had been tackled by 'The Emperor', Lewis instigated the incident with a niggle, but Sydney referee Mick Stone awarded the Maroons the penalty, and stand-in goalkicker Peter Jackson made it 2–0.

For the next 30 minutes, Queensland launched incessant raids at the New South Wales line, without reward. A disallowed Tony Currie try was the closest they got to a score.

Then, just as the match entered its second half hour, O'Connor scored the try which will live with him forever.

It was completely against the run of play. We had absorbed enormous pressure. I remember Noel Cleal took the ball on the left side and went on a diagonal run, and he lobbed it blind above my head and I hauled it in. I had no one in front of me, but the cover was coming across. I crosskicked and beat Allan Langer to the line over about 40 metres.

It's one of the best tries I ever scored. It encompassed every skill I had at my disposal: acceleration, a swerve, chip, chase and re-gather. And it was one of the most important tries I've ever scored because we were under a lot of pressure and it looked like Queensland might score. In the final scheme of things, it was vital to the result.

O'Connor converted his own try from the sideline. Man of the match, New South Wales prop Les Davidson, crashed over four minutes later before stand off Lewis sent his front rower, Greg Dowling, across on the fifth tackle to lift Queensland back into the game just before the break.

But the graceful O'Connor again provided the difference shortly after half-time. Maestro stand off Brett Kenny drew defenders Paul Vautin and Dale Shearer, holding up a pass magically for O'Connor, who scored in the corner.

Again, he added the extras from the touchline.

At 16–6, the game so far represented little more than a very good New

South Wales performance. It was quickly elevated, however, into one of the great Origin struggles. Queensland pegged back the formidable margin, first through full back Dale Shearer and then through winger Currie, who scampered over out wide with four minutes remaining.

Jackson had relinquished the sharp-shooting duties, after missing two goal attempts, to full back Gary Belcher. Belcher converted the Shearer try but could not capitalise on Currie's effort. With three minutes remaining, it was New South Wales 16, Queensland 16.

Sensing a vengeful victory, the crowd became increasingly anxious. The din blotted out any on-field calls in the epic final minutes. A Peter Sterling drop goal attempt missed narrowly with two minutes to go.

Then, a clearing kick by Currie slewed awkwardly off the corner of his boot, and the Blues launched one final attacking raid. Sterling, Kenny and winger Andrew Ettingshausen combined for 'ET's' Cronulla team-mate, Mark McGaw, to steam down the sideline with everyone in the arena on their feet.

McGaw passed inside, but a despairing Currie knocked the ball to the ground. Quick-thinking McGaw toed the grounded ball into the in-goal, ignoring Jackson tugging at the back of his jersey. Several players dived at it, it lolled over the dead ball line and a few seconds waiting for referee Stone's decision seemed like an eternity.

He aimed his outstretched arm at the spot, blew his whistle and awarded McGaw a try. Stone immediately copped emotive abuse from 33,424 Queenslanders – the 33,411 in the stands and 13 on the pitch. Stone responded by calling Jackson and Lewis over and telling them that even if it wasn't a fair try, he would have awarded it.

Jackson would have conceded a penalty try by holding McGaw back.

I think I had one hand to the ball, but I knew that even if I didn't, Mark did. We waited for his decision and, when he gave it, we were just ecstatic. To come back and win like that was incredible.

It was an amazing game. There was so much drama, and I've chosen this one because of the part I played and the fact it was at the peak of my career.

After four successive losses under coach Wayne Bennett, who the following year would coach Brisbane into the Winfield Cup, the Maroons went on to seal the series with a 12–6 win in Sydney and 10–8 back at Lang Park.

But for Michael O'Connor even those two defeats couldn't detract from the memory of that first encounter.

The match had everything; it was magnificent. End-to-end tries, tension, excitement . . .
I was still 'up' about it for days after.

* * *

NEW SOUTH WALES Jack; O'Connor, McGaw, Johnston, Ettingshausen; Kenny, Sterling; Davidson, Simmons, Jarvis, Folkes, Cleal, Pearce. *Subs*: Boyle, Hasler.

QUEENSLAND Belcher; Currie, Jackson, Miles, Shearer; Lewis, Langer; Dowling, Conescu, Bella, Gillmeister, Vautin, French. *Subs*: Scott, Smith.

Scorers New South Wales *Tries* O'Connor (2), Davidson, McGaw. *Goals* O'Connor (2).

Queensland *Tries* Shearer, Currie, Dowling. *Goals* Jackson, Belcher.

Referee Mick Stone (New South Wales).

Martin Offiah

Wigan 74 Leeds 6
Premiership Trophy Semi-Final, Central Park, Wigan
10 May 1992

Born 29 December 1965. Tryscoring freaks like Albert Rosenfeld, Brian Bevan and Tom Van Vollenhoven have graced rugby league at infrequent intervals over its 99-year history. Martin 'Chariots' Offiah, the former Rosslyn Park and Barbarians rugby union wing flyer and currently, at £440,000, the highest-priced player in the professional code, is such a one. Since his unheralded arrival in league in July 1987 for the small fee of £20,000, former Widnes coach Doug Laughton's protégé has, first at Naughton Park and, since his world record transfer to Wigan in January 1992, then at Central Park, commanded the headlines and proved to be world rugby's most lethal tryscorer. In his first four seasons as a professional with Widnes, he topped the league's tryscoring charts, amassing 198 tries, and raced to a fastest-ever 100 tries in just 17 months. At Wigan, where a rigid weight-training programme added a 14½ stones bulk to his gazelle-like speed, he has continued to excite the Central Park faithful with his electrifying dashes down the touchline and added his name to the club's honours board with his record ten-try feat against Leeds. Such exploits in a cherry and white and Great Britain jersey have earned 'Chariots' fame beyond the normal confines of the sport and, in St. George or Eastern Suburbs colours during profitable summers, brought him the respect of the often highly critical Australian public.

At 4.18 p.m. on Sunday, 10 May 1992, panic set in among the normally relaxed contingent of scribes and radio commentators crowded in the press seats in the front rows of the main grandstand at Central Park. There was a decided shuffling of papers and a reaching for record books among the journalists sitting on one end of the benches, while radio commentators, like myself, glanced around nervously and frantically for guidance from their colleagues, aware that something special was happening but unable to break off commentary to find out what.

'Tich' West was a name that suddenly sprang to everyone's lips as being the holder of the record number of tries with 11 in a match. But when did he achieve the feat? What was his Christian name? Further frantic searches were undertaken to confirm rugby league's record holder as George West and, for the benefit of we radio men, now in full throat and anticipating a historic occasion, a slip of paper was pushed under our noses by a friendly journalist. It read, 'George West, scorer of 11 tries in a match for Hull Kingston Rovers v. Brookland Rovers in 1905.' The search was over and, in that calm, authoritative voice that we radio commentators often adopt to impress the listener with our knowledge, it was announced that Martin Offiah, scorer of a staggering ten tries in just 68 minutes, was just one short of equalling rugby league's record number of tries scored by an individual in a match. Almost as an afterthought, the piece of history in the making was added to the name of George West. Sadly for the world's most lethal tryscorer, Martin Offiah had to be content with ten tries, still over half the number of tries yours truly managed in ten seasons of rugby league. But the 26-year-old wing flyer's amazing performance did rewrite the record books for both the Wigan and Leeds clubs and did give those fans present the satisfaction in future years of boasting, 'I was there'.

According to Offiah, he sensed something special about to happen as he arrived at the ground; he felt in tip-top form and capable of punishing Leeds with at least a hat trick of tries.

I knew something special was about to happen. I felt so sharp before and during the match. I just felt electric. In our warm-up before the match I felt so good that I said to our conditioner that I thought I was capable of scoring plenty of tries, perhaps a hat trick. He laughed but, after the game, I reminded him of what I said. Despite that, I would have bet any money against me scoring ten tries against Leeds in a Premiership semi-final play-off.

Wigan's £440,000 investment had been in sparkling form since his much-heralded arrival at Central Park on 3 January 1992, scoring 18 tries in just 14 matches and, only the week before Leeds' humiliation, had just missed grabbing a first-ever hat trick of tries in a Challenge Cup final at Wembley by the intervention of a touch judge. He knew that, in Wigan colours, one day he would be given the opportunity to rewrite the club's and possibly rugby league's record books.

I'd always thought, since joining rugby league, that one day I would score a silly amount of tries. Many a time I've scored a hat trick or five tries, but in the modern game it is very difficult to score because of the speed of the opposition's defence, and usually I'm a marked man. But I knew when I joined Wigan that there would be plenty of scoring opportunities for me. Anything is possible with Wigan. They're one of the best teams in the world.

* * *

Legendary Wigan wings Billy Boston, Johnny Ring and Green Vigo, all of whom had scored seven tries in a match, were erased from the record books, and Leeds' previous worst defeat, a 71–0 thrashing by Wakefield Trinity back in 1946, gave way to Wigan's 74-point tally. But few spectators could have anticipated the events to come, as Leeds, despite the absence of former Wigan skipper Ellery Hanley out injured, threatened to test the champions' reserves of energy after a particularly demanding Challenge Cup final against Castleford just eight days previously. Wigan, however, produced one of their most flawless performances, and Offiah proved just how unstoppable he could be, first against Leeds youngster Leigh Deakin and, for the final 50 minutes, against substitute and former England rugby union back John Bentley.

Within half an hour, Leeds youngster Deakin must have cursed his luck at being selected to face the former Rosslyn Park union player, for Offiah had already celebrated his hat trick, centre Dean Bell had notched two tries, ex-All Black Frano Botica had slotted three goals between the Leeds posts and the home side led by 26–0. Hardly an encouraging start! Offiah displayed his presence of mind and the hunger for tries that all great wings have when, for his first touchdown in the seventh minute, he raced on to the end of a spectacular five-man handling movement to score, and for his third, in the 28th minute, he cleverly supported the master opportunist himself, Shaun Edwards. It was his second try which revealed all the grace and poise we have come to expect of this beautifully balanced athlete. Receiving the ball 60 yards from the Leeds tryline, an electrifying burst of speed swept Offiah clear of the last traces of a Leeds cover defence, enabling him to treat the Wigan fans to the sight of a unique athlete in full flight. The try was a formality for a wing with such superior speed.

Mercifully for Leigh Deakin, making only his fourth appearance for the Yorkshiremen that season, Leeds boss Doug Laughton relieved him of any more pain by substituting him on the half hour with the more powerful and experienced John Bentley. Unfortunately for Bentley, too, there was plenty more suffering to come. Two more tries to Offiah, before half time, courtesy of final passes from Bell and hooker Martin Dermott, plus his own clever support play, and it was obvious that records were there to be broken.

> I didn't know until half time that I was within two tries of the Wigan club record, but someone told me what the record number of tries was so it was always in the back of my mind during the second half. I felt that I could break it if I went looking for tries.

During his first seasons as a professional with Widnes, Offiah, content to be learning the intricacies of the new game, spent most of his time racing up and down the touchlines, eager to finish off any half break by Widnes centres Andy Currier or Darren Wright and always capable of concluding a Jonathan

Davies sidestepping run with a rare turn of speed to the corner. As his
confidence developed and his appreciation of the game matured, so Martin
turned inside for the occasional midfield dash. At Wigan, under Aussie coach
John Monie, he was to be seen more infield, often taking a ball at first receiver
or attempting to break away from the acting half back position, and constantly
linking up on the other wing with David Myers or Jason Robinson. To some
of us he has, of late, appeared to forsake the touchline too much and appeared
to put too much energy into often quite fruitless midfield dashes. But always,
whether at Widnes or at Wigan, his hunger for tries has been unmatched,
with the result that, like Shakespeare's Autolycus in *The Winter's Tale*, he
has become the greatest 'snapper up of unconsidered trifles'. That
characteristic was to haunt Leeds in the final 40 minutes.

As the teams returned to the field after the half-time interval, the roar that
greeted their arrival indicated the expectancy in the air that something special
was about to happen. I cast my mind back to previous playing and spectating
days to remember St. Helens' Tom Van Vollenhoven's and Wigan's own
Billy Boston's six- and seven-tryscoring feats, but never did I expect a figure
of ten tries to be recorded in a match in modern rugby, especially from a
winger. Some months later, Wigan's master of support play, Shaun Edwards,
proved me doubly wrong when he too emulated Offiah's ten-try feat against
lowly Swinton, an achievement perhaps more credible in view of the huge
disparity in ability between the two sides. But ten tries against Leeds in the
tense end-of-season Premiership play-offs bordered on the ridiculous, and
throughout the final 40 minutes I occasionally wondered if the listeners to my
radio commentary actually believed what I was telling them. They certainly
realised very quickly the significance of the afternoon as my voice rose a
notch or two higher and often bordered on the hysterical whenever Wigan's
wing flyer crossed the visitors' tryline.

All of his tries had to be scored. Martin roamed around the pitch looking
for the vital break, he called urgently for the ball to be switched to his wing
and he chased every kick ahead as if his life depended on it. There was no
contrived artificiality about his feat. As skipper Dean Bell indicates, the players
were well aware of the record-breaking possibilities, but no one sacrificed a
try for Offiah, least of all the skipper himself, who grabbed a couple of
touchdowns. As Bell said:

> All the tries needed scoring, and he was running so fast on the day that he
> was going to score whatever anyone did. He popped up all over the place.
> The tries just happened because he anticipated the chances. After about
> seven tries, everyone was looking for the magical ten mark, but no one
> consciously took the ball towards him for a score. You can't do that against
> Leeds. The match was memorable for me because I got a couple of tries. I
> rarely score so many tries, but no one remembers now.

* * *

Offiah's next five tries, much to the delight of a crowd now roused to a passion and an expectancy rarely seen even at Central Park, came very quickly inside 28 minutes. Tries number six and seven were created by the guile of international half back Shaun Edwards within the space of one minute. The first, in the 56th minute, came as a result of Edwards' perfectly flighted 20-yard pass which gave his wing sufficient room to round the cover, and his second, and club record-equalling seventh, illustrated Offiah's roving commission in midfield as he once again was rewarded for his support work of one of Edwards' defence-splitting breaks. The ecstatic supporters cried for more and, with Wigan's midfield quartet of Edwards, Botica, Bell and Gene Miles looking to provide him with tryscoring chances, he duly obliged with another three tries inside ten minutes. Though many tries in his career have been more spectacular, few have given Offiah more satisfaction than that which he scored in partnership with his centre partner of the 1991–92 season, former Aussie Test centre Gene Miles, to whom he admits he owed so much.

The try that really pleased me was the one late on in the game when I moved to acting half back and did a run-around movement with Gene Miles. I went in under the sticks without anyone touching either of us. Gene was a great centre for a winger to have inside him. His basketball background allowed him to get passes to me from the most impossible positions and out of the most unusual situations. He could be held in a tackle, but he was so big and strong he could still get the ball out to me. He was a dream to play with.

For all Wigan's promptings and Martin Offiah's efforts, the elusive 11th try was not to be, David Myers and Martin Dermott were Wigan's other tryscorers and Frano Botica finished with a nine-goal haul. And, in the final nail-biting 12 minutes Leeds did retrieve a little honour before the splendid 18,261 crowd with a last-minute try and conversion from hard-working second row Paul Dixon and hooker Colin Maskill. Amid the after-match congratulations in the dressing room Wigan skipper Dean Bell, a true professional hardened by many seasons of play both in Britain and Down Under, could still not quite believe what he had seen. He could offer no logical explanation for Leeds' complete collapse and his team-mate's ability to take advantage of it. 'I just shook my head at the final whistle. I thought nobody should ever score ten tries in a First Division match, especially against a side like Leeds. I was mystified how anyone could score ten tries. It really was a phenomenal feat.'

A distressed Leeds camp also could offer no explanations for their lacklustre performance and Offiah's punishment of them, but skipper Garry Schofield, forced to play at loose forward in the absence of the injured Hanley, was lavish in his praise of his Great Britain team colleague. 'It was a nightmare for us; nothing went right. I'm glad Martin is on my side when I'm playing for Great Britain. His speed is simply amazing. He has the ability to poach a try out of nothing. A nightmare.'

To Schofield's tormentor, however, the match proved quite the opposite, a pleasant dream.

Insisted Martin:

> I know it sounds a bit clichéd, but the whole afternoon was like a wonderful dream. In the dressing room after the match it felt as though it had never happened. I was pretty high for a long time after the match and the adrenalin was pumping for a few hours after the whistle.

So was I when I scored two tries in a match at Central Park!

WIGAN Hampson; Lydon, Bell, Miles, Offiah; Botica, Edwards; Cowie, Dermott, Platt, Betts, McGinty, Clarke. *Subs*: Myers, Panapa.

LEEDS Ford; Deakin, Edwards, Gibson, Fawcett; Innes, Goulding; Molloy, Maskill, Wane, Divorty, Dixon, Schofield. *Subs*: Bentley, Arundel.

Scorers Wigan   *Tries* Offiah (10), Bell (2), Dermott, Myers. *Goals* Botica (9).
           Leeds   *Tries* Dixon. *Goals* Maskill.

Referee Colin Morris (Huddersfield).

Wayne Pearce

Australia 40 Great Britain 4
First Test, Boothferry Park, Hull
30 October 1982

Born 29 March 1960. Wayne Pearce, or 'Junior' as he was known to the Balmain fans, burst on to the international stage with one defence-shattering tryscoring run in the televised first Ashes Test at Hull Football Club in 1982. His prowess and his threat to British defences over the next decade were appreciated by millions watching BBC television's *Grandstand* programme, while viewers back home in Sydney could announce the arrival of one of the 'greats' of modern rugby league. Despite contracting hepatitis as an 18-year-old and suffering a torn retina of his left eye three years later, Wayne Pearce served the Balmain club with pride and distinction for ten seasons between 1980 and 1990, during which time he represented his country in 18 Tests and in a World Cup final against New Zealand in Auckland in 1988.

Though never gaining a Winfield Cup winner's medal, twice finishing as losing captain to Canterbury Bankstown and Canberra Raiders in 1988 and 1989, he did have the satisfaction of receiving the Rothmans Medal in 1985 as Australia's player of the season. Dedicated to fitness, the 15-stone Kangaroo back row forward epitomised the outlook now adopted by the modern, high-profile league players and, especially in Australia, became the perfect marketing vehicle for the image of the sport. It is a tribute to his approach and his dedication to the sport that, in 1994, he was rewarded with the role of coach of his beloved Balmain club.

As the 1982 Australian championship season drew to a close, 22-year-old Balmain loose forward Wayne Pearce was planning his very first trip overseas. Pearce, a hard-running and superfit rugby player, had represented Sydney in April, had attracted rave reviews all year from critics and had every reason to be well pleased with himself.

Pearce, who was later to become synonymous Down Under with the phrase 'local hero', was a fully paid-up participant for the Tigers' end-of-season trip to Hawaii.

But he was in for a surprise.

Pearce's selection in coach Frank Stanton's 28-man Kangaroo touring squad was but a hint of what was to come over the next three months for this champion forward, on probably the most significant international tour in rugby league's history.

> It was the first time I had ever been out of the country! I had to get a passport organised really quickly. Because [Ray] Price was the established lock and I hadn't even played for New South Wales, I really didn't think I had much of a chance.
>
> I'd only been in the first grade for a year or so . . . I had to find someone to buy the ticket to Hawaii off me at the last minute.

While Stanton no doubt had higher regard for Pearce's Test potential than 'Junior' himself had, he was not there for the opening match on British soil against Hull Kingston Rovers. The game was expected to be tough, Pearce was young, and the judgement proved shrewd. Rod Reddy and Les Boyd were sent off after a nasty brawl at Craven Park.

But against Wigan, Barrow – scoring a try – and Leeds he left British fans marvelling at the depth of Australian rugby league; shaking their heads that they had never even heard of this relentless number 13.

While his on-field performances in the lead-up to the first Test exuded nothing but confidence, Pearce remained starry-eyed at the day-to-day routine on tour with a group of superstars.

> I was the youngest by about six years in the Test pack! They were all very good, they all knew that I was the only one who hadn't played any significant representative football and the guys were great.
>
> The longer you're on tour, the better you get to know one another. The first Test, the feeling was good. When you get towards the back end of a tour, after three months, you start to get on each others' nerves. Everyone starts getting more abrasive, and that comes from living out of each others' pockets.
>
> You're around the same people when you're training, playing, going out, playing cards during the day. It does get pretty hard. But I thoroughly enjoyed it, and for that first Test we had been away for a couple of weeks, we were just getting to know each other and everything was new.

Great Britain's call-up of 33-year-old scrum half Steve Nash from the Second Division was typical of the Lions policy. In the forwards, Les Gorley, Steve Norton, Trevor Skerrett, Jeff Grayshon and David Ward were all well past their prime, although the selection of 19-year-old Hull second rower Lee Crooks was incongruously progressive. While most thought the tourists would win, Pearce says the threat of spitefulness made the Australian room tense beforehand.

* * *

I can still remember the build-up to the game in the dressing room. There was a lot of tension and there was this enormous rush of adrenalin and pride running through me when I was standing to attention out on the field while they played the national anthem, knowing I was about to play a Test for Australia.

I'll never forget that. I made a few breaks during the game so there was plenty to remember. Even though it was 12 years ago, I've got a pretty clear memory of it.

Written off by their own supporters, the British were determined from the outset to show the young, untried Australians they could do what six clubs and Wales previously hadn't.

There was a lot of sledging. That was obviously part of their plan to put us off our game, but they didn't come in with the heavy stuff like we thought they might have.

Pearce says the low incidence of physical violence – although there was plenty of the verbal variety – was an unexpected bonus for the Australians.

We'd had a couple of tough, physical lead-up games. We won comfortably, but they were hard, physically. We were expecting pretty stiff competition. They had picked an experienced, 'old' forward pack and we were expecting them to come out and try to unsettle us and put us off our game.

But they didn't, and they paid the price.

The first Test was still mathematically a contest at 10–4 by half time, but the ease with which Mal Meninga and Les Boyd had scored did not augur well for Great Britain.

Winger Eric Grothe, also an unknown quantity in Great Britain before the tour, scored off a Pearce pass soon after the resumption and, while the Lions complained he had been guilty of a double movement, the try signalled the start of Australia's blitz.

That was really typical of the way it was throughout the series. The margins were pretty close until half time, and then our superior fitness and preparation allowed us to run away with it in the second half.

From that point on I knew we were going to win by a fair margin. They were starting to slow down, they weren't moving up in defence. They were visibly tiring.

Ray Price, Kerry Boustead and Brett Kenny quickly banished any doubt over Grothe's score to the realms of insignificance with tries of their own.

172

Kenny scored after Pearce had burst through the attempted joint tackle by Nash and Norton to find himself in the clear – a situation to which he would become accustomed as the tour wore on.

Then the Balmain rookie got a share of the spoils himself. Australian full back Greg Brentnall had fielded a Nash kick in the tourists' in-goal and ran it back into the field of play. From there, Boustead advanced the ball further and, on the fourth tackle, skipper Max Krilich unloaded to prop Craig Young, who in turn served Pearce with one of his trademark deft passes. Says the loose forward:

> I can recall a break being made by Craig Young, who got the ball off Max Krilich. I was in position after Craig broke away to come up in support, and he gave me the pass and I ran about 30 metres to score.

While British rugby league was at its lowest ebb following the 40–4 embarrassment at Boothferry Park, it did eventually prove to be the beginning of the way back. Australia was able to win the second encounter by just 27–6 and the third 32–8. As a direct result of the shock waves sent through every level of the game in Britain by that first Test, the Lions have battled back to be competing on equal terms with the old adversary again.

Pearce, now a health and fitness author, says Britain's problems were deep seated and, despite opinion at the time, not restricted simply to fitness.

> It was preparation, which goes beyond fitness and takes in a lot of other factors like methods of training, their ages, everything. Our whole preparation was better, and the Pommies paid the ultimate price by being flogged in the series.
>
> They've bridged the gap somewhat, but I believe Australia had a six- or seven-year start on them. In Australia they started to get more professional in the mid-1970s, whereas in Britain they more or less stayed at the same level.

But it was also the beginning of a new era for Australia. Most of Pearce's pack-mates would soon bow out, but the backline would take its country through the 1980s triumphantly.

> There were a lot of young guys in the team that day. There was Brett Kenny, Peter Sterling, myself, Mal Meninga. Eric Grothe was another one who had just hit the international scene. It was really the birth of a new era for Australian rugby league, and full credit must go to Frank Stanton for giving all those guys their opportunities.

But 'Junior' Pearce, who blitzed the old enemy's defences with his powerful

173

unstoppable runs in midfield, concedes that Britain has come a long way since that October day in Hull, and says there is little remaining today from Britain's horrible slump.

I think the number of Australians who've played in Britain and an improvement in the coaching have helped them do that, and hopefully the next series will be even more competitive than the last couple, which have been tight.

AUSTRALIA Brentnall; Boustead, Meninga, Rogers, Grothe; Kenny, Sterling; Young, Krilich, Boyd, Pearce, Reddy, Price. *Subs*: Ella, Muggleton.

GREAT BRITAIN Fairbairn; Drummond, Hughes, Dyl, Evans; Woods, Nash; Grayshon, Ward, Skerrett, Gorley, Crooks, Norton. *Subs*: Heron, Kelly.

Scorers Australia   *Tries* Meninga, Boyd, Grothe, Price, Boustead, Kenny, Pearce, Reddy. *Goals* Meninga (8).
Great Britain   *Goals* Crooks (2).

Referee Julien Rascagneres (France).

Andy Platt

Halifax 19 St. Helens 18
Challenge Cup Final, Wembley
2 May 1987

Born 9 October 1964. West Park Grammar School in St. Helens, before its
sad closure in the reckless advance of comprehensive education, proved a
prolific nursery for rugby league players. Saints former stars Keith Northey
and Peter Harvey, and current Great Britain centre Paul Loughlin all had
occasion to be grateful for their rugby education on the school's much-used
playing fields. Ex-England rugby union internationals and league converts in
the 1950s and 1960s, Warrington's Martin Regan and Barrow's Tom Brophy,
once graced the school's union playing first XV. Wigan and Great Britain
prop Andy Platt, who hails from the same stable, played both codes at school
but enhanced his desires for a career in league by linking up with leading
amateur rugby league club Wigan St. Patricks at weekends. His interest
blossomed and, having made over 189 appearances for St. Helens, during
which time he collected 68 tries, the tough 5 feet 11 inches and 16-stone front
rower was transferred to Wigan in September 1988 for a then club record
£130,000 fee. He has been the cornerstone in the pack for Wigan's
championship and Challenge Cup success in recent seasons.

Acknowledged today as one of the greatest prop forwards in world rugby,
Andy Platt, who began his international career against France in 1985 and
who has twice toured Down Under with the British Lions in 1988 and 1992,
achieved the distinction of becoming only the sixth forward ever to captain
Great Britain when he led his country to success against France at Headingley
in April 1993.

Wigan's and Great Britain's toughest forward Andy Platt has a drawer full
of championship medals and more Challenge Cup final winner's mementoes
than most. If any player has stored up a collection of memories to cushion
retirement, then Wigan's hefty prop has enough to last him to a ripe old age.
Yet, despite unrivalled success with Great Britain and the all-conquering
Wigan side in the past six seasons, his fondest memories centre on a match in
which he freely admits he and his team-mates played the wrong tactics and,
rather than being beaten by the opposition, they beat themselves. St. Helens
v. Halifax at Wembley in 1987 was the occasion of Andy Platt's first visit to

the Challenge Cup final. It was a visit which he cherishes more than any other since.

> Everyone wants to play at Wembley and I was no exception. You never forget your first visit; it sticks in your mind forever. The whole week before and the match itself was the most satisfying time of my career. We had to wait about six weeks after the semi-final win over Leigh, but it was a wonderful time with the pressure off us. I got carried away with the atmosphere before the match and especially on the day itself.

Perhaps Andy Platt and the rest of the Saints team really did get carried away with the atmosphere surrounding the Cup final for, though their younger and faster side was expected to romp away with the Challenge Cup, a stubborn and tactically superior Halifax side surprised them. Tactically, according to Platt, St. Helens were naive in the extreme.

> We seemed to be fated to lose the match. Everyone kept dropping balls and we had tries disallowed, but really we played the wrong game. Our coach Alex Murphy kept telling us in training that they had a strong pack and told us to throw the ball around. We did, but we threw the ball around at the wrong time near our own line and we kept dropping it. We made a lot of mistakes. Perhaps we should have played them more in the pack than we did.

Prior to kickoff few in St. Helens gave Halifax a real chance of victory, such was the pace and flair in the Saints side. Centres Paul Loughlin and Kiwi international Mark Elia as well as exciting scrum half Neil Holding would surely pose huge threats to the Yorkshiremen's slower-moving defence, while there were few better attacking forwards than Saints' Roy Haggerty and skipper Chris Arkwright. And yet Halifax's approach to the final was meticulous and professional, an approach that had begun three years previously when Yorkshire businessman David Brook assumed the chairmanship at Thrum Hall and embarked on an exciting and profitable adventure. The entrepreneurial Brook rocked British rugby league when he introduced several Australian stars into the Halifax side and, when success came the club's way, tempted former Aussie half-back star Chris Anderson to join him as coach. The wily Anderson, 15 seasons in the harsh, competitive Winfield Cup Down Under with Canterbury Bankstown, and a Wembley finalist during his short off-season stint with Widnes in 1975, had all the credentials to plot a Wembley win.

> Chris Anderson had worked everything out before the final and had obviously watched our style of play. He had noticed how we threw the ball

all over the field and played off-the-cuff rugby. His side pressurised us into making mistakes and then they capitalised on them. They kicked better than we did and they kept us close to our line in our 20-metre area. We lost the ball regularly and they picked it up near our line. They retained possession and played a safer brand of rugby. Though we had the better players on paper, they played a much better game.

Halifax may have had the slower team, but Anderson's tactics made good use of the vastly experienced former Australian Test full back, Graham Eadie, half back Garry Stephens and pack stars Mick Scott and John Pendlebury. Their player-coach contained St. Helens in their own half and put a stranglehold on their speedsters, capitalising on their mistakes to such an extent that Saints fans could hardly believe the sight of a scoreboard registering 12–2 at half time in Halifax's favour. A lone 19th minute Paul Loughlin penalty goal was all Saints could offer against tries from wing Wilf George and Irish-born hooker Seamus McCallion, plus two Colin Whitfield goals for Halifax. Far from being too old and too slow, Halifax's ageing stars, notably full back Eadie, were proving the heroes. Twice the Australian number one stopped dangerous Saints thrusts down the flanks, and the vastly experienced loose forward, John Pendlebury, used all his craft to cross the pitch and cover the occasional break. Saints were struggling to haul themselves into the game until speedy centre Elia hit Halifax with just one too many runs immediately after the interval. Andy Platt had the satisfaction of providing the Kiwi flyer with his tryscoring chance.

> We were a little desperate at half time when we were trailing by ten points. We knew we had a lot to do. I was lucky enough to be able to give Mark Elia a pass and an overlap on the wing, just outside our 20-metre line. He made a terrific run and had the pace to go round Eadie at full back. Paul Loughlin added the conversion and at 12–8 we were back in the match.

For the next 20 minutes, fortunes fluctuated and the coveted Challenge Cup looked first to be on its way to Thrum Hall and then to Knowsley Road until the alert Pendlebury struck the dramatic drop goal that was eventually to win the match. Eadie, casting off his advancing years, dashed over for a try and Whitfield converted. Halifax appeared to be coasting at 18–8 in their favour. Saints giant centre Loughlin, using every ounce of his 15 stones, crashed over for a try but failed to add the goal. Alex Murphy's men were edging nearer until Halifax number 13 Pendlebury swung his boot on the hour and placed the ball sweetly between the posts for the goal that was eventually to prove the difference. The seven-point lead meant St. Helens had to score twice. Saints coach Alex Murphy, a shrewd campaigner as a player and a coach at Wembley, gambled with his substitute Paul Round, and his switch paid off when the long-striding second row scored a try to bring Saints just one point adrift of the Yorkshiremen. The game had see-sawed either way and the fans had been treated to two contrasting styles of rugby, of which one style, the Australian way, was to dominate the game's immediate future.

Halifax played methodical rugby, retaining possession, playing for position and using up their full share of the six tackles available to them. They attacked down the middle and were obviously influenced by Chris Anderson's Australian style of coaching. We played 'catch-up' football and took chances, passing the ball all over the field whenever we were on it. We went sideways and were pressured into making mistakes. Some chances came off and some didn't.

From this time, styles were beginning to change, and Halifax realised that they had to make yardage before they threw the ball about. They had thought it out, and their coach Chris Anderson had realised that you just can't afford to give the other side the ball and win. With our style of play, sometimes we were brilliant but at other times we were awful. There was no in-between.

In that final, fatal 14 minutes for Andy Platt and St. Helens, it has always mystified me why St. Helens never attempted one drop goal to level the scores and force a replay at Old Trafford, Manchester. Saints coach Alex Murphy, no stranger to dropping goals himself at Wembley as a player, did shriek such instructions from the coach's bench in that thrilling, closing quarter, but all to no avail as his players took little heed and continued to spread the ball wide in the direction of wings Barry Ledger and Kevin McCormack. The tactics, though fruitless, did come within a whisper of producing a last-minute change of fortune.

Andy Platt, by now firing on all cylinders and hurling his powerful frame at the rapidly tiring Halifax defenders, was beginning to punch holes in the Yorkshiremen's defence. One such thrust down the left wing and he had wing flyer Mark Elia on his outside and with room to score at the corner. His final pass to the Kiwi was ruled forward by referee John Holdsworth. Groans of disbelief from the frustrated Saints fans greeted the decision, but worse was to come for those St. Helens spectators of a nervous disposition. The roar that accompanied Mark Elia's second dive over the tryline in the dying minutes could surely be heard back at Knowsley Road in St. Helens. Saints had snatched the cup from Halifax's grasp, or so their supporters thought until they saw the ball roll clear of Elia's grasp, bobble on the grass and roll into touch in goal. The speedy Kiwi crashed to the floor with Halifax's saviour John Pendlebury beneath him. Pendlebury's magnificent last-gasp effort, and his uncanny ability to knock the ball deliberately out of Elia's hands as he was within a foot of touching down for what would have been the

178

matchwinning try, proved the end for gallant Saints. Andy Platt's eagerly awaited day was to end in despair.

When Mark Elia dived over the tryline, there was only one way John Pendlebury could ever stop him and that was by diving under him and deliberately knocking the ball out of his hands. He did just that. It was a one in a million tackle, something that will probably never happen again. I don't think Alex Murphy has spoken to Mark since.

Both Andy and the Saints fans were upset at referee Holdsworth's ruling of a forward pass in Elia's first tryscoring effort, but the Leeds whistler was right on the spot and has no hesitation in insisting today that the ball strayed forward. He does, however, raise a fascinating talking-point in regards to the second try attempt. Says John Holdsworth: 'The pass from Andy to Mark Elia was definitely a forward pass, but the John Pendlebury tackle raised an interesting point. Under today's rules it would have resulted in a penalty try to Saints, as I would have had to rule ball stealing or raking out in the in-goal area and that warrants a penalty try. As it was, I didn't know until I watched the tackle on the video at home that John Pendlebury had deliberately knocked the ball out of his grasp. I thought Mark Elia had dropped the ball, and so I wrongly ruled a restart on the 20-metre line.'

A deserted Wembley, lifeless save for the occasional attendant picking up paper fluttering in the breeze on the terraces, is a lonely, cold place for players in defeat. No player in the Saints camp was more upset than Andy Platt as he reflected on his day, and yet it was to prove the turning point of his career.

I was really dejected. We had a civic reception, but it was like drinking flat beer. I tried to enjoy it, but I couldn't. I did enjoy Wembley, though. It gave me a taste of the big occasion, and I was determined to return and win. Ironically, I did, two years later, for Wigan against Saints. The game changed my outlook and the match was to prove a turning point in my career.

St. Helens' pack star was forced to wait another two years before, following his then club record £130,000 transfer to Wigan, success came frequently. For Halifax, and the man who had inspired their victory, Chris Anderson, success was immediate as the weary but elated Aussie lifted the Challenge Cup aloft for Halifax for the first time since skipper and loose forward Harry Beverley accepted the trophy from the Earl de la Warr 48 years previously.

HALIFAX Eadie; Wilson, Whitfield, Rix, George; Anderson, Stephens; Beevers, McCallion, Neller, Dixon, Scott, Pendlebury. *Subs*: Juliff, James.

* * *

ST. HELENS Veivers; Ledger, Loughlin, Elia, McCormack; Clark, Holding; Burke, Liptrot, Fieldhouse, Platt, Haggerty, Arkwright. *Subs*: Round, Forber.

Scorers Halifax   *Tries* George, McCallion, Eadie. *Goals* Whitfield (3).
            Drop Goals Pendlebury.
            St. Helens *Tries* Loughlin, Elia, Round. *Goals* Loughlin (3).

Referee   John Holdsworth (Kippax).

Daryl Powell

Sheffield Eagles 34 Oldham 20
Divisional Premiership Trophy Final, Old Trafford, Manchester
17 May 1992

Born 21 July 1965. When Daryl Powell became the only Second Division player to be included in the Great Britain tour party to visit Australia in 1992, it was a fitting reward for one of the game's best clubmen. Sheffield Eagles' first signing in their inaugural season in rugby league in 1984–85, the club captain has achieved his many international honours the hard way. Always giving loyal service on the field, where he holds the Eagles' individual tryscoring record in a match with five tries against the now-defunct Mansfield Marksman, he has consistently helped to raise the impact and image of the fledgling club in Sheffield by doing much good coaching work in the city's schools. But, despite the ups and downs and the frequent movement by Sheffield between the First and the Second Division over the past ten seasons, Daryl Powell has always striven to better himself while continuing to give unswerving service to the club. Playing spells with leading New Zealand club Glenora and top Sydney outfit Balmain have matured this former Redhill amateurs centre or loose forward and helped produce one of the best playmakers and distributors in the British game.

The introduction of a Second Division Premiership decider in 1987 at the end-of-season play-offs and the transfer of the venue to a permanent home at Old Trafford, Manchester, have proved a staggering success story for rugby league. Before crowds of 30,000 and 40,000, clubs like Hunslet, Swinton, Sheffield Eagles and even Third Division pacesetters Workington have enjoyed the full glare of the media spotlight, while many a player has come to the fore and achieved recognition by virtue of his performance there. Oldham's Chris Joynt and Hugh Waddell and Eagles' own Sonny Nickle have all progressed to Great Britain honours after outstanding performances at Old Trafford, and for others, like Sheffield club captain Daryl Powell, the Premiership final play-off has been the setting for confirming his undoubted international class.

The finals day at Old Trafford is a tremendous occasion for the Second or Third Division clubs and a wonderful day out for their fans. An appearance

181

there really is a huge boost for the club, not only in terms of cash rewards either. The effects on morale among the players can be good because many of them have never played, and probably never will again, in such an intense atmosphere and before such a big crowd. It can be a memorable day for them.

Unlike Daryl Powell, for the first half-dozen years of the double-header Premiership finals, I was unable to appreciate the skills and fierce competition among the players at the top of the Second and Third Divisions owing to my duties as the BBC television commentator for the big event, the First Division battle which followed later. Invariably, as I became embroiled in sound checks and vision checks, adjusted headsets, television monitors and microphones and tested talk-back facilities, the activities some way below me tended to pass by rather unnoticed. But always my attention was drawn to the pitch by the roars that frequently greeted or led up to the scoring of a try. Eagles' gifted centre Daryl Powell interrupted my concentration on numerous occasions as, in two finals, he has celebrated his arrival at Old Trafford with a hat trick of tries.

Three touchdowns in Sheffield Eagles' 43–18 defeat of Swinton in 1989 gave him considerable cause for delight, but a further display of his many attacking talents and a second hat trick of tries three years later gave the Eagles classy inside back cause for even greater celebration. Owing to a four-match suspension, Test centre Powell returned to the side for the trip to Old Trafford somewhat apprehensive as to his fitness and his ability to last the full 80 minutes in the intense temperatures which accompanied the finals day.

I had been out for over four weeks previous to the final thanks to a suspension, and I went into the final against Oldham right down on match fitness. The day was so hot, especially down on the pitch where the temperatures rise very high because of the design of the ground, that I was really worried and apprehensive as to whether I would last the pace in the final stages. But Old Trafford just seems to be a very lucky ground for me, and scoring my tries very early on really set me up for the afternoon. I struggled after half an hour in the heat but then I seemed to get a second wind and lasted right through the 80 minutes.

Oldham, who had finished third in the Second Division league table behind champions Sheffield, were contesting their third Premiership final in five years and were no strangers to the big-match atmosphere. With lively Kiwis Iva Ropati and Shane Tupaea lining up in their side, and with future Great Britain and St. Helens second row star Chris Joynt in the pack, Oldham were strongly expected to run Sheffield close for the title. So it proved in a thrilling encounter which both sides looked capable of winning at different stages in the match, but which was eventually settled by Powell's opening three-try blast and aided by Oldham prop Ian Sherratt's foul tackle on the Eagles hero. Within five minutes of the kickoff Daryl Powell was on his way to the Tom Bergin man of the match trophy, an award named in honour of the long-serving president of the Rugby League Writers' Association.

The Sheffield centre timed his run to perfection on to a ball beautifully laid out for him by stand off colleague Richard Price and, with the Oldham cover taken completely by surprise, raced through unopposed for his team's first try of the match. The closeness of the contest could be seen in the manner in which the opposition hit back almost immediately through their powerful 14-stone full back Duncan Platt, who showed a fine burst of speed to accompany his undoubted bulk in a 50-yard dash down the touchline before scoring wide out. But back roared the Eagles and Daryl Powell.

> That first try really came from David Mycoe's break in midfield when he had been stopped just short of the Oldham tryline. Richard Price held the ball up perfectly for me and then put me into the gap. I was able to burst through, stretch over and score. The second try came from a move which we had practised all season and which we had tried to work in many matches, but we never scored off it until this match.
>
> The idea was for the forwards to drive the ball into midfield with three or four tackles and then, using a couple of runners on the open side as decoys, the ball was to be switched back to Richard Price and me on the left. Again, Richard put me through with the perfect pass.

In the 15th minute the move worked exactly as Daryl describes, and with the accompanying two Mark Aston conversions Sheffield were off to a comfortable lead at 12–4. The try, however, once he had received the defence-splitting pass from half-back star Price, had proved no formality.

> When Richard gave me the ball I nearly dropped it. I wasn't looking fully at the ball as I received it, and it popped out of my grasp. The crowd thought that I had lost the ball and that there would be a knock on, but I just managed to reach out, snatch it back and get a firm grasp on it before scoring. It was a close call.

The battle, however, despite the early scores for Sheffield, was far from over, and yet, though gallant Oldham twice fought back to level the scores at 16–16, and, with only ten minutes remaining, at 20–20, the match was effectively settled between the 25th and the 28th minute of the explosive first half. Powell had already come in for some heavy tackling from an Oldham side, conscious that he could prove the vital difference between the evenly matched sides. The high tackle perpetrated by Oldham prop Ian Sherratt on Eagles' elusive centre was to bring about the dismissal of the fiery front row and the removal from the field of Powell himself. Oldham were left to struggle on for the next 55 minutes with only 12 men as the disconsolate Sherratt was made to pay for his sins. But, after a couple of minutes of touchline attention, the still-dazed Powell returned to the fray to deliver yet another killer blow to the Lancashiremen and grab his second consecutive hat trick of tries at Old Trafford.

> After being hit with the high tackle I was dazed and groggy, but there was no way I was staying off the field for long. After a couple of minutes I was OK to resume and, of course, we then had a tremendous advantage with Oldham being down to 12 men, especially on such a hot day.
> Mark Aston opened up Oldham's defences with a well-timed pass just as I was able to burst on to the ball. I managed to sidestep Oldham's full back Duncan Platt and go away from him. I had to run about 40 yards for the try and that's a long distance for me.

To their credit, Oldham refused to yield, playing an exciting brand of rugby despite the loss of Sherratt and with forwards Chris Joynt, Keith Newton and substitute Tim Street causing Eagles' defence plenty of problems. Their clever play created tries for Ged Byrne, wing Scott Ranson and Newton himself, but whenever they threatened to haul themselves back in the game that man Powell struck, as he did late on when he sent youngster David Mycoe racing in for the Eagles' fourth try. The heat, too, played its part as Sheffield's numerical advantage finally told in the closing ten minutes.

As Oldham's threat visibly wilted under the sun, the Sheffield side built on the solid foundations laid by their club skipper, and it was magnificent that their trump cards, two experienced substitutes in Keith Mumby and Tim Lumb, proved the tryscorers in the final hectic flourish. Lumb, a replacement for second row Dale Laughton in the 51st minute, touched down for try number five and, with just seconds remaining, the evergreen Keith Mumby, a player with Bradford Northern in the First Division Premiership final over 14 years previously, celebrated his arrival on the scene with a sixth try.

It was a breathless but overjoyed Daryl Powell who, conscious that the near £50,000 share of gate receipts and prize money would help him and manager Gary Hetherington to continue to cement rugby league in the city of Sheffield, went up to receive his second Premiership winner's medal.

> I was really out of breath at the end of the match. I was shattered. I was delighted to win the man of the match trophy because, before the game, I had fears that my fitness might let the team down. To win the trophy at Old Trafford is a real boost to everyone at a Second or Third Division

Always hungry for tries, Martin Offiah sets off in search of another four points. (*Richard Sellers/Sportsphoto*)

The complete forward. Australia's Wayne Pearce looks for support in midfield during the Ashes series of 1982 when he played his greatest-ever game. (*Colorsport*)

Saints' Andy Platt manages to get his pass away despite the speed of Halifax's cover defence in the close-fought 1987 Challenge Cup final. (*Varley Picture Agency*)

Sheffield Eagles skipper Daryl Powell considers his options in the Divisional Premiership Trophy final at Old Trafford in 1992. (*Varley Picture Agency*)

Victorious Ashes-winning captain Alan Prescott, his broken arm still in plaster, is congratulated after Great Britain's third Test win in 1958 at the Sydney Cricket Ground. (*Varley Picture Agency*)

The sheer speed of Wigan wing flyer Mark Preston takes him past Leeds' despairing full back, Phil Ford. (*Varley Picture Agency*)

A young Mal Reilly receives a hand of encouragement as he prepares to address the crowd at Castleford's Challenge Cup homecoming. (*Varley Picture Agency*)

St. Helens' Kiwi half-back star Tea Ropati in full cry, heading for the tryline. (*Varley Picture Agency*)

New Zealand wing Dane
O'Hara makes sure Great
Britain's record-breaking
centre ace, Garry
Schofield, doesn't add a
fifth try to the scoresheet.
(*Colorsport*)

Powerful Kiwi Test prop
Kurt Sorensen bears the
full force of Great Britain's
defence and still gets the
ball away. (*Varley Picture
Agency*)

Hull's mercurial Aussie half back Peter Sterling sparks a revival and begins to threaten Wigan's hold on the 1985 Challenge Cup. (*Colorsport*)

Mick Sullivan in action for Great Britain against New Zealand in 1961. (*Robert Gate Collection*)

A forceful run out of defence by Widnes full back Alan Tait helps the Chemics to victory in the vital championship decider against Wigan at Naughton Park in April 1989. (*Colorsport*)

Hunslet defenders fail to come to grips with St. Helens' flying Springbok, Tom Van Vollenhoven, as he races for the first of a hat trick of tries in the Championship final at Odsal in 1959. According to some, it was the greatest try ever scored this century.

club, especially to one like Sheffield where we are still introducing the game of league to many new people. I've played in many important Test matches, before even bigger crowds, but I'll always remember this particular match as being one over which I probably had the most influence.

Oldham's Australian coach, Peter Tunks, would no doubt agree with the Sheffield hero's final observation.

SHEFFIELD EAGLES Mycoe; Gamson, McAlister, Powell, Plange; Price, Aston; Broadbent, Cook, Waddell, Laughton, Hughes, Farrell. *Subs*: Lumb, Mumby.

OLDHAM Platt; Ranson, Nicklin, Ropati, Tyrer; Russell, Martyn; Sherratt, Pachniuk, Newton, Joynt, Tupaea, Byrne. *Subs*: Warburton, Street.

Scorers Sheffield Eagles *Tries* Powell (3), Mycoe, Lumb, Mumby. *Goals* Aston (5).

Oldham *Tries* Platt, Byrne, Newton, Ranson. *Goals* Martyn (2).

Referee Stuart Cummings (Widnes).

Alan Prescott

Australia 18 Great Britain 25
Second Test, Exhibition Ground, Brisbane
5 July 1958

Born 17 June 1927. From 1948 to 1960 there were few finer sights for the home fans at Knowsley Road than that of their 16-stone prop Alan Prescott displaying an exceptional burst of speed in a 50- or 60-yard run down the middle of the field. For, though modern rugby league has seen an increase in speed in all its players, few front row forwards today could match this Widnes-born pack star for pace. Originally a wing with the Widnes St. Maries amateur club and a loose forward with Halifax until his £2275 transfer move to St. Helens, Alan Prescott was persuaded to switch to prop forward by Saints coach Jim Sullivan soon after his arrival at Knowsley Road. Sullivan's vision and Prescott's gamble met with huge success. As captain of St. Helens he led the side to its first-ever Challenge Cup final success in 1956 over his old club Halifax and, in doing so, captured the Lance Todd Trophy for his outstanding man of the match performance. Five years later, as coach, he had the good fortune to see his charges triumph over Wigan at Wembley by 12–6. In the international field, the flame-haired number eight achieved even greater distinction becoming, in 1956, one of the few forwards to captain a Great Britain side and, two years later, leading the British Lions to a 2–1 Ashes Test success Down Under. It was during this series that Alan Prescott's name was to be immortalised for his heroic deeds in the second Test, appropriately named the Battle of Brisbane.

The introduction of the substitution rule in 1964, whereby two substitutes per team were allowed for injury up to half time, and then, five years later, allowed for any reason, injury or tactical, changed the very nature of rugby league. The sport quickly became a game of tactical permutations for the rival coaches, with each seeking to use their substitutes to the best effect at the right time in a match. Injuries could no longer hinder too seriously a side's performance, and the flow and pattern of a game could be changed by a single switch of a player. No longer, however, whether rightly or wrongly, do we see the stuff of which rugby legends are made, a player or a team overcoming crippling odds on their way to a famous victory.

It is highly unlikely that we will ever witness again the fighting spirit and the sheer bravery of Great Britain skipper Alan Prescott, who led 12 men to triumph over Australia in a Test at Brisbane despite having broken his right arm as early as the third minute of the match. Today, any Lions captain suffering from a broken arm would surely be whisked immediately to the nearest and best hospital before the final whistle had even sounded and would, no doubt within a week, be on his way home to Britain for further treatment if needed. In line with recent practice, a substitute, flown out from England, would probably be lining up in the Great Britain team before his captain boarded the plane home. Not so in 1958, when the mighty Prescott defied the pain and, dare I say, almost singlehandedly (!) inspired Great Britain to one of the greatest victories in the history of Test rugby.

Though the 1958 tourists numbered among themselves some of the greatest players ever to grace a Lions jersey in men like Brian Edgar, Dick Huddart, Vince Karalius, Alex Murphy, Mick Sullivan and Eric Ashton, they were knocked out of their stride by a convincing 25–8 first Test defeat in Sydney. If the tour was not to fall apart, urgent rethinking had to be given to the make-up of the team for the second Ashes battle in Brisbane and more attention given to its preparation. Once the vote to retain teenage sensation Alex Murphy, who had not had too happy a time against Australia's experienced Keith Holman in the first Test, had been taken and the mistakes in selection rectified, the team was ready to do battle. But not, insists Prescott, before the Aussie press had time to pour scorn on Great Britain manager Tom Mitchell's novel preparation plans.

We lost the first Test through bad selection and that had to be sorted out before we played the second Test. There was also a lobby to drop Alex Murphy, but both I and Tom Mitchell knew what he could do if he used his speed against Holman and we fought to keep him in the side. We knew we had to win this Test or we would be flying home as failures.

To lift everyone's spirits, we moved to Surfers Paradise to do our training and we even, for the first time ever on a tour, trained at Surfers on the beach. The Aussie press laughed at us because the holiday resort is well known for bikini-clad girls, gambling, night-clubs and every distraction you can think of for young, fit men. But the lads buckled down to the training and, though Tom Mitchell told everyone that should anyone step out of line he would be sent home, nobody did. It proved the ideal preparation and we were ready for anything.

However, even Alan Prescott and the 32,965 spectators packed into the Exhibition Ground, Brisbane, were not prepared for the happenings that were to pass into rugby league folklore on that eventful Saturday in July 1958. Within three minutes of the kickoff, skipper Prescott was to break his right arm in a tackle on Australian second row Rex Mossop, now a very successful television commentator, and, in the 17th minute, Wigan stand off David Bolton was forced to leave the field for good suffering from a broken collarbone. To add to the Lions' woes, both centre Jim Challinor (shoulder) and loose forward Vince Karalius (back) were suffering from injuries and were forced to visit hospital after the match. It was a difficult time, to say the least.

The match started disastrously for us. Dave Bolton was very quickly forced to leave the game with a broken collarbone and, as early as the third minute, I knew I had broken my right arm. I tackled Rex Mossop, and as I raced to get up after the tackle my arm just buckled under me. It was very painful, but I carried on for a while until I went off to get our coach, Jim Brough, to put tape around the arm and strap it up. It was very silly of me really because there could have been so much damage.

I knew it was broken because I had heard and felt the crack in the tackle, but I don't think Jim Brough realised it was broken. In my opinion, I just had to battle on, especially when David Bolton left and we were down to 12 men. If I had called it a day then, that would have been the end of us.

Team-mate Alex Murphy agreed with his courageous captain:

I realised very early on that he had broken his arm as I could see the pain he was suffering whenever I put the ball into a scrum. If he had gone off the field then, I think we would have collapsed, but they would have had to shoot him to get him off the pitch.

He was a very brave man. He acted like a real leader who led us from the front. He didn't shirk a tackle, never hid anywhere on the pitch and he even went to the acting half-back position and took the ball up to the Aussies at all times. His attitude inspired everybody, especially Vince Karalius, who was injured himself, and without his leadership we would have lost the Ashes.

Fortune did favour Britain, however, before Alan Prescott departed temporarily for running repairs to his arm. Brilliant half-back star Murphy, told by Prescott to use his speed more in this Test and run away from the Aussies, sparked the Lions into life and helped to lift any depression in the camp. In only the fourth minute of the match he revealed what a threat his acceleration and eye for a gap would be when he raced away and combined with stylish centre Eric Ashton to put Jim Challinor over for the opening try at the corner. The captain's spirits lifted.

Jim Challinor's try at the corner did more for us to win this match than anything. It came just at the right time and gave us all heart. And my

188

support for Alex to be kept in the side was more than justified, for, after this try, the Aussies just couldn't hold him, and he went on to devastate them with his breaks from the scrum and midfield.

With Great Britain, after the opening quarter, effectively reduced to 11 fit men and with St. Helens loose forward Vince Karalius, christened the 'Wild Bull of the Pampas' for his rampaging deeds, settled into the stand off position in place of the absent Bolton, few waving the Union Jack on the terraces contemplated victory, especially as the Australian side contained one of the toughest and most powerful packs of forwards in their history – Davies, Kearney, Marsh, Mossop, Provan and O'Shea. Further shocks for the Kangaroos, however, were in store.

Live-wire scrum half Murphy, now revelling in his midfield role, shot away from yet another scrum, leaving the slower Keith Holman grasping thin air and aware of his advancing years. The Lions number seven found prop Brian McTigue, who had broken quickly from the scrum. He then passed on to the strong-running Sullivan, who went over for one of his record 41 Test tries in a Great Britain jersey. Two goals from the reliable full back Eric Fraser and the Lions amazingly trooped off the field at half time leading 10–2. But, with even the most optimistic in the British camp aware that fatigue would set in and that Australia's numerical advantage could prove decisive, the five-minute rest period not only proved dramatic but vital to the outcome of the Test series.

Alan Prescott explains:

At half time the Australian doctor took a look at my arm and told me that I must come off. But I looked around the dressing room and I knew that the lads wanted me to stay on. They weren't aware that it was fully broken. Spirits were high despite our problems, and I knew the loss of another player could send those spirits low. I had to stay on; there was no way I was leaving the match. The Aussie doctor washed his hands of me, and our manager Tom Mitchell told me it was my decision. I thought to myself, 'I can be of nuisance value: the Aussies will have to run round me'.

The die was cast. Twelve-man Great Britain would return with their skipper carrying a broken arm and forced, in his own words, 'to tackle with my left shoulder, lead with my left side and pass with my left hand'. Though the mercurial Murphy, within four minutes of the resumption, paved the way for extending the Great Britain lead to 15–2 with yet another blistering burst of pace past the Kangaroos' cover, setting up a try for wing Ike Southward and a conversion from Fraser, Australia, as expected, roared back. Tries from Marsh, Carlson and Dimond, plus a second goal from Clifford, with just a reply from Great Britain's Southward and a fourth goal from the reliable

Fraser, edged the home side nearer at 13–20. With ten minutes remaining, for all Alan Prescott's brave, excruciatingly painful plunges in midfield, Karalius's awesome tackling display and Murphy's magic, the Lions were tiring rapidly in the face of constant attacks from the Aussies. For once, Alan Prescott was to be thankful for the pain in his right arm.

There was ten minutes left of the match and referee D'Arcy Lawlor ordered a scrum on our 25-yard line. I knew this was the most dangerous time of the match and I knew that, playing under the unlimited-tackle rule as we then did, we must win the ball at this scrum. If we didn't I sensed that we would go under.

As we packed down for the scrum I shouted to the lads, and especially to Dick Huddart, who was in the second row behind me, that we must have a huge push, that we desperately needed the ball. Remember we only had five forwards in the scrum with Vince Karalius, our loose forward, having to play at stand off. If we won the ball I felt we could hold it for a lengthy period and put a halt to Australia's constant barrage of our line.

Suddenly Dick Huddart rammed himself into the scrum behind me like a raging bull. He was all fired up, and he swung his arm around to bind me in the pack. But he grabbed the wrist of my broken right arm. I thought he had pulled my hand off the arm. I have never known pain like it in my life, it was unbelievable. I screamed, catapulted forward and pushed like I have never done in my life. We won the scrum, kept the ball and, though Australia's Keith Holman scored a try in the dying seconds, we scored another try from Karalius to win the match.

The Battle of Brisbane had been won and, two weeks later, following the Lions' massive 40–17 annihilation of Australia, skipper Prescott was chaired aloft around the boundary of the Sydney Cricket Ground, his arm in a plaster cast, and waving with his good left arm in response to the cheers of both British and Australian fans alike. The Australians, though the toughest and most merciless of opponents, respect a battler and a winner. Saints' fiery red-haired prop earned their respect over the most painful 80 minutes of his life, and yet he too will always be most respectful of his opposite number Brian Davies for not taking advantage of his sorry predicament and for not, possibly, putting an end to the Great Britain captain's glorious career.

My opposing prop Brian Davies could have ruined my career and put me out of rugby for good if he had tried intentionally to have a go at my arm. He knew it was broken and that it was just hanging loosely outside the scrum. Brian McTigue, the other prop, and myself switched over at every scrum, so that I didn't push with my right arm on the inside of the scrum.

I was afraid of the pack collapsing on it. I will always be grateful to Brian Davies for leaving my arm alone.

Alex Murphy and his colleagues on the 1958 Lions tour only too willingly acknowledge their own gratitude to the Great Britain captain:

Alan's injury was so bad that the Australian doctor called him a 'Pommie maniac'. He didn't even have a pain-killing injection to help him overcome the pain. His bravery won the second Test and we wouldn't have been in a position to win the third Test but for Alan. His bravery won the Ashes series for us. Today, no player would be allowed to play on with such a bad injury, and the substitute rule would allow an injured player to be replaced. But Alan's courage inspired us to win the series, and nobody can take the Ashes win away from him. It's in the record books.

AUSTRALIA Clifford; Kite, Hawick, Carlson, Dimond; Brown, Holman; Davies, Kearney, Marsh, Mossop, Provan, O'Shea.

GREAT BRITAIN Fraser; Southward, Ashton, Challinor, Sullivan; Bolton, Murphy; Prescott, Harris, McTigue, Huddart, Whiteley, Karalius.

Scorers Australia   *Tries* Marsh, Carlson, Dimond, Holman. *Goals* Clifford (3).
          Great Britain   *Tries* Southward (2), Challinor, Sullivan, Murphy. *Goals* Fraser (5).

Referee D'Arcy Lawlor (Australia).

Mark Preston

Wigan 20 Halifax 16

John Player Special Trophy Second Round, Central Park, Wigan
26 November 1988

Born 3 April 1967. Pace is the essential requirement of any aspiring winger, and Mark Preston amply illustrated that he was blessed with the attribute when, as a schoolboy, he frequently raced down the touchlines at Kirkham Grammar School. The addition of a deceptive swerve and, on occasions, a telling hand-off gave him the ideal credentials to make rapid progress in rugby union once he had left school. After a season with local club Preston Grasshoppers and then a move to near neighbours Fylde, the short but powerful threequarter quickly came to the attention of the England rugby union selectors. An appearance in March 1988 for England 'B' against Italy indicated that the selectors had higher things in mind for the Fylde flyer, but the 20-year-old Preston, a schoolboy fan of Wigan, had other ideas.

Later that month, Mark Preston was delighted to switch codes and join Wigan where, firstly under Kiwi coach Graham Lowe and then Aussie boss John Monie, he enjoyed three highly profitable seasons. Differences between himself and John Monie over the style and role of a winger resulted in his chances becoming less frequent at Central Park, with the result that, in 1991, he moved across the Pennines to continue his tryscoring at Halifax.

In the mid-1960s, when the then secretary of the Rugby Football League, Bill Fallowfield, had the vision to understand that television would eventually be the medium to promote any sport, many clubs took the opposite view. A decision to allow up to 35 matches a season to be shown live on BBC television aroused considerable controversy in the north, where many club treasurers could envisage only a loss of revenue through the gates and could not understand the increased receipts in sponsorship and advertising which would be gained. Nor could such parochial management foresee the advantages for the spread of the game and the cultivation of a worldwide audience as rugby league enjoys today. Indeed, the mighty Wigan were fined £500 for refusing to allow the cameras to be installed at Central Park. How times change!

Wigan, whether on BSkyB, ITV or BBC, are now one of the leading attractions on television and have possibly done more than most to promote the 13-a-side code and raise its image to levels beyond the wildest dreams of even Mr Fallowfield. The marketing of the game, and especially its players, is now done via television, and no one knows that better than the likes of Martin Offiah, Ellery Hanley or Garry Schofield, now household and international names by virtue of their activities on the small screen. It did not take long for Mark Preston, a professional with Wigan for barely eight months, to realise that if he wanted to progress in the game then a good performance when the television cameras were at Central Park was needed. His first, nervous appearance under the BBC cameras and a superb two-try matchwinning performance gave him the kick start he needed in his new professional career and, naturally, proved the highlight of his career to date.

I had only signed for Wigan in March and had only just broken into the first team when I was selected to face Halifax on TV. It was my first ever appearance on TV and I knew that I had to make the most of it. A good game would help me progress at Wigan. The game would be watched live by millions at home and abroad, any tries would be replayed on the news at night, and I knew that a good performance could do a lot for me. I daren't have a bad game. It was the most important game so far for me. Luckily, it proved to be the breakthrough I needed.

To arrive at a rugby league club on one's first training night is always a nervous time for any rugby union convert, especially if, like Mark Preston, he has been a supporter of the professional club all his life. Suddenly, your heroes on the field, Ellery Hanley, Shaun Edwards, Andy Gregory and company, are hanging their clothes on the very next peg in the dressing room. The union convert has to prove to them that he is worth his fee and, quickly, he has to learn to adapt to his new rugby life. Mark Preston's dapper suits, his flashy ties and his immaculate hairstyle, with never a hair out of place, helped him to become part of the team.

I was very nervous when I signed league. Wigan is not the easiest of places to come into from rugby union. I had always watched Wigan as a kid and, though I wasn't overawed, I wondered what I was doing among players I had once worshipped.

I was lucky in that I enjoyed a good laugh with the players, and especially Joe Lydon, who christened me James Bond because of the way I dressed. Even at training I used to turn up in a suit and tie with gel on my hair. Somehow the jokes helped to break the ice.

But it was his performance on the field which would determine the success of his switch to league, not his friendships in the dressing room. As Mark Preston walked down the tunnel at Central Park and on to the pitch to face Halifax he knew that the television cameras were filming and the next 80 minutes would determine his immediate rugby future at Wigan. At least he was put at ease by the banter around him and the pre-match ritual which Joe Lydon and himself were accustomed to practise before kickoff.

> As we stepped out I used to turn to Joe and ask him to look after me. He would always reply, 'Don't worry, I'll look after you, Bond.' It was always reassuring and was just a little thing we laughed about between ourselves.

Under Aussie coach Ross Strudwick, Halifax had been making good progress in the league, and their accompanying army of fans, estimated at around 3000, expected much from them. Australian centres Bob Grogan and Tony Anderson had developed a good understanding in midfield, and the back row trio in the pack, Neil James, Paul Dixon, and former Wigan favourite John Pendlebury, had proved troublesome to opposition defences. It was still a surprise, though, when, after 23 minutes, Wigan were trailing by 14–2, both Anderson and Pendlebury had scored tries, and ex-Wigan star, full back Colin Whitfield, had landed three goals. Hardly the score the Central Park faithful expected, and they let their favourites know. For Mark Preston those opening 23 minutes did not go as planned.

> Before the match, though I was nervous, I thought that things would go my way. But things began to go badly wrong and nothing seemed to go right for me or the team. When Halifax were leading 8–2, Shaun Edwards passed a long ball to me and gave me a little space in which to chip kick over Mark Taylor's head. I re-gathered and scored, but the referee blew his whistle and awarded us a penalty for a previous offence. I thought that it just wasn't going to be my day. At 14–2 the crowd began to jeer and call at us. At that moment I wished I wasn't on TV.

In any world-class side, when the odds are stacked against them, there are always the two or three individuals who, with one pass, sidestep or swerve, can turn a match and rekindle the fire in the belly. Wigan's Kevin Iro, Joe Lydon, Shaun Edwards and Andy Gregory were such players. On the half hour, with the home supporters baying for action, Wigan's rugged scrum half Gregory decided to take matters into his own hands and, having made a break in midfield, scampered clear. Half-back partner Shaun Edwards, as if guided by radar, was at his elbow within seconds and in receipt of the ball. He moved deep into the Halifax half where, having sidestepped the full back Colin Whitfield, his pass gave Mark Preston the easiest of runs to the corner for Wigan's opening try. Preston's day was beginning to brighten, especially when the powerful Kiwi, Kevin Iro, converted and, five minutes later, added a penalty goal to send Wigan into the dressing room with a hint of respectability and a scoreline of 14–10 in Halifax's favour.

A try and a penalty goal from Joe Lydon and, in reply, a penalty goal from Halifax's lively stand off Peter Coyne tied the scores at 16–16 as the referee and the spectators began to look at their watches and count down to the final whistle. Five minutes remained, and all thoughts turned towards a replay. Not so Mark Preston, who still yearned to add to his growing reputation with a matchwinning try.

Nobody wanted a replay at Thrum Hall. The Halifax ground had a fearsome reputation as a burial ground for visiting sides, and it was very difficult for wingers who were not used to the slope on the pitch. Joe Lydon used to say that he wouldn't send a letter there.

Little did the ex-Fylde union star realise that he would be the one to bring millions of viewers to the edge of their seats with one of the best tries of his career and one which established him very quickly as one of the most dangerous runners in the game. His 75th minute 75-yard spectacular took Wigan into the third round of the John Player Special Trophy and gave him the media coverage he desired.

Our team were lined up very flat and throwing the ball all over the field, rather like touch rugby, in an effort to score the winning try. Andy Gregory threw a long speculative pass on our 25-yard line to Joe Lydon, who ran about five yards before passing to me. I noticed that my opposite wing, Mike Taylor, had dropped back too deeply and given me more room than usual. I rounded the Halifax prop Dan Staines and set off upfield. I managed to cut inside Mick Taylor and then, suddenly, I saw two Halifax defenders, one of whom was David Holmes, a former England 'B' rugby union team-mate, standing in front of me.

I had in mind to pass to Ellery Hanley, who was racing up alongside me on my inside, and I did go through the motions of passing the ball. But just as I had the ball on my fingertips ready to part with it, both players moved towards Ellery. I changed direction, kept the ball, and veered back out towards the touchline to score at the corner. We missed the goal but the match was won and I'd proved the matchwinner. I was thrilled at what I'd done.

So were millions of viewers who, having seen the try once, twice, replayed in slow motion and highlighted on Saturday evening news programmes, were well aware of the Wigan wing. The fans on the terraces and the viewers at home had been treated to the classic winger's try, a perfect example of the use of speed on the outside to beat opponents. According to Mark Preston, this was his favourite ploy.

* * *

Some coaches want their wingers to have bulk, but I think speed is the biggest asset a winger can possess. I'm blessed with pace, and I always like to make the best use of it by going round an opponent. Some wingers tend to overdo coming inside and have to thread their way through defenders. I think a wing should have confidence in his speed.

Sadly for Mark Preston, though he had impressed everyone with his try of the season, the arrival of new coach John Monie the following year was to cause problems and do little for his confidence. His reputation as a tryscorer continued, and he had the pleasure of registering two tries at Wembley in Wigan's 36–14 triumph over Warrington in 1990, but always there were long spells in the Alliance team away from the limelight, thanks to a difference of opinion on wing play between the coach and the player.

In 1989–90 I was Wigan's top tryscorer with 33 tries, but I was still not the sort of winger John Monie wanted. He wanted his wings to drive into midfield and help the forwards out in the middle. This was all very well, but when the ball came your way on the wing your legs were tired and there was little running in them. When I scored a lot of tries he kept me in the side, but when he signed Frano Botica I was left in the second team.

There was no way I wanted to play in the second team, so I jumped at the chance to move clubs.

Ironically, he moved to Halifax, the team against whom he scored the most rewarding try of his career and celebrated his first television appearance with an eye-catching performance.

WIGAN Hampson; T. Iro, K. Iro, Lydon, Preston; Edwards, Gregory; Case, Kiss, Shelford, Potter, Platt, Hanley. *Subs*: Betts, Lucas.

HALIFAX Whitfield; Taylor, Grogan, Anderson, Hutchinson; Coyne, Holmes; Fairbank, McCallion, Staines, James, Dixon, Pendlebury. *Subs*: Simpson, Ramshaw.

Scorers Wigan   *Tries* Preston (2), Lydon. *Goals* K. Iro (3), Lydon.
           Halifax   *Tries* Anderson, Pendlebury. *Goals* Whitfield (3), Coyne.

Referee Kevin Allatt (Southport).

196

Mal Reilly

Castleford 11 Salford 6
Challenge Cup Final, Wembley
17 May 1969

Born 19 January 1948. A total of nine international caps for his country, all earned in one hectic, crowded 12-month spell in 1970 against Australia (5), New Zealand (3) and France, fail to do justice to the impact Mal Reilly had on the game for 15 seasons both in Britain and Australia. The dynamic loose forward burst on to the scene with Castleford in 1967, having signed from the Kippax Welfare amateur club, and, after winning a couple of Challenge Cup winner's medals against Salford and Wigan and shattering the best of Australia's forwards on the Lions tour of 1970, he left to link up with top Sydney league club Manly. His departure cost him many Test caps, but his then overseas record £15,000 transfer fee to the Aussie club provided him with the satisfaction of becoming the only English player to be on the winning side in two Australian Grand Finals against losers Eastern Suburbs and Cronulla in 1972 and 1973.

An absence of four seasons Down Under hardly diminished Mal Reilly's skills when he returned home to Wheldon Road in 1975 as Castleford's player-coach, an experience that was to help him sharpen his coaching techniques in anticipation of his selection as Great Britain coach in 1988. For the past six seasons, the former Castleford, Leeds and current Halifax coach has guided Great Britain's fortunes both at home and abroad, achieving memorable Test wins in Sydney, Melbourne and London against the world champions Australia and defeating New Zealand in three Test series.

All sports are littered with the names of famous venues, grounds or arenas which, once mentioned, immediately arouse fond memories to the devotees of a particular sport. Rugby league is no exception, especially for a globetrotter as famous as former Great Britain loose forward and current coach Mal Reilly. The tiny, compact stadium at Goroka, nestling on the green and wooded hillsides of Papua New Guinea and packed with excitable fans, seemingly hanging in the air in the surrounding palm trees, has an atmosphere all of its own. The futuristic Sydney Football Stadium captures the lively, brash atmosphere that is Australian rugby league, while the quaint wooden grandstand and the grassy banking of Auckland's Carlaw Park typify the

197

homely setting of Kiwi rugby. Nowhere, however, is there a finer, more traditional venue for rugby league than Britain's own Wembley Stadium, an arena which can hold terrors for many but which can inspire some, like Mal Reilly, to great deeds.

> My first visit to Wembley Stadium was when I was just 20 to watch the Leeds v. Wakefield Trinity match. At the time I was watching the match I could appreciate the unique atmosphere and I was determined to return as a player. I just wanted the chance to play there, everything about the stadium was so impressive. When I eventually did play there for the first time 12 months later, I felt about nine feet tall when I walked out and on to the pitch. You can sense that you are playing in a special arena the moment you walk out. There is nowhere like it for rugby league anywhere in the world.

Within two years of his first trip to Wembley, Mal Reilly had two cup-winner's medals on his mantelpiece at home and was the proud possessor of the Lance Todd Trophy, awarded for his outstanding man of the match performance in the 1969 Challenge Cup final between, at that time, two of the most exciting sides in the country, Castleford and Salford. And, on his return to Wembley as a player, he was more than ready to play his part in the history of the famous stadium.

> I couldn't wait to play the match. I was psychologically right for the game and absolutely prepared for Salford. I felt right for days before the match and, without being too sure, I was very confident of playing well and winning. Salford were the glamour side of the game at that time and were a huge challenge for a homespun side like Castleford.

Under the astute guidance of chairman Brian Snape, Salford had emerged out of the shadows of their more famous neighbours, soccer giants Manchester United, to become one of the strongest teams in rugby league. Their capture of David Watkins, the gifted prolific points-scoring half back from the world of Welsh rugby union at a record £14,000 fee, and the acquisition of England rugby union forward Mike Coulman ensured the club national headlines. The arrival of league internationals Colin Dixon, Bill Burgess, Chris Hesketh and Ron Hill gave them the experience they needed to capitalise on their glamour buys. The bookmakers rightly installed them as favourites to lift the cup for only the second time in their history.

Castleford, in stark contrast, had a collection of players equally as skilful and as gifted as any in the Salford ranks, but their sources for recruitment were more centred on the small Yorkshire town itself and the surrounding league amateur clubs. Great Britain stars Derek Edwards, Alan Hardisty,

Keith Hepworth, Dennis Hartley and Mal Reilly himself had all graduated to Wheldon Road via such a background. The local boys of Castleford and the cosmopolitan Salford were renowned as two of the most attractive, attacking footballing sides in the country, and it was no surprise that they attracted a capacity 97,939 crowd to Wembley. It was a surprise, however, that the Challenge Cup final failed to live up to the attacking delights most of the fans expected they would be offered.

> We had some very classy and fast players, especially at half back in Alan Hardisty and Keith Hepworth, and we had a good footballing pack. They had exceptional pace out wide and, in Watkins, had one of the top points-scorers of the day. Many people were surprised that it was such a hard, low-scoring game and not the high-scoring, all-action match everyone expected. There were plenty of players blessed with attacking skills, but I think the two teams were so concerned at each other's tryscoring potential that both concentrated very heavily on defence. Perhaps each side was too intent on stopping the other. Whatever the reasons, it was a very tough, physical battle.

Two Ron Hill penalty goals for Salford and a try for Castleford centre Keith Howe were all that both teams had to show for a hard slog in the opening 40 minutes. Indeed, the exchanges had been tough and torrid at times, with Salford's Great Britain wing, Bill Burgess, being flattened in the opening minutes and with the Yorkshire side lucky to have 13 players remaining on the field. Loose forward Reilly, in one exciting dash in the 32nd minute, did give the Castleford fans a glimpse of possible success when he roared through a gap and engineered the decisive break which led to try hero Howe crossing Salford's line to score. Thirteen minutes into the second half, it was Reilly again who stamped his class on the match and provided a try for Castleford stand off Alan Hardisty and, after second row Mick Redfearn's conversion, an 8–4 lead.

> I picked up a clearance kick from David Watkins and set off running upfield. There were some gaps in the broken play which I managed to break through until the Salford scrum half came up high to tackle me. I carried him on my shoulders for about ten yards and then threw him off, but as I was falling I sensed that someone was nearby. I couldn't see Alan Hardisty, but I could hear him racing alongside, and when he shouted to me I just passed the ball in the direction of the shout. Alan had such tremendous anticipation and acceleration that he was on the ball in a flash and was over the tryline.

Former Castleford favourite Ron Hill did hit back with another penalty goal

199

for Salford when Cas hooker Clive Dickinson was pulled up at the scrum by keen referee Derek Brown for a 'loose arm' offence. There was, though, no stopping the stronger Castleford pack, and superbly led by number 13 Reilly, prop Dennis Hartley and lively hooker Johnny Ward, they stormed the Salford line in the final quarter to clinch the game with a try from Hardisty's half-back partner, scrum half livewire Keith Hepworth – a try which, according to Mal Reilly, took the tiny Hepworth by surprise.

> There were only a couple of minutes remaining in the match when our hooker Johnny Ward put Keith Hepworth in for a try. He sold two dummies to the Salford defence and, after the first dummy, Keith Hepworth thought he had the ball and carried on running for the corner. But he didn't have the ball, Johnny had it. He dummied again before finally passing it to Keith, who went on to score the try that clinched the game.

The game had hardly proved a classic, perhaps, as Reilly has indicated, there being so much at stake in Castleford's first appearance at the stadium in 34 years and Salford's first since the pre-Second World War glory days of skipper Gus Risman, Alan Edwards and Billy Watkins. Yet Reilly's ferocious tackling, his powerful running and his ball-playing skills shone brightly, as did the fierce rivalry and duel between Reilly and the ex-Castleford loose forward, Salford's own Ron Hill. The old gunslinger had been challenged by the young ambitious fighter and it proved an absorbing shootout. Mal Reilly emerged the winner, by virtue of carrying off the coveted Lance Todd Trophy, but he was lavish in his praise of the man whose jersey he now wore.

> Ron Hill had been a fine loose forward for Castleford, and playing against his old team put a little extra bite in him. He played well above himself and really tested us. I had to be wary of him, but his presence playing opposite me really motivated me. As the man who had taken over his number 13 jersey at Castleford, it really put me on my mettle.

Salford's ex-British Lions union star, David Watkins, was equally lavish in his praise of Mal Reilly's man of the match performance.

> He was simply awesome. He was so fit and strong that his sheer physical strength just brushed some of our big forwards aside. He played behind some big prop forwards who gave him the room to display his running and handling abilities. He also had perfected a tactic I had never seen a forward use in rugby union, that of the chip kick over the opposition defence. In the final he rushed up a couple of times, and just when we thought he was going to run into us or pass he fooled us by kicking over our heads. He really was the difference between the two sides.

* * *

Sadly for Castleford, Great Britain's future loose forward was not to remain long in the number 13 jersey for, following another successful Wembley appearance 12 months later against Wigan, he was soon to board a plane for Australia and yet more honours with the top Sydney league side Manly. In the 1969 and 1970 Challenge Cup finals, Castleford had proved themselves to be a great team, one fit to grace any era, and one destined to dominate the sport for a decade. That it was not to be proved a disaster for the town as the side began to break up with many, including Reilly himself, departing hastily for elsewhere. Though it was an ecstatic Mal Reilly who celebrated his cup-winning feat in 1969 by saluting the Castleford fans in a lap of honour on the pitch, today there is more than a hint of regret as he laments the demise of the team that could have been spoken of alongside the greats.

> I can remember all the excitement of the lap of honour at the end, and yet within a couple of seasons there was little left of the team. I went to Australia, Alan Hardisty and Keith Hepworth left for Leeds, Brian Lockwood joined Widnes and some just faded out. It was sad, because if the side had been kept together then it could have developed into a really great one. It was a formidable team, one which played good rugby and threw the ball about all over the field. It was a great loss to Castleford.

Castleford's loss was Aussie giants Manly's gain as the Yorkshire club pocketed a then massive £15,000 cash sum for his departure from Wheldon Road. And more starring roles were in prospect as, along with legendary Australian Test stars, current Kangaroos coach Bob Fulton and former full back Graham Eadie, he helped Manly storm to two Sydney Grand Finals. The Sydney suburb, in four seasons, had full value for their record outlay, while Castleford fans could only bemoan the loss of an extraordinary talent and wonder at the team that might have been.

CASTLEFORD Edwards; Briggs, Howe, Thomas, Lowndes; Hardisty, Hepworth; Hartley, Dickinson, Ward, Redfearn, Lockwood, Reilly. *Subs*: Harris, Fox.

SALFORD Gwilliam; Burgess, Whitehead, Hesketh, Jackson; Watkins, Brennan; Ogden, Dickens, Bott, Coulman, Dixon, Hill. *Subs*: Prosser, Smethurst.

Scorers Castleford   *Tries* Howe, Hardisty, Hepworth. *Goals* Redfearn.
Salford   *Goals* Hill (3).

Referee Derek Brown (Preston).

Tea Ropati

Otahuhu 13 Wynnum Manly 32
Challenge Match, Carlaw Park, Auckland
10 October 1984

Born 7 September 1965. One of seven rugby-playing brothers, of whom four – Joe, Peter, Iva and Tea himself – have represented New Zealand at varying levels, Tea Ropati had little option but to become a rugby league player. And a very good one too.

After showing early promise with the Otahuhu club, the powerfully built centre or stand off joined Aussie club Newcastle Knights for one season in 1988 as part of a young Kiwi development scheme before linking up with top Auckland side, Mangere East. That early promise soon fulfilled itself in international honours and a place on New Zealand's touring party to Great Britain in the autumn of 1989. While on tour in Britain, his outstanding form soon attracted the attentions of a host of leading First Division clubs, notably St. Helens, for whom he signed in the November immediately after the Kiwis' visit.

Though a serious knee injury restricted him in his first season at Knowsley Road, Tea has proved an outstanding bargain in whatever role. His powerful tackling and strong bursts down the middle have helped St. Helens to major honours and earned him the reputation as one of New Zealand's toughest competitors in the British game.

Whatever talent a youngster may possess, he will achieve little in rugby league until he gains the confidence to use his skills to the full. A fear of not wanting to make mistakes can hold a youngster from taking the initiative on attack, while any doubts over his ability can restrain an apprentice from accepting the responsibility of attempting something himself. A teenager making his debut can hold in such awe the star names lined up against him in the opposition, or even those players alongside him, that he can freeze on what should be his big day. But, if the skills are there, it can take just one good performance to make the player aware that he has what it takes to reach for the top in rugby league.

Such a performance and such a match came along for the 19-year-old Auckland teenager Tea Ropati when his club Otahuhu were chosen by the New Zealand league to represent his country in a grand challenge match at

Carlaw Park against Wynnum Manly, the winners of the Brisbane league in Australia. With two of Australia's greatest-ever midfield backs lining up in the Brisbane side, Wally Lewis and Gene Miles, and with seasoned internationals like Colin Scott at full back, the nervous Ropati knew that the match would be a huge challenge.

Eager to prove himself in front of his friends, he could hardly contain himself at the prospect of facing his boyhood heroes in what was to prove one of the most influential games of his career. The bustling centre's performance that night in Auckland gave him the confidence to go on to an illustrious international career.

I was really excited at the prospect of Wynnum Manly coming to New Zealand to play against us. I had only seen Wally Lewis and Gene Miles on the television, and to play against them was beyond my wildest dreams. But it was what I needed at that stage in my career. All my mates came to watch me play against these legends. It was really good for me and, as it turned out, proved to be just the boost I needed.

For Otahuhu to play against Wynnum Manly, then one of the top sides in Australia, was also a good boost for New Zealand rugby league. Then we were all amateur players, and the game was very much in the shadow of the rugby union. But games such as these helped to create an upsurge in public interest, and it was at this time that league really began to develop in New Zealand. The match certainly did a lot for me.

For Tea Ropati a boost to his confidence before kickoff came in the shape of the charismatic figure of Graham Lowe, one of the most influential figures in New Zealand rugby league in the past 20 years. The former Kiwi, Wigan and Manly coach has been, until ill-health forced his retirement from coaching in 1992, one of the foremost innovators and thinkers in the modern game. His visit to one of Otahuhu's pre-match training sessions and his chat with the nervous Ropati did much to put the teenager in the right frame of mind to approach the match.

Graham Lowe visited us at one of our training sessions and helped with the tactics. He was at the top then and was an inspirational figure in New Zealand rugby league. I had a lot of respect for him, and I really appreciated him giving up his time to talk to me. He gave me the confidence to play well against Wynnum Manly.

Though the Brisbane champions were eventually to win the challenge by 32–13, thanks to tries by Miles, Butler, Dawes, Bullock and Green (2) and four goals from full back Scott, the contest proved to be far more than an end-of-season outing. When a big crowd is on hand at Carlaw Park, the noise generated by the fans on the steep concrete terracing along the touchline and that generated from within the tiny, somewhat archaic wooden stand opposite can be quite intimidating, especially for Australian visitors. But the confidence for which Otahuhu's young Ropati was searching was there for all to see in the calm, assured play of Wynnum Manly's experienced international duo, Gene Miles and Wally Lewis. In the words of a local scribe: 'Wally Lewis' hallmarks – hard tackling, long passing and swift running – were there when necessary.' The Kangaroos and Wynnum Manly skipper paraded around the pitch as some superior being, involving himself here, involving himself there when necessary and always prompting play and directing those around him towards the Otahuhu tryline. Sixteen-stone centre Gene Miles was his accomplice in the backs, battering down the tightest of defences with a thundering run down the flanks or inflicting pain on Otahuhu's forwards when, occasionally, he moved infield to assist his pack with a charge at the play-the-ball. Both players commanded the respect of Tea Ropati but, after Kiwi boss Lowe's help, he was not afraid of them.

Wally Lewis and Gene Miles are two of the greatest-ever players to represent Australia and, at that time, they were probably at the peak of their abilities. Lewis could control a game with his passing and kicking and was a difficult player to pull down. He was much bigger than people think.

Gene Miles was so strong that if you didn't hit him right in the tackle then he would go right through you. He was a good centre for a winger; he could create openings for him. I was nervous, but when the kickoff arrived I couldn't wait to play against them. I wanted to know just what I could do against them and measure myself against them.

The talented youngster did enough to convince himself and those watching that, given the right encouragement, New Zealand would, a few years later, have need of his services in the heat of many a tough Test battle.

Lining up in the centre, directly opposite the huge bulk of Gene Miles, Tea Ropati could hardly have dreamed of a better start to his senior career. His strong tackling performance, his clever support play and, above all else, his two opportunist tries against the mighty Aussie duo soon had the name of Ropati ringing around the terraces. His first try came courtesy of Otahuhu's shrewd ball-playing hooker, Rene Nordmeyer, who timed his pass to perfection to meet the young, bustling centre's powerful burst.

Rene Nordmeyer, our hooker, cut across field with the ball and threw out a very wide pass in my direction on the flank. The pass cut out a couple of players, and I was able to time my run and burst on to the ball. I timed my run just right because I was able to fly straight between Miles and Lewis for a try. They were not very pleased, but it was a great thrill for me to score.

Ropati's second try illustrated the characteristics of his play which, later with New Zealand and St. Helens, were to become the powerful Kiwi's trademarks. His acceleration off the mark and his instinct for a gap, allied to his determination and strength to go for it regardless of the consequences, have resulted in many a try. So it was against Wynnum Manly.

To score one try against Gene Miles was a thrill, but to score two tries gave me a real buzz. Especially in front of all my mates from junior rugby who were spectators at the match. The second try was similar to the first in that I received a short pass out wide on Wynnum Manly's 25-yard line and I straightened up quickly. Both Miles and Lewis held back for a split second and I was able to cut through them again. I was even more pleased to have the room to run around Colin Scott at full back before touching the ball down. Two tries in the match, I couldn't believe it.

In recent seasons Tea Ropati has faced many of the world's finest midfield backs, Australia's Mal Meninga and Laurie Daley, Great Britain's Garry Schofield and Shaun Edwards and his fellow countrymen Dean Bell and Kevin Iro, and has invariably proved a tough and resilient opponent. His surging runs in midfield and his instinct for a tryscoring chance have transformed many a championship match in Britain. Little wonder then that he has proved such a valuable acquisition to St. Helens in their search for honours in the past five seasons. He has fulfilled the rich promise that he displayed that night against Wynnum Manly at Carlaw Park, and it was his never-to-be-forgotten performance that made him realise that, given the confidence in himself, he had the skills to succeed.

The game against Miles and Lewis gave me the confidence I needed. I knew from then on that, if I worked at it, I could do it. I knew that I had played against two of the best players in the world and had done the job well. The next time I came up against such players I was not overawed or nervous. That one match brought the best out of me and made me determined to succeed.

Though the softly spoken Kiwi has made himself a firm favourite with the St. Helens fans at Knowsley Road and finds his style of fast attacking play so suited to the British style, he has found it difficult to resist the temptation to return home to Auckland and play with the newly formed Auckland Warriors in the Australian Winfield Cup in 1995. Coach John Monie, in his days as manager of Wigan, was a big admirer of the St. Helens number six, and knows well the threat he can pose on attack. Whatever his future at home in New Zealand, there can be little doubt that Tea Ropati has been one of his country's most successful exports in the past decade.

OTAHUHU Tul; Magatakia, Muller, Ropati, Pakieto; Lee, Morrison; Tinitella, Nordmeyer, Piriol, Wright, Simons, McGahan.

WYNNUM MANLY Morgan; Eastley, Scott, Miles, Butler; Lewis, Dawes; Kajewski, Green, Polmon, Walsh, Dowling, Jemmott. *Subs:* Bullock.

Scorers	Otahuhu	*Tries* Wright, Ropati (2). *Drop Goals* Lee.
	Wynnum Manly	*Tries* Miles, Butler, Dawes, Green (2), Bullock. *Goals* Scott (4).

Referee Dennis Hale (New Zealand).

Garry Schofield

Second Test, Central Park, Wigan
2 November 1985

Born 1 July 1965. When Garry Schofield left for Australia with the Great Britain touring team in the summer of 1984 as, at 18 years 10 months, the youngest-ever player to accompany them, he had already displayed two attributes which were to stamp him above others of his generation. His outstanding captaincy of the British youth team to New Zealand a year earlier was eventually to be complemented by the captaincy of the full Great Britain side. Second, his 38 tries in his first season made him the youngest player ever to top the tryscoring lists in a campaign and were an indication of his ability to take advantage of the slightest scoring chance. Originally a Hunslet Parkside amateur player, Garry took the circuitous route to Headingley and Leeds via Hull who, for financial reasons, were forced to release him to his home city for a then world record £178,250 fee in the 1987–88 season. Honours accompanied him as, following his debut Lions tour Down Under in 1984, he returned on three more occasions in 1988, 1990 and 1992 to visit Australia, New Zealand and Papua New Guinea.

Such success was bound to attract the interest of the giant Sydney league clubs, and it was no surprise when Great Britain's talented stand off returned to Australia for two short summer contracts in the late 1980s as the guest of Balmain.

When a youngster is trying to break into the top flight and establish himself at international level, many are the pitfalls, and harsh is the criticism which is often levelled against him. Unlike the continentals or the Americans, who adore their sporting peers, we English seem to take a perverse delight in seeing our heroes fail to live up to their promise or prove unable to match our early expectations of them. Spectators often take satisfaction in being able to turn to their companion on the terraces and, with a smug expression, utter those oft-heard words, 'I told you so, he's not as good as people think he is'. Garry Schofield, with less than two years' professional rugby league experience under his belt, but with five international caps already in his cabinet, was accustomed to hearing such disturbing comment, especially after his display in Great Britain's 22–24 first Test loss to New Zealand in the autumn of 1985. The 20-year-old Great Britain centre expected to be dropped for the second Test clash at Central Park, Wigan, and feared the worst

> After the loss at Headingley I took plenty of flak from the critics and the supporters. I missed a tackle on the Kiwis' Dane O'Hara in a movement which eventually led to my Hull team-mate James Leuluai clinching the game with a last-minute try. Our coach Maurice Bamford spoke only briefly to me after the match, and I was convinced he would drop me. But he never did; he stood by me despite all the abuse, and put his confidence in me. I wanted to repay him.

Great Britain boss Bamford, though upset at the time, remained convinced that Schofield's talents would still have a part to play in determining the outcome of the next two encounters:

> We had the first Test won when we scored a try with just a few minutes to play. Then Deryck Fox kicked directly to New Zealand's Dane O'Hara on the wing. All week in training I had made doubly sure that the chasers of the kicks made the first tackle and didn't allow play to develop. Garry lined Dane up on the touchline, had his hands on him, but then missed him, with the result that Leuluai soon scored the matchwinner at the other end of the field.
>
> I went into the dressing room and pulled Garry to one side with our captain Harry Pinner and told him that if he had made that one tackle then we would have won the first Test. It shook him, but I never had any intentions of dropping him. I was convinced his talents would blossom.

The desire to repay the trust of his coach and to prove to himself and his harshest critics that he could, despite his tender years, handle the pressures of international rugby spurred Schofield on to his greatest individual achievement at Test level and provided him with one of the most rewarding moments of his glittering career.

> I had to prove myself in the second Test. I had made quite a name for myself on tour with Great Britain Down Under in 1984 and had scored a lot of tries with Hull in my first season. The match itself, for Great Britain, was a do-or-die situation. One slip and we could have lost the Test series. Many people said that I couldn't handle Test rugby, that I had done too much too early.
>
> I just had to prove a few people wrong, and it was very satisfying to prove the knockers wrong by scoring a record four tries.

The 11th New Zealand tourists had been one of the most eagerly awaited teams ever to visit our shores for, in the mid-1980s, their performances had reached a level previously unknown at international level. They had destroyed Great Britain's hopes in a Test series at home just 12 months previously by three Tests to nil, and had recorded a defeat on the almighty Australians. Their party did indeed contain names that were to become synonymous with all that is best in Kiwi rugby league and players who were, in later years, to excite the crowds at Wigan, Warrington, Widnes, Cronulla and North Sydney. The Kiwis paraded possibly one of the greatest packs of forwards they had ever assembled, featuring the fearsome Sorensen brothers, Kurt and Dane, the powerful Kevin Tamati, two inspirational captains Mark Graham and Hugh McGahan and the current New Zealand coach, hooker Howie Tamati – an awesome gathering. Behind, in Gary Kemble, James Leuluai, Dean Bell, Dane O'Hara and livewire stand off Olsen Filipaina, they had the pace and the craft to take advantage of the powerhouses before them.

The raw power in the pack and the clinical finishing of the backs had shocked Great Britain in the first Test, not least Garry Schofield himself, and it was no surprise that coach Graham Lowe's men were immediately installed as favourites to win the series. The odds were stacked against Great Britain and especially the young Schofield.

> They were a great side, a blend of sheer strength and pace. I knew all about Leuluai, Ah Kuoi, O'Hara and Kemble from playing alongside them at Hull, and I knew that, above all else, they were quick and could score. In Graham Lowe they had one of the most shrewd coaches in the world, who had the ability to fire up his players and make them play above themselves. We knew it would be difficult to come from 1–0 behind in the series and beat them.

Great Britain's record at Test level had been shaky, to say the least, having lost their last ten successive Tests to Australia and New Zealand with respite only coming from none-too-convincing wins over France and Papua New Guinea. Yet a combination of determined and spirited forward play, plus the precocious talents of Great Britain's young centre, not only beat off the Kiwi challenge but sent them back to their base at Leeds with their tails between their legs and gave coach Graham Lowe an outsize headache ahead of his selections for the vital third and deciding Test at Elland Road, Leeds. The veteran Jeff Grayshon, John Fieldhouse and David Watkinson withstood all the Kiwi charges in the pack, while, at loose forward, captain Harry Pinner paraded all his handling skills and displayed his uncanny ability to create a gap in the tightest of defences. Above all, however, it was the lethal finishing and deadly tryscoring ability of Schofield, determined to make his critics eat their words, which destroyed Kiwi hopes of a series win. The 'Poacher', as I labelled him in one of my BBC television match commentaries after yet another of his tryscoring feats, devastated the visitors with his support play, his quick thinking and his speed off the mark on his way to four matchwinning tries. Before Billy Boston's own fans at Central Park, Schofield equalled the great Welshman's record four tries in a Test against New Zealand which had been set in Auckland 31 years earlier and propelled himself down the path to one of the most successful international careers in the history of the game.

Though the match, as is customary with most Test clashes, proved extremely tight in the opening 15 minutes, with both sides having to settle for a goal apiece from Joe Lydon and New Zealand's Olsen Filipaina, such were the gifted attackers on the field that the excited crowd were soon treated to a rugby feast. Indeed, the open nature of the game and the extent of the broken-play running can be gauged by the small incidence of scrums in the match, there being only ten occasions when the forwards locked shoulders in the whole of the 80 minutes. New Zealand, confident in the pace on their wings, were also keen to move the ball wide at every opportunity and contributed to the type of play in which a centre as alert and as inventive as Garry Schofield revels. He exploded into action in the 16th minute and proceeded to baffle the Kiwis with a hat trick of tries in 24 magical minutes.

With skipper Harry Pinner prompting in midfield and with centre partner Ellery Hanley using his impressive upper body strength to good effect, Schofield gave Great Britain the lead with the first of his four record-breaking tries.

> Ellery and I worked a crossover move behind the scrum. He used his strength and pace to suck a couple of defenders on to him, hold them, and then ride the tackles before giving me the ball in the gap he created. I gratefully accepted the pass and only had to shoot through to score. It was a perfectly timed pass, and I just managed to hit the ball at the right time.

Though it is an art in itself to hold oneself up in the tackle, as Hanley did, before offloading the ball at the precise moment, there is an equal art in arriving on to the pass at just the right time. Schofield has the ability to do just this and, as he showed 14 minutes later, the knack of always being in the right place at the right time. A centre's main function is to create space and tryscoring opportunities for his winger, but, whenever a break is made in midfield, he must be on hand to continue the break or finish it off with a try of his own. When hard-working Great Britain prop John Fieldhouse surprised New Zealand's marker defence by scurrying away from the acting half-back position, it was only to be expected that Garry Schofield should follow him.

> The second try was quite a simple affair. John Fieldhouse started the movement when he broke clear at the play-the-ball and raced upfield. I ran towards him, knowing that if he could get the ball out to me then I would

have a good chance to score. He managed to pass and, running over 35 yards, I was able to avoid Graeme West, who was covering back. With Joe Lydon's two goals we had a healthy lead of 12–2.

That Great Britain went into the dressing room at half time confident of victory and leading 18–12 came courtesy of the classy centre's third try, but not before skipper Pinner had illustrated his ability to prise open the tightest defences with a perfectly flighted pass.

The modern era of rugby has created strong-running, all-tackling, tryscoring loose forwards in the mould of Australia's Wayne Pearce, New Zealand's Hugh McGahan and Great Britain's Ellery Hanley, at the expense of the ball handling constructive number 13 of yesteryear like John Whiteley and Derek Turner. The St. Helens and Great Britain captain, though small in stature for a forward, was one such practitioner who delighted to run, pass a ball and devise openings for others. Few have a greater estimation of his worth to a side than Garry Schofield himself.

Many criticised Harry for not being a rough-tackling forward, but he always did his share. He expected the front five forwards to do the tackling, while he created play and schemed openings for all of us. He was a superb captain and a brilliant ball handler who could time and deliver a pass better than any forward in the game. It was a delight to run on to his passes.

Schofield did just that on the stroke of half time when Pinner and an equally gifted ball player, stand off Tony Myler, combined in a run-around movement in midfield. Their ploy quickly opened up the Kiwis' centre defence and drew inside James Leuluai and Gary Prohm sufficiently to allow Garry Schofield the extra yard of space he needed to burst through the gap. The try was a formality, as was the third of Lydon's four successful kicks of the afternoon.

Tony Myler and Harry combined in midfield about 45 yards from the New Zealand tryline and got their centres back-pedalling a little. Tony was big for a stand off, and he had a good pair of hands on him. Both created just sufficient room for me to escape the tackles, and the final pass was a beauty.

Any player would have been content with a hat trick in a Test match, but not the 20-year-old Hull midfield star. Though Kiwi wing Dean Bell and Olsen Filipaina raised the visitors' hopes with a try and a goal early in the second half, the eager Schofield complemented skipper Pinner's late drop goal with his record-equalling fourth try five minutes from the final whistle. The strength of Tony Myler and Ellery Hanley again played a prominent part in those closing but historic final minutes.

* * *

Tony Myler was proving unstoppable, and he was able to draw the defence yet again, hold the ball for a vital split second before launching Ellery towards the line. I only had to race alongside him, accept the ball and, with only 15 yards to cover, beat Gary Kemble to the tryline.

Great support players like Leeds' Garry Schofield and Wigan's Shaun Edwards score plenty of tries which are made to look easy and which appear to leave them with very little running to do. The skill is in anticipating the break or the vital pass and being in the right place to accept the opportunities presented. Support play is finely tuned, usually by experience and an appreciation of the necessary angles for running. Garry Schofield, with less than three years in the professional game, was already blessed with assets that invariably take many years to acquire. He had used them to answer his critics, prove his ability at international level and provide him with the most satisfying performance of his career.

The match was particularly satisfying for me because we had had our backsides smacked in all three Tests in New Zealand in 1984. We were really outplayed then, but in this match we had completely turned the tables on New Zealand. For British rugby it was memorable because I think it was the turning point of our international fortunes. We started to become a Test force again.

For me it was a great experience to score four tries in a Test match and equal the great Billy Boston's record. I had proved to the knockers that I wasn't too young for international rugby, and it restored my confidence in my own ability.

Great Britain coach Maurice Bamford, despite Schofield's doubts, never had anything but the utmost confidence in his talented centre:

I kept him in the side because I knew he had the ability. I have always had confidence in him. After all, it was me who, two years later, when I was coach at Leeds, paid Hull a world record fee for him. You can't have more confidence than that.

GREAT BRITAIN Burke; Drummond, Schofield, Hanley, Lydon; Myler, Fox; Grayshon, Watkinson, Fieldhouse, Goodway, Potter, Pinner. *Subs*: Edwards, Burton.

NEW ZEALAND Kemble; Bell, Leuluai, Prohm, O'Hara; Filipaina, Friend; K. Sorensen, H. Tamati, D. Sorensen, West, Stewart, McGahan. *Subs*: Ah Kuoi, Cowan.

* * *

Scorers Great Britain *Tries* Schofield (4). *Goals* Lydon (4). *Drop Goals*
Pinner.
New Zealand *Tries* Bell. *Goals* Filipaina (2).

Referee Barry Gomersall (Australia).

Kurt Sorensen

Australia 12 New Zealand 19

Second Test, Lang Park, Brisbane
9 July 1983

Born 8 November 1956. For 21 seasons, since his first outing as a 15-year-old for Mount Wellington in Auckland, Kiwi Kurt Sorensen has struck fear into the opposition. Weighing over 16 stones yet barely 5 feet 9 inches in height, his powerful, squat frame proved an awesome sight as he hurled himself at top speed against a nervous defender or crashed into a hesitant runner in midfield. He was a fierce competitor and, following his first appearance for Auckland at the tender age of 17, such was his reputation for tough, uncompromising forward play that his services were in great demand worldwide. Amid playing duties with Wigan, Cronulla, Eastern Suburbs and Widnes between 1976 and 1993, the pacy prop found time to be the cornerstone of many a great New Zealand pack.

Before departing from Naughton Park to assume the coaching duties at Whitehaven in the summer of 1993, Kurt Sorensen achieved his lifelong ambition of playing in a Challenge Cup final at Wembley. Sadly, after achieving Championship, Regal Trophy and Premiership success in Widnes colours, he tasted defeat against cup-holders Wigan in his last match for the Cheshire club.

The months of June and July 1993 proved a hectic time for the followers of both codes of rugby in New Zealand, with the Kiwi rugby league team locked in a gripping three-match Test series with Australia and the All Blacks rugby union squad involved in an equally absorbing contest with the visiting British Lions. The interest throughout the North and South Islands was intense, as New Zealand battled for supremacy on the two fields of play, but by far the greater interest for the 13-a-side code was the battle for supremacy in the television ratings and the resultant standing of the sport within the country. That the viewing figures actually recorded for the two Test series revealed a far greater share of viewers for the rugby league transmissions is an indication of the healthy respect which the game now commands. It was not always so as, in the past two decades, the professional code has fought hard for parity with the union code in the media. Both now, quite rightly, enjoy equal attention and time from

214

the media, but rugby league owes its new image and increased support to one telecast from Lang Park, Brisbane, on the night of 9 July 1983 when the Kiwis defeated Australia for the first time in 12 years.

That win, attracting almost a million viewers, illustrated New Zealand rugby league at its best, galvanised the game's administrators into life and projected the sport to a public who, in the past, had been largely unaware of its attractions. For Auckland-born Kurt Sorensen it was to prove the match of his life. He had been set one of the biggest challenges of his rugby career and had proved himself to be equal to the task; above all, he was proud to have elevated the sport he had loved since he started with Mount Wellington Juniors as a five-year-old to a new peak in the New Zealand public's consciousness. No more would league be looked upon as inferior to union in New Zealand. His performance and that of his team-mates proved the launching-pad for the renaissance of New Zealand rugby league.

> I always look upon this particular match as the most enjoyable and most rewarding match in which I ever played. The game represented a huge personal challenge to me, one which I had to win to prove myself to myself and my friends. I was so proud to beat Australia, not just for the win but because the game proved the breakthrough that New Zealand rugby needed. Today, the game is appreciated throughout the country and is as popular as union, and I like to think that on that night in Brisbane we all did something for the game. I have never experienced such satisfaction from any match before or since.

The rise of New Zealand rugby league had had its beginnings in the appointment of former Wigan and New Zealand half-back great, Cec Mountford, as coach to the Kiwis in 1979. The crafty half back's patient and innovative coaching and authoritative approach to the job quickly brought results and fostered a pride among his players in the black and white jersey. The appointment of the more extrovert Graham Lowe to the job four years later and the relaxation of the ban on Kiwi players playing abroad if they did not play for their country gave a further boost to the development of the sport. For Kurt Sorensen and his brother Dane, the relaxation of the ban ended a six-year period of exile from Test rugby and, in the first Test of 1983, a chance to prove to Kurt himself and New Zealand that he was still the power that he once was.

> My brother and I were having a lot of trouble with Cronulla, for whom we were playing in Sydney. Though there was no written law to stop a player playing for his country, Cronulla stuck to the rule of the International Board and neither of us could be selected for New Zealand. After the relaxation of the rule I returned immediately to Test rugby for the first

time since 1977 and obviously my selection for the first Test in Auckland represented a big challenge to me.

Sadly for Kurt Sorensen, his return to international rugby was not accompanied by the success he had hoped for, because, despite an enthusiastic 15,000 crowd roaring him on at Carlaw Park in his native Auckland, the rugged prop had a nightmare match as Australia swept to a 16–4 victory. Though Dean Bell and Ron O'Regan occasionally troubled the Aussies with a burst of speed in midfield, Kurt Sorensen had failed to live up to his reputation earned in the tough Sydney league with Cronulla. He was bitterly disappointed.

We had great expectations before the first Test, but nothing went right for me. I was very disappointed with my performance, and I really can't say why I didn't perform. Graham Lowe had no option but to drop me for the second Test in Brisbane, and I felt pretty low, having waited so long to resume Test rugby.

Fate, however, intervened to give the Kiwi prop a chance to show his true ability when, in the week prior to the second Test at Lang Park in Brisbane, powerful second row Mark Graham was ruled unfit and Sorensen was reinstated alongside new skipper, Wigan's Graeme West, in the second row. Auckland's goalkicking full back Nick Wright was also drafted into the team for the injured Gary Kemble. For Kiwi coach Graham Lowe the two inclusions fitted into his overall pre-match team plan, for he intended to 'work on our defence in training. Our tackling will be much harder. Kicking was one area in Auckland where we were weaker, and I expect Nick Wright to strengthen this department.'
For his reprieved pack star it was a heaven-sent last chance to prove his true worth, especially to himself.

Mark Graham hurt his knee in the first Test and during the week was ruled unfit. I was pleased to be recalled from the substitutes' bench to the team, and I was more determined than ever to wipe out the memory of that last match and set the record straight. But I was given a real rocket by our coach, Graham Lowe, who told me that if I didn't perform in the first ten minutes then I would be pulled off the field. I had to play well and was put under tremendous pressure, perhaps deliberately so, by Graham.

It was generally agreed that New Zealand had let themselves down badly in the first Test and that many matchwinning opportunities had been missed. They would have to raise their game considerably if they were to put a halt to Australia's run of 16 consecutive Test victories and upset an Australian side which, only nine months previously, had amassed an embarrassing 99 points

216

in three Ashes Test wins against the best of Great Britain. The Australian selectors, obviously anticipating huge support on the terraces of Lang Park, had selected nine Queensland players in the team, the highest number from that state for almost 60 years. The city of Brisbane was ready to give their country cousins from New Zealand their comeuppance.

I have never known the Australians to be so blasé about a Test match. Everyone in Brisbane where we trained was full of confidence about an Australian win, and I have never experienced a feeling quite like it. The whole city seemed to think it had a divine right to win and that we were just going along to the match to make up the numbers. Their over-confidence really got through to me, and I don't think, in all my career, I have ever wanted more to win a match. I was desperate to play well and win.

Kiwi coach Graham Lowe's tactics, however, won the day, and his 'rocket' to Kurt Sorensen paid off immediately as the big prop, Mark Broadhurst, Graeme West and Howie Tamati immediately set out to tackle and hustle Australia out of the match. Their powerful drives had Australia's forwards Wally Fullerton-Smith, Brad Tessman and Paul Vautin reeling backwards and dumped to the floor with a ferocity not encountered in the first Test in Auckland. In the centres, Australia's two giants, Mal Meninga and Gene Miles, were cut down by the smaller but faster Kiwis James Leuluai and Fred Ah Kuoi, who used their pace well to head off their opponents from the side. Full back Nick Wright, possibly for the first time in a Test match, kicked repeatedly at great length to the Australian tryline and established such a territorial advantage over the Kangaroos that they became frustrated and made mistakes. Kurt Sorensen and hooker Howie Tamati, who topped the match tackle count with 37 tackles, stormed into the green and gold jerseys with crunching and at times painful tackles. There was no danger of New Zealand coach Graham Lowe calling his prop from the field. Sorensen wouldn't have heard his call, he was so engrossed in the match.

Our pack was really fired up, and it was a very big one with plenty of pace. In the first 20 minutes I had a strong tackling game and, along with Mark Broadhurst, Howie Tamati, brother Dane and Graeme West we held them mostly in their own half and forced them on to the defensive. Our front row did a lot of damage to them, and, behind, Nicky Wright kept driving them back with his long kicks. We got the upper hand right from the beginning of the match and rarely lost it.

The Australian fans' confidence soared when exciting wing Eric Grothe grabbed a try after just four minutes' play but, instead of capitulating as they had done in the first Test, New Zealand slowly but surely gained the advantage.

217

Full back Wright started the scoring with a penalty goal, and skipper West rocked Australia with a try typical of his innovative Kiwi coach Graham Lowe. In his coaching career at Wigan and Manly, Lowe surprised his fans with the occasional inspirational gamble or shrewd move which fooled his opponents. In his entire career he never planned a better try than the one scored by Graeme West in the 25th minute of this absorbing Test thriller. When referee Robin Whitfield ordered a scrum outside Australia's 20-metre line, stand off Gordon Smith moved into the loose forward position, Gary Prohm moved from number 13 to full back and Nick Wright assumed the half-back role. Confusion reigned in the Australian ranks when Prohm burst on to the ball from full back, only to be tackled by Australian halves Wally Lewis and Steve Mortimer. With both Australian halves tied in at the tackle, Kiwi centre Fred Ah Kuoi dashed forward from the acting half-back position and put West in for New Zealand's opening try with a precision pass. The Australian defence had been completely fooled and, following Wright's conversion and a drop goal, the Kiwis led 9–6 at half time.

Within three minutes of the resumption, a Shane Varley break from the scrum gave James Leuluai a try and Wright the chance to add his third goal of the match. At 15–6, after 43 minutes, in their favour, New Zealand were in a commanding position. Eight minutes later, thanks to Kurt Sorensen and Joe Ropati, New Zealand's chunky, nuggety wing, the game was as good as over and the Kiwis were on their way to an historic victory. The skills and the power missing in the first Test were never better exhibited by Kurt Sorensen than when he burst his way past two tacklers, swept imperiously upfield and drew Australian full back Colin Scott before delivering the match-clinching pass with the poise and perfection of a half back. A subtle delay in the pass to the supporting Joe Ropati drew Australia's wing Eric Grothe infield just a yard too far. That yard enabled Ropati to hand off his Aussie opponent, round him and score at the corner. Kurt Sorensen remembers that pass.

> That final pass to Joe Ropati was the best moment in the match for me. I drew Colin Scott right on to me, and Eric Grothe moved inside towards me. When Joe got the ball, he launched himself for the tryline and just shrugged off Grothe. I've never experienced a feeling like it. I knew then that we would win.

Australia's substitute back Steve Ella did score a late try, and the mighty Meninga added his second goal of the match, but there was no denying New Zealand their first win in Australia for 12 years. There was no denying the Sorensen brothers their celebrations as Howie Tamati suddenly led his team-mates into an impromptu performance of the Haka, a ritual dance, specially for the viewers back home. Coach Graham Lowe had put New Zealand rugby league back at the top with his first outing on the international scene. He was

218

naturally full of praise for his players: 'The team did all that I asked. They tackled, tackled and tackled, and that is just what I wanted. Our game plan worked perfectly and this time we finished off our moves.'

Genial Aussie coach Arthur Beetson, too, was generous in his praise for the Kiwis: 'My blokes bumbled their way through the game. The New Zealanders played very well and stuck to their game plan. People haven't stopped saying what a great thing for league the win by New Zealand has been. That may be the case, but I wish to hell it had been someone else they'd beaten.'

The silent Queensland crowd filed out of Lang Park at the final whistle shocked at the treatment handed out to their heroes in their own back yard. Kurt Sorensen, as is his wont after a match, sat silently on the bench in the victors' dressing room slowly undoing his bootlaces and contemplating the scope and importance of the win. The memories remain.

> Beating Canberra Raiders with Widnes in the World Club Challenge at Old Trafford and clinching our first Division One Championship with a 66–14 defeat of Hunslet at Elland Road were special moments for me in my career, but the win over Australia in Brisbane rates the highlight with me. I'd been exiled from Test rugby for six years when I played in the first Test. Beating Australia was as sweet as any moment I've ever experienced in league. The team ranks with the best I've ever played in, and the team spirit was unbelievable.

NEW ZEALAND Wright; Ropati, Leuluai, Ah Kuoi, D. Bell; Smith, Varley; D. Sorensen, Tamati, Broadhurst, K. Sorensen, West, Prohm. *Subs*: O'Regan, I. Bell.

AUSTRALIA Scott; Boustead, Meninga, Miles, Grothe; Lewis, Mortimer; Tessman, Krilich, D. Brown, Vautin, Fullerton-Smith, Price. *Subs*: Ella, R. Brown.

Scorers New Zealand   *Tries* West, Leuluai, Ropati. *Goals* Wright (3). *Drop Goals* Wright.
          Australia   *Tries* Grothe, Ella. *Goals* Meninga (2).

Referee Robin Whitfield (Great Britain).

Peter Sterling

Wigan 28 Hull 24
Challenge Cup Final, Wembley
4 May 1985

Born 16 June 1960. Every era, whether it be in Australia or Britain, throws up a club which, by virtue of its style or play, its achievements and, above all, the charisma of its players, stands above all others. Such a club Down Under in the 1980s was Parramatta, a club which dominated Australia's Winfield Cup competition and which had, at its centre, perhaps the greatest scrum half ever to represent Australia, Peter Sterling. The tiny, blond-haired, midfield maestro tormented defences with his precision passing, his uncanny kicking and his lightning bursts through a gap to such an extent that he appeared as a puppet-master in total control of everyone around him. That control earned him 18 appearances at Test level for Australia between 1982, his first tour of Great Britain, and 1988, and saw him dominate in 13 State of Origin games for New South Wales.

Such was Peter Sterling's reputation in Britain that he became a leading target for the top clubs, with the battle for his services being won by Hull. Between 1983 and 1985 the outstanding number seven made 36 appearances for the Humberside club, steering them to a Wembley showdown with Wigan in May 1985 and helping himself to nine tries. Though a serious shoulder injury brought about his premature retirement in 1992, his work as a successful television commentator still illustrates his shrewd rugby brain.

Late in 1983, a blond-haired Australian called Peter Sterling was lying on the beach in Sydney, thinking only of three more months doing the same. His future was rosy, but it was unlikely anything would top what had occurred in the past two years.

At 21 years old he had inspired Parramatta to its first-ever Premiership victory, an event of such significance that supporters ceremonially burnt down the Eels home ground Cumberland Oval to mark the beginning of a new era. Parramatta had established itself as a great team by again bagging the title in 1982, and Sterling had won selection on what was to be an historic Kangaroo tour.

Going to Britain as understudy to the illustrious Canterbury scrum half Steve Mortimer, Sterling had displaced him in time for the first Test against

Britain and proceeded to make the green and gold number seven jumper his own on an unforgettable journey through England and France. And, just a few weeks before he found himself lazing at Bondi, he had celebrated his beloved 'Para's' third successive Premiership, sealed with an 18–6 Grand Final win over Manly.

Yes, good times were ahead, but Sterling had every right to believe that – even at just 23 – the greatest moments of his career were already behind him. Then, with indigestion and the state of Randwick racecourse the only things this junkfood-loving punter thought he had to worry about, a telephone call came from his manager, John White.

Sterling, now a highly successful television personality, recalls:

I never had any great designs on playing in England, and it was only after the Kangaroo tour in '82 that my manager at that stage had said, 'Would you like to go back?' I was lying on the beach when he rang up and planning to do that for the next three months. The thing I remembered was that Hull had given the 1982 Kangaroos their hardest game, including the Tests. I think we'd sneaked home 13–7 with a late try to Eric Grothe. I liked the passion of the people there, the supporters were great and I said, 'Yeah, OK, I will go back'.

Sterling's date with one of the game's most famous days was still a year and a half off, but a seed had been sown. He put away his swimming trunks and packed his bags for Yorkshire.

I only went back for a very short season. I think it was only ten games or something, which I think were fairly successful. We won eight or nine of them, and I signed up to go back the following year. It wasn't even something I'd planned to do for a long time. It just came out of the blue, and I guess when things happen like that the more spontaneous things are often the most satisfying.

In signing to play for two years, full time, in Britain, Sterling effectively surrendered the Australian shirt that was set to be his for as long as he wanted it. He would not re-establish himself in the national side until 1986.

Upon his arrival in Britain, the dynamic schemer soon became aware that the Challenge Cup was barely comparable to the beer and skittles floodlit competition at home.

Over there in Britain Wembley is such a big thing. It's probably a little bit out of proportion. If a side only wins five matches all year and that happens to be all the Challenge Cup games and a win at Wembley, it's considered to be a very successful season even if they've lost 30 club games.

So much emphasis is put on Wembley, and, I guess, winning it as well. The expectations are very, very high.

Sterling remembers the 1984–85 Challenge Cup campaign in detail – and says two draws made the climax all the more special.

We had a couple of early wins which weren't much trouble – we played, I think, against Carlisle and Halifax.

Our first real test came against Widnes, who had a really strong side that year with the likes of Tony Myler and the two Hulme brothers; I think Kurt Sorensen was playing for them at the time. I actually missed the game against them, which was played at Hull, through injury, and I remember sitting on the sidelines going through fingernails galore.

We ended up sneaking away with a pretty unconvincing draw, and then we had to go to Widnes to play the replay in a night game. We played pretty well. I played; I was back from injury. We got through that one fairly comfortably, which was always going to be tough.

We ended up meeting Castleford in the semi-final. We played them at Headingley, and we had a draw there in a game I thought we should have won. We had a lot of chances early on, they came back at us.

I'll never forget the final couple of minutes . . . They had a very good ball player called Barry Johnson. He was a front rower who had magnificent ball skills, and he used to combine with a very clever hooker, Kevin Beardmore. I remember with 60 seconds to go, the scores were tied, they did a runaround move and I was completely fooled by it, and I ended up missing Kevin Beardmore eight metres out from our line. He got straight through a tackle and I just remember thinking, 'Oh, jeez, after all the effort and everything . . .'

I turned around, and Gary Kemble came up with the greatest trysaving tackle you've ever seen, ball and all, and stopped him from scoring the try. Probably in my entire career there aren't too many other times when I've felt such enormous relief, through missing a tackle and seeing someone come up with a trysaver like Kemble did that day. We drew in that game, played the replay at Headingley in a night game and absolutely went straight through them, had no problems.

And it was in that second semi-final that Sterling became embroiled in the controversy of the season.

That was the night that I had a few problems with Malcolm Reilly. His fingers found their way into my eyes, and I made a big statement in the paper and I ended up nearly getting sued and everything.

Years on down the track, it was eventually smoothed out, but I was pretty rope-able that night. That sort of tempered the feeling that we'd actually got to Wembley.

For a young Australian from the western suburbs of Sydney, the next few weeks were more eye-opening than all the Grand Finals and Test matches in history. In choosing the most memorable game of his career, Sterling said losing at Wembley was 'easily' as good as winning the 1981 Grand Final for his beloved Eels against Newtown – and probably better.

It is such a special time, not just the 80 minutes, but the week leading up and even the couple of days after. I remember things like the fact we were completely outfitted for the Wembley trip. You know, new blazers, new everything. We actually had new jerseys made up, and the English jerseys are fabulous. The insignias are hand-woven.

The preparation was very, very good. It was difficult not to get caught up in the excitement of it all. But I guess there was a bit of experience in the side which probably helped in a lot of ways.

Hull got off to a magnificent start before a 97,801 crowd which had paid record receipts, with Welsh winger Kevin James scoring after Sterling shed a tackler with sheer strength.

I felt very good from the word go. We kicked off and Freddie Ah Kuoi came up with a tackle five metres out from their line, which was just bone-crunching. It was just the ideal way to start such an important game.

Kevin James scored for us after some good lead-up work, and then they came back very strongly.

Chicka [John] Ferguson scored a try out of absolutely nothing. He basically tiptoed down the sideline, got outside Dane O'Hara, to score the try. Then Brett Kenny ran nearly the length of the field from the scrum base.

Kenny's 28th minute try for Wigan, in which he skirted wide and straightened up to slice through from 60 yards out, was one of the most exhilarating and memorable in Wembley history. Sterling says no one would have stopped him.

A sensational try. If you have a look at Brett, it was him at his very best. In that 60- or 70-metre run, there was everything there. There was the in-and-away, the sidestep, it was just great. You'd have preferred it to have been someone on your side and not in the side you were playing against, but it was hard not to sit back with incredible admiration for what he did.

* * *

Henderson Gill scored again for Wigan before half time, and Kenny sent Shaun Edwards over following the re-start, which meant the score was 22–8.

> They ended up getting away to a very big lead. Even early in the second half, they scored pretty much straight away, which looked like it was going to be the final nail in the coffin. But we came back at them.

And how!

Sterling ran diagonally towards the blindside almost immediately afterwards, sucking in three defenders before unloading one-handed to centre Steve Evans, who scored. That tactic, running the blind and opening up centrefield, began working for Sterling at regular intervals.

> That probably describes every run of my life, I suppose . . . [But] the momentum turned around and we started to find a few holes, and James Leuluai started to come into his own and Fred Ah Kuoi put him away a couple of times.

Wigan wing Ferguson helped to ease the Riversiders' nerves with a converted try in 51 minutes to take the score to 28–12. But Hull were not finished as Leuluai scored. Replacement forward Gary Divorty joined in the revival, scoring the only forwards' try of the match, and Ah Kuoi put Leuluai over to make the scores 28–24 and set up a dramatic finale. But, for Hull, time ran out. Sterling says the reasons were straightforward.

> Arthur Bunting, who I had great respect for as a coach and who is a very, very close friend, who was the coach of Hull, would probably look back and say he made the wrong choice because he left Garry Schofield on the bench . . . which probably wasn't the best thing he's ever done. He put Steve Evans at centre, who was a fine player, but Schofield was a little bit 'out of the box'. When he and Gary Divorty, who was a very good young back rower, came in, they made a bit of a change. The momentum, and the fact that we had some new faces out there . . . I think players can sort of smell tiredness and fatigue. They [Wigan] were getting tired. Apart from making the mistake of thinking they had it won, they were starting to get a little bit weary too. That's another thing about Wembley – it's a very tiring ground. It's spongy and it has wide open spaces and it's very difficult to play on, and maybe that got to them a little bit as well.
> In the end we ran out of time and we had no one to blame but ourselves . . .
> If we'd gone another five minutes, we would probably have won the game.
> We just allowed them to build up too much of a lead, unfortunately.

Goalkicking was a problem, too; I think we had two from seven.

The photograph of Sterling sitting on the Wembley turf, head in hands, while his Parramatta club-mate Kenny performed the victory lap is one of rugby league's most enduring images.

But, almost a decade on, the legendary half back says the pain was short lived.

I was extremely disappointed in losing the game . . . This may sound a bit strange, but going to Wembley . . . it's the first time I ever felt successful being on a losing side. Just being there and being part of the occasion, for an Australian, was good. I was devastated by the loss, but I was more devastated for people like Steve Norton, Dane O'Hara and Gary Kemble; these guys who had been to Wembley a couple of times before and never got the result.

I still felt like 'this is something that I will remember'. Probably one of the regrets of my career is that I never got the chance to go back and change the scoreline and rectify that. If I'd gone back and got beaten again, it would have been much more devastating.

I truly believe that if Brett Kenny hadn't played that day, we would have won by ten or fifteen points. And, again, I guess that softened the blow of losing; the fact it was Brett who really proved the difference. I coped with the loss a lot better because I just had incredible admiration for him.

And if you're going to get beat, you might as well get beat by one of the champions of the game.

For Peter Sterling, Wembley Stadium was a place apart. It had always been his dream to play there. To win would have simply been icing on an already irresistible cake.

I remember walking out of the tunnel there . . . and I looked at the far end of Wembley, and all you could see was red and white. And I remember thinking, 'What the hell's going on here?' And when I got to the end of the tunnel, the noise from behind almost knocked us over, and I turned around and that's where the Hull 50,000 were standing. I'll never forget that, turning around and this noise propelled you forward.

How many times in your career do you get the opportunity to go out in front of this many people and show what you can do? That was great and, again, when you're young, you see Wembley as something unattainable and the international ban made it more so.

I sat at home as a seven-, eight-, nine-year-old, and I used to watch FA Cup finals, and it was always a magical ground. They only ever seemed to play two or three games there a year of any code. It always looked spectacular and a magical place.

While some big-money imports since the lifting of the international transfer ban in 1983 have been perceived simply as hit-and-run moneygrabbers, Sterling had a real passion for British rugby league, and these days, when he lazes around, it's the Boulevard he dreams about, rather than the beach.

I've got to give the fans a mention too. I've got a record at home of a club song over there, that they sing; it's called 'Old Faithful'. It sounds like this old cowboy song. You've got to hear it. They sing it during the games, and every time I hear it the hair on the back of my neck stands up. It just sends a tingle through the body.

And you can imagine at Wembley, with 50,000 of them singing this song. It was a sensation like . . . it must be like backing a 100–1 winner or something. It's that kind of adrenalin rush. That's one thing I'll never forget is the singing of this song 'Old Faithful'. As I said, I brought the record home to play it.

Whenever I feel depressed, I just put it on and it lifts me straight away.

HULL Kemble; James, Evans, Leuluai, O'Hara; Ah Kuoi, Sterling; Crooks, Patrick, Puckering, Muggleton, Rose, Norton. *Subs*: Schofield, Divorty.

WIGAN Edwards; Ferguson, Stephenson, Donlan, Gill; Kenny, Ford; Courtney, Kiss, Case, West, Dunn, Potter. *Subs*: Du Toit, Campbell.

Scorers Wigan   *Tries* Ferguson (2), Gill, Edwards, Kenny. *Goals* Gill (3), Stephenson.

Hull   *Tries* Leuluai (2), Evans, James, Divorty. *Goals* Crooks (2).

Referee Ron Campbell (Widnes).

Mick Sullivan

France 12 Great Britain 16
World Cup Final, Parc des Princes, Paris
13 November 1954

Born 12 January 1934. Any player who figured in two world record transfer fees, as did Mick Sullivan in 1957 when he moved from Huddersfield to Wigan for £9,500 and then in 1961 from Wigan to St. Helens for £11,000, must have had special qualities. Mick Sullivan had, for, though he stood only 5 feet 10 inches and weighed barely 13 stones, he was one of the toughest wingers I ever played alongside, and certainly one of the most deadly finishers down the flanks. His all-time record of 46 appearances for Great Britain, including a record run of 36 successive outings, and 41 tries bears testimony to his skills between 1954 and 1963, the date of his last Test appearance against Australia.

It was in Australia that the former Shaw Cross Boys amateur player enjoyed his greatest successes and aroused the most controversy for his tenacious approach to his Aussie opponents. On the 1958 Lions tour, Great Britain's left wing recorded over 38 tries, still a record for a tourist Down Under. Though Mick Sullivan's greatest achievements were performed with Huddersfield, Wigan and St. Helens, he also enjoyed playing spells with York and Dewsbury, where, in the loose forward role, he inspired them to a Challenge Cup semi-final against his former club, St. Helens. Always willing to accept a challenge on or off the field, he joined a rebel club, Junee, playing in a breakaway Australian league at the end of his illustrious career.

In the autumn of 1995 the sport of rugby league will celebrate its centenary with the staging of the tenth World Cup finals, an event eagerly anticipated by players and fans alike. When, in 1954, Paul Barrière, the president of the French Rugby League, donated a silver trophy valued at three million francs and suggested the holding of a tournament between the then four league-playing nations, Great Britain, Australia, New Zealand and France, few, however, were enthusiastic. Australia, having won a tough Ashes series in the summer, were hardly in the mood to travel 12,000 miles to compete, while many of the top British players were either injured or simply declined selection and yet, at the insistence of the French, the inaugural World Cup became a fixture on the calendar.

Under the leadership of former Hawick and Scotland rugby union star, Huddersfield loose forward Dave Valentine, Great Britain were considered 'no-hopers', with many young players like Mick Sullivan and David Rose getting their first taste of international rugby. Mick Sullivan, then a 20-year-old unknown who had just broken into the Huddersfield team, recalls the mood in the country as the 18-man squad set out across the Channel for France:

> I never expected to be selected. I was merely a kid who had just broken into the Huddersfield side, playing centre to the great Lionel Cooper. I hadn't even played for Yorkshire. I was plucked from nowhere. Everyone said I wasn't big enough or good enough, but I knew I could tackle and I had confidence in myself.
>
> We were slated as a team, and even before we had got to France we had been written off by everyone. We were just a bunch of novices with one or two 'old heads' like Gerry Helme.

The novices, however, surprised the rugby league world in pulling off one of the biggest shocks in World Cup history by beating France in the final, not Australia, as everyone expected. The tournament, watched by millions on Eurovision TV, proved a huge success, launching many, like Hull's John Whiteley and the unknown Sullivan, firmly on to the international stage. To be plucked from obscurity to the final of the World Cup at the Parc des Princes Stadium in Paris exceeded the wildest dreams of the young Sullivan, but the British selectors knew well the mettle of their raw, new recruit. And that mettle was there for all to see in Great Britain's opening match in the league format against the all-conquering Australians, a match which was to guarantee the young Huddersfield wing his place in the final.

> When we played Australia in the league in our opening match at Lyons, I cut my eye badly and I had to leave the field. Our manager wanted me to stay off for the rest of the match, but I knew that if I did then I might never play any further part in the World Cup finals. I insisted on going back on to the field.

Young Mick Sullivan's arrival back on to the pitch, coupled with his outstanding performance and courageous display against the odds, ensured that there was no way he would ever be left out of a Great Britain team for the foreseeable future. Always a battler, he resumed the fight with gusto, helping the 'unknowns' defeat the red-hot favourites by 28–13.

> I had stitches inserted above my left eye, and a doctor covered the gash by wrapping a huge bandage around my head. I was just 11 stones 7 pounds

at the time, and was marking their 15-stone centre Harry Wells. I knew I had to prove myself or it would be the end of my World Cup. Things went well for me, though, and I had a good game and impressed everybody. That game gave me my chance of playing against France in the final.

The term 'final' for the concluding match of the World Cup is, however, a misnomer, for there was, in fact, no World Cup final, rather a play-off between the two teams who headed the league table after all the contestants had played each other. In the absence of an outright winner, and with Great Britain and France finishing on five league points each, a play-off was arranged for 13 November 1954 at the famous Parc des Princes Stadium in Paris. And, after the tense 13–13 draw between the two teams at Toulouse just a week before, Mick Sullivan and his team-mates knew that they were in for a tough battle.

Before we left for France everyone thought Australia would be the favourites. In Keith Holman, Harry Wells and Clive Churchill they had some of the world's greatest players. But France, at that time, were a major force in rugby league with one of the finest full backs anywhere in Puig Aubert, a big strong-running wing in Raymond Contrastin and a very formidable pack. We prepared for a really tough match before a fanatical French crowd, and we were proved right.

Inspired by France's brave performance in the previous match and their surprise 15–5 win over Australia, a 30,368 crowd rallied behind the host nation and, if they were not rewarded with the win they desired, they had the satisfaction of seeing their favourites take Great Britain right to the final whistle. Restored to the wing, the 20-year-old Sullivan was set to mark local hero Contrastin, whose try in the dying seconds had foiled Great Britain's win in the previous encounter and who was one of the finest wingers produced by France.

He was a big-game player, very strong, tricky and fast, and he had shown excellent form in the earlier matches. I knew I had to look after him and mark him very closely or he could do a lot of damage. I was nervous of the occasion, but I was confident I could do the job.

A big task for the Huddersfield youngster, but such was his own growing reputation that, without touching the ball, he was able to play a part in what proved to be the vital try of the match.

Roared on by cries of 'Pipette, Pipette', the nickname of the French full back and captain Puig Aubert, France took an early 2–0 lead when the number one slotted a penalty goal between the posts. Great Britain had a battle on their hands, especially in the forwards, where France's powerful pack trio

Save, Pambrun and Verdie were proving difficult to hold. Behind, however, Great Britain had the sharper cutting edge with Gerry Helme and Gordon Brown at half back and loose forward Dave Valentine carving out openings, from one of which Leeds centre David Rose scampered around French wing Cantoni and in for the opening try. His Leeds colleague Gordon Brown obliged with another and, despite fierce resistance from the French pack, Great Britain led by 6–2 at half time. Suddenly, however, the match seemed about to slip away from them.

Flying wing Cantoni eluded the cover and, using his speed to good effect, crossed for France's first try. Puig Aubert's conversion and penalty goal shortly after gave France a 9–6 lead and Great Britain looked vulnerable. Not, though, according to Mick Sullivan.

> I don't think the referee, Charlie Appleton, was doing us any favours. I told him I thought he was a Frenchman. But there was a great spirit in the side and everyone pulled together. Once we had the ball among our backs I always felt it was only a question of time before we would score again.

That vital try came courtesy of Warrington's scrum half maestro, Gerry Helme, but the reputation of Sullivan was to play its part as the tiny number seven touched down over the French tryline. Helme, Lance Todd Trophy winner in the Challenge Cup final draw between Warrington and Halifax just six months earlier, was in sparkling form and a menace to the French around the scrums. Using his uncanny acceleration off the mark, he shot away from a scrum and, selling two of the most outrageous dummies, one to Sullivan, he scored beneath the posts. Ledgard added the conversion and gave Great Britain the lead they never lost.

> Without doing a thing I had a hand in the try of the match. Gerry Helme shot through a gap and sold a huge dummy towards me. I thought I had the ball, the dummy was so good. Two Frenchmen came in very quickly, hit me hard and knocked me flat to the floor. Gerry was through and under the posts for the try. Nobody laid a hand on him, only on me.

It was Jimmy Ledgard, the Leigh full back, who, with France now trailing by two points, sealed their fate with a final pass for Gordon Brown's try at the corner and a further goal. A few Union Jacks unfurled in the Parc des Princes in anticipation of an historic first World Cup win. The trophy was on its way across the Channel as reward for a magnificent display of courage from Great Britain's novice outfit. A try from the great French wing Contrastin in the closing minutes ensured a dramatic finale, but Great Britain were home. Against all the odds, Great Britain's much-ridiculed squad had proven their critics wrong against a very strong French outfit. That three weeks in France was also to prove the launching-pad for the young Mick Sullivan, who was to play a prominent part in the next two World Cup tournaments held in Australia and England in 1957 and 1960.

> France had a great side in the 1950s and they were always capable of playing brilliant, exciting rugby. Their two wings Contrastin and Cantoni were as good as anyone in the game at the time. Australia were a very experienced side full of seasoned internationals, but we had a tremendous team spirit and lads who wanted to do well, many of us had so much to prove to the knockers. I enjoyed myself throughout the whole of the tournament, especially in the play-off which was the most memorable game of my life. It meant so much for my career.

Great Britain will be looking for another unknown youth like Mick Sullivan when the next World Cup kicks off in England in October 1995.

FRANCE Puig; Contrastin, Merquey, Teisseire, Cantoni; Jiminez, Crespo; Krawzyk, Andoubert, Rinaldi, Save, Pambrun, Verdie.

GREAT BRITAIN Ledgard; Rose, Jackson, Naughton, Sullivan; Brown, Helme; Thorley, Smith, Coverdale, Robinson, Watts, Valentine.

Scorers France *Tries* Contrastin, Cantoni. *Goals* Puig (3).
  Great Britain *Tries* Rose, Brown (2), Helme. *Goals* Ledgard (2).

Referee Charlie Appleton (Warrington).

Alan Tait

Widnes 22 Wigan 18
Stones Bitter Championship, Naughton Park, Widnes
16 April 1989

Born 2 July 1964. Alan Tait pocketed a Premiership final winner's medal after taking part in only his third game of rugby league since his decision to switch codes in April 1988. And, since his tryscoring appearance for Widnes against defeated near-neighbours St. Helens, the former Kelso and Scotland rugby union centre has rarely been out of the headlines. Persuaded to forsake Scotland, for whom he gained eight union caps, by Widnes coach Doug Laughton, the canny, pacy centre assumed the role of the attacking full back in Widnes's plans for success. Within months he had confirmed Mr Laughton's wisdom in splashing out a £100,000 fee for his services when, after a series of exciting displays in the Widnes number one jersey, he joined the ranks of those players who have achieved international recognition at both league and union.

A starring display for Great Britain against France on his international debut at Wigan in January 1989 led to his selection for the Test series against New Zealand later in the autumn and the tour by the Lions to Papua New Guinea and New Zealand in the summer of 1990. Sadly for the Widnes fans, Alan Tait's stay at Naughton Park was somewhat short-lived for, following the shock departure of his mentor Doug Laughton to assume the coaching duties at Leeds, the ambitious Scot left to join him at Headingley in September 1992.

The scoreline of Widnes 10, Wigan 12 on the scoreboard at the corner of the tiny, compact Naughton Park ground indicated the evenly balanced nature of the match and the tension among the players and the fans. All 17,323 spectators, a Division One record crowd for the Widnes ground, sensed that the next mistake could prove decisive in determining the winners of the last Stones Bitter Championship clash of the season. When, shortly after half time, Wigan lofted a huge, towering kick in Widnes full back Alan Tait's direction, the Widnes fans in the tightly packed crowd held their breath. They remembered the ex-Scottish union star making an awful mess of a couple of such kicks in the John Player Special Trophy final, also against Wigan, just four months earlier. Alan Tait also remembered those nightmare kicks as the ball seemed to go higher and higher before beginning its descent. He stood motionless beneath the ball and reflected on that day in January when he had dropped a couple of high balls and allowed Wigan to mount their attacks. He remembered Ellery Hanley's words to him then as he swept past him and on to the ball: 'You were lucky there. There's more of them to come.' The Wigan captain had tried to unnerve him and shatter his confidence.

Alan Tait waited patiently and confidently before making the leap to catch the ball, conscious that three months of practising the art of catching a high ball had given him the confidence to field such an awkward kick. Hanley, sporting a wide grin, thundered into him, hitting him with such force that he was propelled back to the ground with a sickening thud. But the ball held in his arms. Alan Tait was ready for the Wigan skipper. 'Are there any more to come? I've been practising,' the Scot snorted.

The stakes were high, personal battles were being waged, but Alan Tait and Widnes were not found wanting and, within minutes, were to sweep to victory in the final and decisive match of the 1988–89 championship chase.

I'd had some problems under the high balls in the John Player final and had misjudged a couple near our own line. I hadn't been practising and Wigan had sensed that I was vulnerable. When I fluffed a bad one, Ellery Hanley raced up to me and tried to unnerve me. He told me how lucky I'd been that he didn't score off my mistakes.

I was ready for him at Widnes, though, and when I caught a really high one and he hit me, I couldn't resist laughing at him and telling him that I'd been practising.

After one or two unpleasant experiences early in the season, 16 successive wins had tempted Wigan's huge army of travelling fans to Naughton Park for what they hoped would be the climax to a Division One Championship title chase. Both the team and their fans wanted to send Kiwi coach Graham Lowe, who was returning Down Under to coach the top Sydney league club Manly, away from Central Park with another winner's medal. And those fans who had fancied a flutter on the bookmakers' pre-season odds of 7–4 had visions that by 4.30 p.m. on Sunday, 16 April they would be due their reward. The little matter of a record £25,000 prize money to the winners of the title race was also a matter of some consideration, especially for the directors of the two clubs.

Widnes, pre-season at odds of 4–1 to win the title, had been confident of winning the Championship earlier in the season, but a hectic ten matches in just over a month and Wigan's successful late flourish had pegged them back to just one league point ahead of their rivals at the top of the First Division table. A draw would give the Chemics the title; a win for Wigan would take the trophy back to Central Park. As Alan Tait approached the ground before kickoff, he had experienced no atmosphere quite like it in his short league career.

* * *

233

It was a winner-take-all situation and everyone knew that, the players and the fans. It was the end of my first full season and I was within sight of my first Championship medal. Widnes and Wigan were the two best clubs in the game at the time, and the crowds expected something special. The streets around the ground were a blaze of colour, all black and white and cherry and white, and the noise was terrific.

Everyone was excited because the club had even erected a temporary stand and balcony above the players' tunnel where the trophy was on display and where the winning captain would receive it. It was a do-or-die situation.

Wigan, led by Hanley, about to be voted the world's greatest player, kicked off in typical fashion and stormed the Widnes line with such ferocity that within half an hour they seemed to be coasting away with the game at 12–4 in their favour. International forwards Andy Platt and Andy Goodway had touched down for tries, and Joe Lydon, assuming the kicking duties, had landed two goals. A try from wing Martin Offiah, created by Tait, was Widnes's sole reply and the outlook was looking decidedly bleak.

Many of us had thought that the Championship was in the bag, but Wigan had other ideas and, in that first half hour, they hit us with everything. The pressure was really on us, but we kept in touch with them with Martin's opening try. I raced across the pitch and did a 'drop off' with him. I gave him the ball and he cut inside and around Steve Hampson to score.

Widnes coach Doug Laughton, once a roving loose forward himself, had, however, assembled a pack of forwards with pace, power and exceptional handling ability. In hooker Phil McKenzie, giant Tongan second row Emosi Koloto and loose forward Richie Eyres he had three speedy ball-handling forwards who, if given room in which to work, could create havoc with any opposition defences. Wigan gave them the room, and the trio ran riot for the next half hour. Martin Offiah, eventually the season's leading tryscorer with 60 tries to his credit, suddenly revealed just why he has proved a sensation since his arrival in the professional code from Rosslyn Park rugby union club. He raced in for one of his classic tries, and former Welsh union skipper Jonathan Davies, playing on the other wing and still feeling his way in the game after his £150,000 signing just three months previously, added the conversion to send Widnes in at half time trailing by only two points.

Alan Tait today still experiences more than a touch of excitement at 'Chariots' Offiah's magnificent touchline dash.

I don't think I have ever seen a better try than Martin's second try. I still get a tingle up and down my spine when I think of him racing at full speed down the touchline, no one able to catch him. He is a majestic sight when in full flight. At half time we knew that that try had pulled us right back into the game and, if we could use our extra pace, we knew we could win the match and the Championship.

The Widnes full back's pace and his uncanny understanding with the even faster Offiah were perhaps the biggest factors in the defeat of Wigan, according to Widnes coach Doug Laughton:

Alan has tremendous pace that enables him to fly into the attack from behind the threequarter line. He is lethal when he times his run perfectly, and it is very difficult for anyone to stop him pushing through a gap out wide. Against Wigan, Alan and Martin were a class act.

Martin was one winger who could keep up with Alan when he went for a break, and he could read exactly where Alan wanted him to be, either inside or outside him. They devastated Wigan down the left touchline.

Wigan were then a great side, but we had that extra yard of pace and everything we tried on attack came off for us on the day. We proved ourselves better on the day.

The speed of the Widnes backs, the thrust of Tait from full back and the deadly finishing ability of the amazing Offiah put Wigan to the sword with three tries in nine minutes in a wonderful second half spell from the Chemics. Another piercing, darting run from the Widnes number one put skipper Kurt Sorensen in for a try and, minutes later, the ex-Rosslyn Park flyer scorched down the touchline to complete his hat trick of tries, much to the delight of the Widnes fans in the highly excitable crowd. Offiah's third try was truly a majestic effort as he evaded the clutches of Wigan's giant Kiwi wing Tony Iro and centre Dean Bell, rounded forlorn full back Steve Hampson and, with a burst of blistering pace, just beat off the attentions of Wigan's own wing flyer Mark Preston to score his third try. Strong-running scrum half Paul Hulme powered over beneath the posts to complete the home side's three-try blitz of an ailing Wigan. The mercurial Davies, having a terrific impact at Naughton Park in his first season, added two goals and, with Widnes leading 26–12, the Championship trophy, on display on the temporary stand, appeared to be stayng put in the town. But Wigan were not yet finished.

The loss of forward Emosi Koloto, dismissed by referee John Holdsworth for a high tackle in the final quarter, proved a severe blow to Widnes's fortunes. Any side reduced to 12 men is in difficulties, but a side so reduced and facing Wigan is in serious trouble. So it was for Widnes. Ellery Hanley, summoning up all the power and appetite for tries that made him one of the world's greatest players for over a decade, led the charge for glory with a typical Hanley burst and try beneath the posts. Joe Lydon added his third goal of the match and, though still 26–18 in Widnes's favour, there was more than a hint of edginess in the Widnes team.

> We thought we were home and dry when we went 14 points in the lead, but the loss of Emosi Koloto hit us hard, not only on defence but in attack. When Hanley scored beneath the posts, Wigan sensed they could still snatch the game and I think we wobbled a little. But our defence held out and everyone worked for each other.

Widnes's defensive pedigree that season could not have been better, holding the best defence record in the first division with just 345 points recorded against them. And, when called to account in those final desperate ten minutes, they not only responded with an exhibition of terrier-like tackling but had the cheek to nip in for one more try, a sixth, from lively Aussie hooker Phil McKenzie and a fourth goal from the irrepressible Davies. The Championship was theirs and Kiwi skipper Kurt Sorensen proudly received the trophy for only the third time in the club's history. They had pipped their deadly rivals Wigan by just three league points to take the Stones Bitter Championship for a second successive season, thus joining Swinton, Bradford Northern and Hull Kingston Rovers as the only teams to have done so at that time. Wigan have, of course, since joined that illustrious quartet, but their coach Graham Lowe was the first to admit the better team had won.

For Widnes boss Doug Laughton it was the fulfilment of plans laid over the previous two seasons and brought about by his blending of top union signings and local, home-grown league talent. His plunges into the world of rugby union for leading international stars Martin Offiah, Jonathan Davies, Alan Tait and Emosi Koloto had provided that little extra ingredient to make Widnes into Great Britain's premier side. How sad that, within four seasons, over £1½ million-worth of talent in Offiah, Tait, Currier, Eyres, McKenzie and Davies had been lost and sold to relieve the pressure on the financially crippled club. A tragedy for the good folk of Widnes.

WIDNES Tait; Davies, Currier, Wright, Offiah; D. Hulme, P. Hulme; Sorensen, McKenzie, Grima, M. O'Neill, Koloto, Eyres. *Subs*: Dowd, Smith.

WIGAN Hampson; T. Iro, Bell, Lydon, Preston; Hanley, Byrne; Lucas, Kiss, Shelford, Platt, Potter, Goodway. *Subs*: Dermott, Betts.

Scorers Widnes *Tries* Offiah (3), McKenzie, Sorensen, P. Hulme. *Goals* Davies (4).

Wigan *Tries* Platt, Goodway, Hanley. *Goals* Lydon (3).

Referee John Holdsworth (Kippax).

Tom Van Vollenhoven

St. Helens 44 Hunslet 22
Championship Final, Odsal, Bradford
16 May 1959

Born 29 April 1935. When Tom Van Vollenhoven, the Springbok flyer, made his debut at Knowsley Road, St. Helens, on 26 October 1957 against Leeds, 23,000 fans were packed on the terraces. All had heard and read how the powerful 22-year-old, two years previously, had humbled the British Lions rugby union team and their great Irish wing Tony O'Reilly with a spectacular hat trick of tries. Rumours had spread of the South African wing's phenomenal pace down the flanks and his strength in the thighs when bursting through a tackle. They were not to be disappointed for, in just 80 minutes 'Voll', as he was affectionately known to the fans, gave his admirers glimpses of the speed and power which were, over the next ten seasons, to stamp him out as one of the game's greatest-ever wingers.

In those ten seasons at Knowsley Road he recorded 392 tries, and his 62 tries in the 1958–59 season still stand today as the club's record number of tries scored by any player in a season. Against Wakefield Trinity (1957) and Blackpool Borough (1962) he had the distinction of twice collecting six tries in a match, quite a feat for one so closely marked by the opposition as Tom was. At the end of his testimonial season in 1967–68 he left for home in Springs, near Johannesburg, where today he is actively involved in helping to promote the spread of rugby league as president of the local Springs Gladiators club.

By the end of my first year at Leeds University in 1959 most of my friends had tired of me telling them how Tom Van Vollenhoven was the world's finest winger in both codes of rugby. Yet a dozen of them, some from London, South Wales and Coventry and with no knowledge of rugby league, accompanied me to the end-of-season Championship final at Odsal, Bradford, along with another 52,560 fans, ready to put my boast to the test. The Springbok wing ace was to be the mighty St. Helens' trump card in their battle against what the pundits considered to be merely a workmanlike Hunslet side. After 20 minutes' play, and with St. Helens trailing by 12–4, I was in danger of suffering acute embarrassment, especially since the world's greatest wing (in my opinion!) had not touched the ball. The jibes from my student

237

pals flew thick and fast as even I, then a diehard Saints fan, had failed to realise the ability of the Hunslet team. Tom Van Vollenhoven had never underestimated them.

> Many people viewed Hunslet as the underdogs, and people seemed to forget that they had defeated Wigan, the Challenge Cup winners, at Central Park in the semi-final play-offs just a week before the final. In that opening 20 minutes they threw everything at us and we were really taken by surprise. Their forwards, Geoff Gunney, Harry Poole and Brian Shaw were finding the gaps, and they put us under real pressure. They had no real stars, but they played as a team, and when Jim Stockdill and Kevin Doyle scored two tries and their full back Bill Langton landed three goals we were in real trouble.

St. Helens fielded one of the most star-studded sides in the club's history with a combination of pace and power on the wings in Vollenhoven and his Springbok partner Jan Prinsloo. Few centres were as crafty or as adept at timing a pass as the veteran Doug Greenall, while the mercurial Murphy at scrum half was in a class of his own. In the forwards, Great Britain skipper and prop Alan Prescott had one of the fiercest, fastest and most skilful back row trios in the game behind him in Dick Huddart, Brian Briggs and Vince Karalius. The bookmakers had laid them as odds-on favourites to lift the Championship trophy, but around 3.20 on that hot, sunny Saturday in May both they and I looked to have miscalculated. And the fickle Saints fans who had trekked over the Pennines in their thousands were none too pleased either.

> Our own spectators in the crowd were starting to call us and say that the team had let them down at the last hurdle again. The players were starting to lose heart when I got the opportunity to do something. Doug Greenall just whipped the ball out to me and set me running in the right-hand corner about ten yards from our own tryline. It was the greatest try I ever scored in my career. For that try alone the match proved the most rewarding of my league career.

Most rewarding, too, for a 19-year-old student battling to save his reputation on the terraces.

Though seemingly hemmed in on the touchline and with less than a yard in which to manoeuvre, 'Voll' received Greenall's despairing pass almost at standstill. His instant acceleration and swerve to the outside immediately confused a couple of menacing defenders and left them, red-faced, in a heap over the touchline. The crowd, tightly packed on the steep terracing of the vast Odsal bowl, suddenly sensed they were witnessing something special, and the roar from their throats increased a decibel or two. A feint inside, before a sudden burst of speed propelled him to the edge of the touchline, saw Van Vollenhoven leave Hunslet full back Billy Langton diving despairingly behind him. The Saints tryscoring machine was free, running easily, but with Hunslet cover defenders Brian Shaw and Jim Stockdill bearing down on him from across the pitch. A combination of upper body strength and a devastating hand-off dispatched Hunslet's tough, uncompromising loose forward, Shaw, to the floor. Now with his head cocked to the side, a mannerism of Tom's whenever he raced into top gear, Saints' hero swept past the forlorn Stockdill and completed his length-of-field touchline dash by touching down for a sensational try at the foot of the posts. He had left five men trailing in his wake and never once, save when he crossed Hunslet's tryline, did he veer inside more than a yard from the touchline. A magical piece of running, a combination of pace, power, swerve and a hand-off – yet, as Tom Van Vollenhoven insists, it was all done by instinct.

> People have asked me how I beat Langton, Shaw and the other Hunslet players. You do it instinctively. You have the ball and you just do what comes naturally at the time. I've never really tried to analyse any of the tries which I've scored, why I sidestepped or swerved. It just worked.
>
> I never knew what I was going to do when I got the ball, and this try was no different. All I wanted as a wing was to get the ball in my hands. I never had a plan of how to beat a particular winger. I was fortunate to be blessed with pace, and I was quite strong in the hips and the legs which enabled me to ride and break a tackle. Things just happened for me when I received the ball.

Things just happened for the Saints and their fans after Van Vollenhoven's dramatic intervention. Young full back Austin Rhodes converted the try and landed a penalty goal minutes later to bring St. Helens to within one point of the Yorkshiremen. The team's spirits were lifted and, more importantly for the outcome of the match, Tom had proved to himself that he was indeed fit to play. For days beforehand, one of the most closely guarded secrets at Knowsley Road was the extent of the damage to Van Vollenhoven's leg injury incurred in the final match of the season. Saints Welsh coach, Jim Sullivan, realised the value of his prolific points-scoring winger and persuaded Tom to take a gamble with his niggling hamstring problem, a gamble which thankfully paid off but which caused Van Vollenhoven considerable discomfort afterwards.

> What gave me the greatest thrill about the opening try was that I went into the match suffering from a bad hamstring pull. I was very doubtful of playing right up to the kickoff. After the match I returned to South Africa

239

for a holiday, and for the first ten days I could hardly walk, my leg was black and blue.

For all Hunslet's opening salvo and the earnest efforts of their forwards, especially the second row pairing of Geoff Gunney and Harry Poole, once half back star Alex Murphy began to direct operations behind the St. Helens pack and bring into play the pace of Prinsloo and Vollenhoven on the wings, the Yorkshiremen had no answer. The effervescent international scrum half was simply too fast and too clever for Hunslet, giving Saints the lead with a brilliant solo try in the 33rd minute and having a hand in a magnificent cross-field handling movement which resulted in Prinsloo diving over for a try at the corner. And, not to be outdone, Jan Prinsloo's ex-Springbok colleague threaded his way through for a second try on the stroke of half time to leave Hunslet trailing by 24–12 and looking decidedly weary. As Van Vollenhoven commented:

> Once Saints got in front it was all over for Hunslet, as well as they played. Doug Greenall was the perfect foil for me; he could time a pass beautifully and knew exactly when to give me the ball. Alex Murphy, the greatest scrum half I have ever seen in either code, had a brilliant game, scoring two solo tries, and Jan Prinsloo ran so strongly on the wing. In front of us all, Vince Karalius at loose forward was so strong that he blocked up the middle with his tackling.

Within two minutes of the resumption of the second half 'Voll' was flying down the touchline to record his hat trick of tries and, despite gallant resistance and further tries from Hunslet hard-working second row duo Poole and Gunney, Saints cruised home by 44–22 with Wilf Smith, Alex Murphy and Dick Huddart completing the try tally. Future international Austin Rhodes, making only his second appearance at full back, crowned a memorable display with a Championship final record ten goals. The match had proved a classic, with Saints' Van Vollenhoven capturing the accolades of the crowd, not just for his hat trick of tries and his brilliant first touchdown, but for the manner in which he scored them. Rarely did the Saints wing need to forsake the touchline; on even rarer occasions did he need to kick and chase, for always he relied on his blistering speed and his swerve on the outside to beat his man. He never lost sight of the fact that a winger's job is to score tries.

> I enjoyed scoring tries and I always considered that was my job. I liked to be on the wing when the ball came across. Now and again you have to come inside and, if you have the talent, then you can do it. But, for me, the nicest try to score is one where you run around your opponent on the outside. That's the classic winger's try. I could use an inside swerve and a

sidestep when I needed it, but I preferred always to beat a man on the outside. That's why I was so pleased about my first try at Odsal. I beat them all on the touchline on the outside.

Contrary to early opinion during the match, Saints did not fail their fans nor did the fans let down their heroes when the victors paraded the trophy on the town hall steps before a crowd of thousands on their return from over the Pennines. Mr Harry Cook, the St. Helens chairman, and the mayor were both unable to speak until the crowd's idol, Tom Van Vollenhoven, had held the microphone. Many who thronged in the town's main square that night would, two years later, witness the 90-yard Wembley spectacular, created by Ken Large and finished by 'Voll', and would argue that his Challenge Cup final try against Wigan was Van Vollenhoven's finest.

But the scorer himself would disagree; and I would agree with him. For sheer audacity and the ability to create a try out of nothing, the 25th minute spellbinder at Odsal on 16 May 1959 will rarely be equalled. For Tom Van Vollenhoven the try and the match remain a treasured memory from a long and illustrious career.

Many people say that the try which I scored at Wembley against Wigan in 1961 and which is often shown on television was my best. But once I had the ball it was a case of straight running and swerving away from Wigan's skipper Eric Ashton at the end. Emotionally, to the fans, I suppose it was one of the most important tries I scored, but the try in the Championship final had to be scored and there was always a player in front of me. That was my best.

Writing in the *Guardian* newspaper 34 years later, 'Centipede', assessing the merits of the greatest-ever tries scored in both union and league, not only agreed with 'Voll' but proclaimed his tryscoring dash as 'the try of the century'.

Writes 'Centipede':

And from league comes the try of the century, which has to be scored from the most individual of positions, wing threequarter, with your team down, the cover closing, hope slim and the line 75 yards away: thus Tom Van Vollenhoven of South Africa and St. Helens, playing against Hunslet in the 1959 Championship final.

Vollenhoven beats five men, one after another, down the touchline, using change of pace, swerve and hand-off. Having crossed the tryline, he then takes on and beats a sixth player to score near the posts. It was the nonpareil of verve, nerve, balance and strength, skill and speed. William Webb Ellis would have been proud.

241

* * *

ST. HELENS Rhodes; Van Vollenhoven, Greenall, McGinn, Prinsloo; Smith, Murphy; Terry, McKinney, Prescott, Briggs, Huddart, Karalius.

HUNSLET Langton; Colin, Stockdill, Preece, Walker; Gabbitas, Doyle; Hatfield, Smith, Eyre, Poole, Gunney, Shaw.

Scorers   St. Helens *Tries* Van Vollenhoven (3), Murphy (2), Prinsloo, Smith, Huddart. *Goals* Rhodes (10).

        Hunslet   *Tries* Stockdill, Doyle, Poole, Gunney. *Goals* Langton (5).

Referee Mr Wilson (Dewsbury).